The Choice
Controversy

The Choice Controversy

Edited by
Peter W. Cookson, Jr.

CORWIN PRESS, INC.
A Sage Publications Company
Newbury Park, California

For information address:

Corwin Press, Inc.
A Sage Publications Company
2455 Teller Road
Newbury Park, California 91320

SAGE Publications Ltd.
6 Bonhill Street
London EC2A 4PU
United Kingdom

SAGE Publications India Pvt. Ltd.
M-32 Market
Greater Kailash I
New Delhi 110 048 India

Printed in the United States of America

Library of Congress Cataloging-in-Publication Data

The choice controversy / [edited by] Peter W. Cookson, Jr.
    p. cm.
    Includes bibliographical references and index.
    ISBN 0-8039-6029-8 (cl) —ISBN 0-8039-6030-1 (pb)
    1. School, choice of—United States.   2. Educational change—
United States.   3. Education and state—United States.
I. Cookson, Peter W., Jr.
LB1027.9.C49   1992
371—dc20   92-17348
                                                          CIP

The paper in this book meets the specifications for permanence of the American National Standards Institute and the National Association of State Textbook Administrators.

92 93 94 95 10 9 8 7 6 5 4 3 2 1

Corwin Press Production Editor: Tara S. Mead

Contents

Preface

Few educational reforms have ignited the public imagination as much as "school choice," and few reforms have aroused so much public controversy. Despite the fact that *school choice* is in reality a generic term that covers a wide variety of governance options, at its core, the school choice "option" rests on the fundamental assumption that public education will not improve until it becomes more competitive, less bureaucratic, and more consumer oriented. School choice is a policy perspective, but it is also a philosophical and political perspective. Those favoring choice argue that greater school choice will liberate American elementary and secondary education from the iron grip of bureaucracy and create the conditions for an educational renaissance. Those who oppose choice—especially unrestricted choice—argue that deregulating the public school system will lead to a fragmentation of the entire educational system and irrevocably dash the dream of a truly common school for all American children. Without doubt, school choice has become infused with emotion because it is an educational reform that goes directly to the heart of an American dilemma. What is the correct balance between individual and family freedom and the rights of the community? All of us have strong feelings about how to resolve this dilemma. It is not surprising that school choice has become a kind of reform Rorschach where people read into the choice rhetoric their own feelings about the relationship between school and society.

The school choice controversy engages us at several levels; it touches our heads as well as our hearts and compels us to ask questions about the fundamental purposes of education. School choice is not just about school improvement, it is also a metaphor for how we should live our lives. Because this issue is so volatile, it is not surprising that much of what has been written about school choice has lacked intellectual depth and rigor. With some exceptions, the literature concerning school choice has been either ideologically driven or empirically weak and often both. This has been problematic from an analysis and policy point of view because school choice raises critical issues of constitutionality, feasibility, equity, and educational productivity. There is a danger that school choice policies will be implemented throughout the country before there is an understanding of how these policies affect student achievement, institutional stability, and equal educational opportunity. It is apparent that there is a real need for thoroughgoing analyses of the origins of the school choice movement, the kinds of plans that have been proposed and implemented, the educational and social consequences of these plans, and the philosophical suppositions that underlie the argument that more freedom of choice leads to greater student achievement and social equity.

The chapters in this book represent some of the most contemporary and scholarly thinking about the issues mentioned above. Taken as a whole, these chapters provide an overview of school choice that has been previously lacking. Yet, each chapter is distinctive and can be read as a self-contained discussion. This book is intended for scholars, policymakers, educators, graduate students—indeed, for everyone who has an interest in the relationship between school choice, society, and educational reform. It is my hope that *The Choice Controversy* will be used in and out of the classroom. As a supplemental reader, this book could be used in graduate school courses dealing with school policy, educational reform, and school and society.

The book is divided into two parts. Part I, "Democracy, Choice, and Markets," centers on the political and philosophical issues related to school choice in the United States today. Mary Anne Raywid, who is a philosopher by training and a longtime advocate of greater freedom of choice for parents and students, illuminates clearly the distinctions between education-driven, economics-driven, policy-driven, and governance-driven forms of school choice policies in the first chapter, "Choice Orientations, Discussions, and Prospects." She provides us with a method of conceptually organizing school choice polices and then makes a number of informed speculations about the future of school choice.

Chapter 2, by sociologist Kevin J. Dougherty and educator Lizabeth Sostre, "Minerva and the Market: The Sources of the Movement for School Choice," is an analysis of the political context of the choice movement. What are the origins of the choice movement and what role does the state play in the choice movement? Dougherty and Sostre provide us with an outstanding descriptive overview of who the main choice players are, and they also provide us with a solid sociological lens by which to examine the politics of the school choice movement.

Chapter 3, "Choice: The Fundamentals Revisited," by the philosopher Jeffrey Kane, draws our attention to some of the fundamental issues underlying the meaning of choice in a democracy. This chapter challenges us to go beyond the conventional ways of discussing school choice and to examine our unspoken and often unacknowledged confusions about the nature of freedom in a democracy.

Chapter 4, by sociologists Amy Stuart Wells and Robert L. Crain, "Do Parents Choose School Quality or School Status? A Sociological Theory of Free Market Education," is a unique contribution to the school choice debate because it examines the underlying rationale for the competitive model of educational reform. Wells and Crain point out that choice is contingent on culture and class and in that sense choices are never entirely "rational."

Chapter 5, "The Ideology of Consumership and the Coming Deregulation of the Public School System," is my analysis of the rise of the school choice coalition and its connection to the Reagan revolution of the 1980s. I argue that there is a powerful coalition of interests that is challenging the legitimacy of traditional public institutions, including public education. If the free market wing of the school choice coalition were to triumph, the idea of the common school would most likely disappear from American civic culture.

Part II, "Private and Public School Choice," provides us with a number of alternative ways of examining the school choice issue. Chapter 6, by political scientist John F. Witte, "Public Subsidies for Private Schools: What Do We Know and How Do We Proceed?" is a very clear presentation of one of the key issues within the school choice debate. During the 1980s, a number of researchers claimed that private schools outperform public schools and therefore private schools should be subsidized with public funds. There are few aspects of school choice that are as controversial as supplying public funds for private schools. Witte's discussion helps us to con- textualize and understand this issue.

Chapter 7, by Albert Shanker and Bella Rosenberg of the American Federation of Teachers, "Do Private Schools Outperform Public Schools?" is a close analysis of some of the data that have been used to suggest that private schools are institutionally superior to public schools. This issue is of importance because many private school researchers have claimed the reason that private schools outperform public schools, if indeed they do, is because they are market oriented.

Chapter 8, "Private Citizenship and School Choice" by Michael Johanek of Teachers College, is an investigation of how the distinctions between the public sphere and the private sphere have shifted since World War II. Johanek develops the novel concept of "private citizenship" and applies it to the school choice debate.

Frank Brown, who is former Dean of the School of Education at the University of North Carolina, provides us with an important international comparison in Chapter 9, "The Dutch Experience With School Choice: Implications for American Education." The Dutch have used school choice as a way of organizing their school system for a number of years; Brown examines the Dutch system and assesses its applicability to American education.

The last chapter, "Issues of Choice: Canadian and American Perspectives" by Stephen B. Lawton, Professor of Educational Administration, points out the critical differences between the Canadian and American educational systems as they relate to policies allowing for greater freedom of choice. Clearly, one of the unique features of American education is the very strong boundaries that are drawn between church and state. Lawton's chapter places the American experience in an international context and also gives us insight into the politics and structure of Canadian education.

This book would not have been possible without the intellectual contributions and good cheer of its authors. I am indebted to them for their hard work and for their help in identifying some of the major issues underlying the school choice controversy. I am also indebted to the editors at Corwin Press for their support and expertise, particularly Gracia A. Alkema and Ann McMartin. This project began several months ago and I want to thank the editors of *Educational Policy* for their enthusiasm and daring. Carla Hernandez of Adelphi University provided the kind of secretarial support that is indispensable. Finally, I want to thank my colleagues in the School of Education at Adelphi University for sharing their thoughts with me about school choice and being tolerant of my relentless interest in this topic.

Peter W. Cookson, Jr.
Adelphi University

About the Authors

Frank Brown is the Cary C. Boshamer Professor of Education and Director of Educational Research for the Institute for Research in Social Science at the University of North Carolina at Chapel Hill. He is also the former Dean of the School of Education at the University of North Carolina at Chapel Hill and has held professorships and administrative positions at the City College of New York and the State University of New York at Buffalo. He holds a Ph.D. in Policy, Planning, and Administration from the University of California at Berkeley and is a graduate of the Institute of Management at Harvard University. He has published numerous books and articles, and he has held major positions with the American Educational Research Association and the National Organization for Legal Problems of Education, specializing in administration, policy studies, and school law.

Peter W. Cookson, Jr., is the Associate Dean of the School of Education at Adelphi University. He received his Ph.D. in the sociology of education from New York University. He is the coauthor of

Preparing for Power: America's Elite Boarding Schools and has authored and coauthored numerous scholarly articles on private schools, educational policy, and research. Currently, he is completing three coauthored or coedited books: *The International Handbook of Educational Reform, Exploring Education,* and *Making Sense of Society.* In the field of school choice, he has written or cowritten articles in *Education and Urban Society* (spring 1991), *Educational Policy* (forthcoming), and *Teachers College Record* (fall 1991) and is the coauthor of a chapter in *Empowering Teachers and Parents: School Restructuring Through the Eyes of Anthropologists.* He is also writing a book on school choice for Yale University Press. His chapter in this volume will also appear in a future issue of the *Journal of Educational Policy.*

Robert L. Crain is Professor of Sociology and Education at Columbia University's Teachers College and an expert on school desegregation and race relations. He is first author of *The Politics of School Desegregation* and coauthor of five books, including *Making School Desegregation Work.*

Kevin J. Dougherty is Associate Professor of Sociology at Manhattan College and Visiting Professor of Sociology of Education at Columbia University's Teachers College. His research has focused on the politics of education and of economic development. The chapter in this book arises from a research project, funded by the Spencer Foundation, on the political sources of the educational excellence movement of the past decade. Prior to this research, he wrote many articles on the political origins and socioeconomic impacts of community colleges in the United States. He is also the coeditor (with Floyd Hammack) of *Education and Society: A Text/Reader.* Currently, he is serving as Deputy Editor of *Sociology of Education.* In 1992, he will be beginning research on the political forces shaping the development of state government policies to foster economic growth.

Michael Johanek, a doctoral student in History and Education at Columbia University's Teachers College, focuses on urban precollegiate education. His current research involves schooling and community in East Harlem, New York City, from roughly 1930 to 1960. An instructor at Teachers College, he directs both the Fellows In Teaching and the Urban Scholars programs and is a graduate of the former. He also coordinates the Mellon Fellowships Collaborative, a new national teacher recruitment effort directed at minority liberal arts graduates. A high school history teacher for seven years, he has most recently taught in Lima, Peru. A magna cum laude Phi Beta Kappa graduate in Economics and Philosophy at Georgetown University, he later completed his initial graduate work at Teachers College.

Jeffrey Kane is Dean of Adelphi University's School of Education. He received his Ph.D. from New York University in the philosophy of science and is the author of *Beyond Empiricism: Michael Polanyi Reconsidered*. His interest in epistemological issues extends to the study of the relationship between the development of human intelligence through the formal means of schooling and the nature and responsibility of government in a democratic society—the subject of his monograph, *In Fear of Freedom: Public Education and Democracy in America*. Recently, he assumed editorship of an emerging educational quarterly, *Holistic Education Review*.

Stephen B. Lawton is Professor in the Department of Educational Administration, the Ontario Institute for Studies in Education, where he specializes in the finance, governance, and economics of education. Author of *The Price of Quality: The Public Finance of Elementary and Secondary Education in Canada*, and coeditor of *Scrimping or Squandering? Financing Canadian Schools*, he recently commenced a second term as international member of the board of directors of the American Education Finance Association; he has also served as program Cochair of Division A of the American Educational Research Association and as Vice-President of the Canadian Association for the Study of Educational Administration. Before moving to Canada in 1970, he earned a Ph.D. in Educational Administration at the University of California, Berkeley, and served as a high school teacher in the nearby Richmond Unified School District. His current research is concerned with methods of funding decentralized educational systems, especially those emphasizing school-based management. With colleagues, he has recently completed studies into provincial, school district, and school policies affecting student retention in high schools and into administrative practices of local school districts.

Mary Anne Raywid is Professor of Administration and Policy Studies at Hofstra University, Hempstead, New York. The sociopolitical context of education has been of long-term interest to her. Over the past several decades, she has focused on school reform policy, including choice and school-based management as strategies for restructuring education.

Bella Rosenberg is Assistant to the President of the American Federation of Teachers, where she deals with a variety of education reform issues and AFT policy initiatives. Prior to coming to the AFT, she was a Research Associate at the National Institute of Education in the Educational Policy and Organization Unit. Her undergraduate work in social and behavioral sciences at Queens College of the City University of New York earned her membership in Phi Beta Kappa, and she pursued doctoral studies in education and social policy and educational history at the Harvard Graduate School of Education, where she was also editor of the *Harvard Educational Review* from 1974 to 1976. Among the issues she has written about are education history, Chapter 1, public school choice, and the privatization of education.

Albert Shanker is President of the 780,000-member American Federation of Teachers (AFT) and has been reelected to that position every two years since 1974. He also serves as a Vice President of the AFL-CIO, as the President of its Department of Professional Employees, and as the President of the International Federation of Free Teachers' Unions. From 1964 to 1986, he was President of New York City's United Federation of Teachers, which under his leadership was the first organization in the United States to win collective bargaining rights for teachers. Widely known as the pioneer of the American teacher union movement, he has also had a long career as an advocate of public education and a leader in its reform through his weekly Sunday column in *The New York Times*, "Where We Stand," as well as through numerous articles, speeches, and television appearances. He has also long been involved in national and international organizations dedicated to promoting civil and human rights, including the A. Philip Randolph Institute, the National Endowment for Democracy, and the Committee for the Defence of Soviet Political Prisoners. He holds numerous honorary degrees, is on the advisory boards of many national organizations, and is the first labor leader to be elected to the National Academy of Education.

Lizabeth Sostre is Acting Coordinator of Parent Information Services for the Office of Alternative Schools, Community School District Three, in New York City, implementing the district's choice initiative, adopted in April 1991. She is the editor of the District's Middle School Directory, a collaboration between the district and Manhattan Institute's Center for Educational Innovation. She taught English in the New York City public schools at the junior high school level for 20 years. She is a MetLife Fellow at Columbia University's Teachers College, working as part of a team documenting and participating in the planning and implementation of the Wadleigh Secondary School in Harlem. She presented a paper, *Variations on the Implementation of an Organizing Model: The Wadleigh Schools* at the April 1991 meeting of the American Educational Research Association. She is currently working on her doctorate in the Department of Educational Administration at Columbia University's Teachers College. The working title of her dissertation is *School Choice and Equity: Complement or Contradiction?*

Amy Stuart Wells is Assistant Professor of Education at the University of California, Los Angeles, Graduate School of Education. She received her Ph.D. in sociology and education from Columbia University's Teachers College in 1991 and has been a frequent contributor to *The New York Times* Wednesday education page for the past four years. She is coauthor (with Edward B. Fiske) of *How to Get into the Right College: The Secrets of the College Admissions Process.*

John F. Witte received his B.A. degree from the University of Wisconsin—Madison in 1968. Following three years as a naval intelligence officer, he attended graduate school at Yale University, where he received an M.A. in philosophy (1974) and a Ph.D. in political science (1978). Since 1977, he has been Professor in the Department of Political Science and the Robert La Follette Institute of Public Affairs at the University of Wisconsin—Madison. He has been a fellow at the Russell Sage Foundation in New York and at the Center for Advanced Study in the Behavioral Sciences at Stanford. His research interests include education and tax policy and politics. In 1984-1985, he was the Executive Director of a governor's task force studying the quality and equity of the Milwaukee metropolitan public schools. In 1988, he was awarded (with William Clune) grants from the Bradley, Spencer and Joyce foundations to organize a conference, "Choice and Control in American Education." That conference, held in May 1989, produced two volumes on educational choice published by Falmer Press. In addition to these two edited volumes, he has written three other books and numerous articles or book chapters. In 1990, he was named as the state evaluator of the Milwaukee Parental Choice Program. A study of that program through June 1994 is being funded by the Spencer Foundation.

PART I

Democracy, Choice, and Markets

1

Choice Orientations, Discussions, and Prospects

MARY ANNE RAYWID

The idea of inviting family choice among public schools is not a new one, having been around now for almost a quarter of a century. Of course, it can be argued, as some do, that choice is really far older than that and indeed has been a feature of American education from the start: choice, that is, between public and nonpublic schools, and as to residence location, hence school assignment. The focus in this chapter, however, is the contemporary choice movement currently producing an array of policy initiatives at federal, state, and local levels. This kind of interest in choice dates from the 1960s and has been manifest in four fairly distinct though parallel forms representing different sponsorship, conceptual lenses, and agendas. We have in effect spawned four different species of choice proposals. Differing

AUTHOR'S NOTE: This chapter previously appeared in *Educational Policy* (in June 1992); copyright © 1992 by Corwin Press.

influences and impacts can be linked to the four as well as waxings and wanings—although, as several have coexisted for much of the period, the four can hardly be viewed phases or evolutions.

But, if the idea of choice is not new, its burgeoning is a relatively recent development. Over the past several years, a variety of choice proposals have been set forth, producing a scene of considerable complexity. This chapter attempts a broad mapping of today's choice terrain. It sketches four different routes whereby people have come to choice—hence four distinct orientations marking the choice movement. It identifies several of the more arresting features of today's choice discussion. And, finally, it ventures some predictions about the likely course of the choice movement for the coming decade. Such purposes call for broad strokes in preference to detailed mapping and fine-grained analysis. They also direct attention to exploring the situation rather than assessing it, even though the proposals clearly are not of equal merit and might all be challenged. The purpose here is rather to introduce some of the initial clarifying that might desirably precede critical assessment.

The four approaches identified here are distinguished by the primary orientations they bring to choice—what they are trying to accomplish and the conceptual resources they bring to bear. As distinguished in this way, there are *education*-driven choice advocates, *economics*-driven espousers, specific *policy*-inspired advocates, and *governance*-oriented proposers. The types reflect central tendencies rather than sharp differences and are not mutually exclusive. Some espousers seem inspired by more than a single orientation. Nevertheless, distinctive tendencies are often discernible, even when proposals might superficially appear similar—such as in the voucher espousal of Milton Friedman and Christopher Jencks. Both have urged the use of vouchers, but for quite different purposes, with economist Friedman bespeaking the economically oriented case and Jencks urging equity, or a policy-driven case. But, despite the fact that the categories are not finely honed and mutually exclusive analytic sets, they may still be useful in understanding the different voices of today's choice movement, in recognizing the sorts of assumptions leading advocates to their positions and defining their nonnegotiables, and in projecting and interpreting policy proposals.

Because analysts of the choice discussion, as well as advocates, also find some concerns more salient than others, and select conceptual lenses and tools for their analyses, the four approaches may also help in understanding the sorts of ways the choice movement is being studied and interpreted. Thus the pages that follow make reference to choice analyses as well as to proposals.

Education-Driven Choice

Of the four varieties of choice advocacy, the educational orientation was the first to emerge. It was initially inspired by the alternative schools of the 1960s and captured in the counterculture's expansive invitation to "Let 100 Flowers Bloom" (Graubard, 1972). The idea of an array of options among which to choose was not really very central to much of the discussion of those times, however, and indeed a number of the early alternatives considered themselves not an "alternative" to conventional schools but the vanguard that would eventually replace them. The argument that there was room for, and even merit in, sustaining a *variety* of schools was initially articulated by Mario Fantini. In his role as foundation officer and later as academic, Fantini had ties to alternative education as well as to policy circles. The dust jacket of his *Public Schools of Choice* (1973) bore the description on the cover: "A Plan for the Reform of American Education." Fantini proposed the deliberate diversification of schools on the grounds that differences among youngsters, as well as among teaching styles, recommend the provision of differing school environments and classroom orientations in preference to a single standard type. His argument was buttressed with the appearance of historian David Tyack's *The One Best System: A History of American Urban Education* (1974). Tyack's book traced the emergence of the uniformity dominating public education—as to structure, organization, and practice—and he documented the problems it brought. The book's title quickly became a slogan for education-oriented choice advocates, who used it to allude to the arbitrarily narrow character of school practice.

Fantini's argument remains the essential core of the education-inspired case for choice, although it has been elaborated and substantially extended since. His argument for students' need for diversification was based almost exclusively on differences in learning style and in the amount of structure youngsters need. Other differences—notably, in student interests—have now expanded the educational case for student choice. Moreover, Fantini had said little of parent entitlement to choice, or of the case for educator choice, so the argument has now been supplemented. A recent summary of the educationally oriented case for choice summed up the grounds for *student* choice this way:

> (1) There is no one best school for everyone. Accordingly, (2) the deliberate diversification of schools is important to accommodating all and enabling each youngster to succeed. Moreover, (3) youngsters will perform better and accomplish more in learning environments they have chosen than in environments which are simply assigned to them. (Raywid, 1989, p. 14)

The case for *parent* choice is summarized this way (Raywid, 1989, pp. 16-17):

> (1) There are many viable, desirable ways to educate, and (2) no one best program can prove responsive to the diverse preferences a pluralistic, democratic society accepts as legitimate. Hence, (3) the diversification of schools to accord with family value patterns and orientations is desirable.

The educationally oriented case for choice also includes an argument for teacher choice, identifying it as an effective vehicle for arriving at the professionalism now widely sought (Nathan, 1984). Schools of choice, it is asserted, render teachers more collaborative, less isolated, more autonomous, less role bound, and more efficacious than do conventional schools. It is also claimed that teachers are happier in, and more committed to, the programs they have chosen.

The educationally oriented case argues, then, that choice among schools is desirable in that it makes education work better, and to the greater benefit and satisfaction of the participants. This approach dominated the choice discussion of the early 1970s, perhaps because there wasn't much discussion. This was the period overwhelmed by the discovery of how little difference so many of the innovations of the previous decade had made. Thus there was a distinctly diminished audience for "A Plan for the Reform of American Education." Even, however, as general receptivity to reform warmed late in the decade, the education-driven argument for choice never managed to claim much attention. The concern of the late 1970s and early 1980s with raising standards makes that understandable, with standards urging the case for uniformity, not diversity. But it is more notable that, even in the late 1980s, as reform talk in educational circles turned to seeking many of the traits most salient in the choice arrangement—such as school-home value agreement, school responsiveness to individuals, student motivation, teacher empowerment, school-level autonomy—the choice idea claimed scant attention from educators.

Economics-Driven Choice

As understood here, the economics-oriented case for choice enjoys the most varied sponsorship of the four types. The orientation is reflected by those who urge various forms of privatization in the interests of forcing public schools to compete with private schools and those who talk of competition, consumer satisfaction, and markets that will drive bad schools out of business. The economic orientation is also reflected by those who are not choice advocates but who accept and pursue the market analogy in discussing education and who employ it as a root metaphor for explaining public situations and events, and thus for recommending solutions. This means that many who are advocates neither of vouchers nor privatization nevertheless fall within the economics-inspired genre. In a bit more detail, here are three prochoice orientations that all appear economics-driven in some significant sense.

In an obvious sense, some (though not all) voucher and tuition tax credit advocates can be deemed economics-driven choice advocates. Those who prefer nonpublic schools for their children, or those who operate schools outside the public system, might understandably fall within this category. Thus one of the first voucher proposals came from a priest who reasoned that, because government subsidizes the education of children attending public schools, it ought to extend comparable subsidies for those who attend nonpublic schools (Bloom, 1958). State governments might extend vouchers to students and the federal government might extend tax refunds to those paying tuition to nonpublic schools. The argument has continued to be carried on in much the same terms, holding that public support should be understood as a benefit to children rather than to institutions.

A second and more fundamental version of the economics-driven position on choice is reflected in the effort to make the ends and purposes of commerce foremost in public school aims and also to model business's orientation and methods in operating schools. This is an economics-driven case for choice in a sense quite similar to that in which Raymond Callahan (1962) found public education to be dominated by the spirit of business, having imbibed its criteria and overall orientation.

Critics have charged that *A Nation at Risk,* the influential product of Education Secretary Bell's National Commission on Excellence in Education (1983), was a prime example, making the economy's needs paramount in judging and reforming education. President Reagan's well-known belief that competition is the best organizing principle for almost any collective endeavor is another such example, and critics have attributed a similar outlook to President Bush.

Such an orientation is surely familiar, but perhaps two illustrations will suggest just how it can govern a conception of educational purpose and organization. The first comes from a sheet detailing the U.S. Chamber of Commerce position on "Choice in Education" (1991). The first item reads: "Incorporating competitive forces into our nation's schools can lead to a higher caliber work force and increase productivity and economic growth."

A second example comes from a Select Committee on Educational Reform named by Arizona's business community. Its report, *Better Schools for Arizona* (1990), suggests the extent of the guidance the business/market analogy can yield in recommending school structure. Although the report backs school-based management as well as choice, it qualifies its recommendation for the former this way:

> We take exception to one practice prevalent in school-based management—giving parents who serve on site councils equal participation in making educational decisions . . . we would not let customers set our budget, determine our manufacturing or service-delivery processes, or determine which employees we should hire—and we don't think the schools should either. (p. 15)

These examples suggest an economics-driven perspective in that economic concerns supply the ends and means of schooling and its operation. But there is a separate, third sense in which some perspectives on educational choice appear to be economics-driven: It consists of the acceptance of the basic concepts of the discipline of economics as a guide to understanding and perceiving human affairs. Thus some have applied those concepts to interpret individual human motivation, and some have applied it to interpret the behavior of the role takers who operate organizations and institutions. Accordingly, some attribute public schools' shortcomings to their noncompetitive, monopolistic, and no-incentives status and look to market solutions to cure these ills (e.g., Kearns & Doyle, 1988; Kolderie, 1985a, 1985b).

Others appear simply not to have considered the appropriateness of treating school choice in market terms rather than placing it within an alternative theoretical framework. This seems a strong tendency for a number of scholars. For example, even in a work subtitled "The Theory of Choice and Control in American Education," the question of the aptness of the market analogy to understanding school choice goes unraised (Clune & Witte, 1990). Not all of the authors employ the analogy, but all who do use it without examination or question—despite the fact that challenges have been brought to such an "economization" of schools in particular and of other institutions as well (see, e.g., Callahan, 1962; Etzioni, 1988; Garner & Hannaway, 1982).

Policy-Driven Choice Initiatives

A third sort of sponsorship has come as choice has been selected to implement major policy directions. Through the 1960s and much of the 1970s, equity was a primary commitment of national domestic policy. Choice early became a way to pursue equity with respect to school finance. In *Private Wealth and Public Education*, Coons, Clune, and Sugarman (1970) argued that, as a matter of constitutional principle, the quality of education offered in a particular school or district must not vary from that of other schools within the state as a consequence of differences in wealth. The authors spoke, too, not only of district-to-district equity but of family-to-family equity. Coons and Sugarman (1978) subsequently elaborated their "family power equalizing plan" designed to enable families to choose both the school their children would attend and the amount of tuition assistance they would receive. Families would receive vouchers to purchase education from private or public schools. The vouchers were to vary in amount, depending on the school's tuition, the family's income level, and the family's willingness to invest in education (with taxes owed varying according to all three factors).

The voucher idea lacked sufficient political viability, even when linked to equity; but it early became clear that the choice arrangement well served equity interests of a different sort. It was a politically advantageous response to school desegregation orders—advantageous in the sense that it was almost universally preferred to the forced busing otherwise imposed. Thus the magnet school monies made available by the federal government subsequent to 1976 have offered incentives and assistance to the development of choice. The purpose of the new arrangement was made quite explicit by then Assistant Secretary of Education Mary Berry. She told reporters that magnet school support was a civil rights matter, not a school improvement initiative—and indeed that there was no evidence of the educational effectiveness of magnet schools (Middleton, 1977).

Yet, in the interval, there had been efforts to yoke the choice arrangement to the orienting policy commitment that succeeded equity: that of excellence. The State of Massachusetts provides a good illustration of how choice was seen to fit both purposes sufficiently to be selected as the major instrument for implementing both. Charles Glenn, the former director of the state's Bureau of Educational Equity, used the influence of his office to urge choice as a primary means of school desegregation and, subsequently, as a major route to school improvement. Glenn believed choice the most effective means yet found for "breaking the link between residence and access to educational opportunities" (1990, p. 156). In oral testimony to the Hearings of the National Governors' Association in 1985, he also espoused choice as "our most powerful single force for improving education".

Choice has been brought to bear by others, as well, as an instrument for achieving educational excellence. Policy analyst Ted Kolderie (1985b), for example, has asserted that the opportunities and incentives created by choice are the essential leverage for almost everything sought in the way of change and improvement in the schools" (p. 5).

But the link between choice and excellence has appeared less clear and direct for many than the connection between choice and equity. Choice was obviously a clear means of equalizing the opportunities of families to find a good school—or of enabling a youngster to escape a bad one; but it seems that fewer have been able to find it a means for improving the quality of schools. Thus, as national focus shifted to replace equity with excellence as the major target of domestic policy, interest in choice was initially eclipsed by a preoccupation with curriculum, standards, and teacher qualifications. Although the interest in choice certainly revived, with some form of choice legislation now in effect in more than half the states (Consortium for Policy Research in Education, 1991), that legislation far more typically is geared toward enabling individuals to find better or more appropriate schools than toward improving school quality or excellence. And when a recent move in Congress sought to make magnet school monies available in the interests of enhancing school excellence apart from desegregation purposes, it could not muster sufficient support to pass.

Governance-Driven Choice

A governance-oriented case has been part of the choice discussion throughout the past several decades, advanced first by libertarians, then fueled by populist sentiments, and more recently taken up by new sources.

The libertarian case for choice rests on the desire to remove education from the arena of collective decision and return its control to individuals. John Stuart Mill has often been quoted to express the risks to freedom of public schools. Mill (1859) was highly dubious about such schools, concluding that "an education established and controlled by the State should only exist, if it exists at all, as one among many competing experiments." His fears about the coercive potential of such schools have been mirrored by those currently recommending school choice in the interests of restoring freedom to individual families. Placing schooling under market control in preference to political control is perhaps one of the most assured routes to such a goal. Accordingly, economist Milton Friedman "put Mill's analysis into modern economic dress" (Coons & Sugarman, 1978, p. 20) and recommended that all youngsters receive vouchers spendable in any state-approved school, public or private (Friedman, 1962).

Not all libertarian arguments move in the direction economists take them, however. Stephen Arons, for example, is disposed to supporting the choice position in legal and political terms rather than in those of economics. For example, "The majoritarian assumption transformed the public schools into a battleground for determining public orthodoxy" (Arons, 1982, pp. 24-25). "By requiring that the majority decide how all children should be socialized we in effect require that people contest the most intractable issues of individual conscience" (p. 29). "The current structure of education in the United States is broadly inconsistent with the values advanced by the First Amendment" (p. 30).

But not all governance-oriented choice advocates have been libertarians. Some came to the choice idea as parents' rights advocates who asked why it was necessary that school assignment be determined by officials. The 1960s revolt against urban school governance highlighted the conflicting interests of families and school officials; and the later failure of school advisory councils to empower parents very significantly underscored the difficulty of extending not just voice, but influence, to parents. It is not surprising then that a demand for the power to choose and to reject a school occurred to some as a solution.

But there were other, somewhat different versions of the governance-oriented case. For instance, some made much of accountability, suggesting that schools where families could "vote with their feet" were accountable to their constituents in ways schools cannot be when families constitute a captive audience. The resulting accountability to families as well as to bureaucratic superordinates was claimed to constitute a significant modification in school governance.

Choice was also argued as a way to restore a more appropriate balance of power between families and schools, on the grounds that our traditional commitment to a division of powers, and to checks and balances, called for a restoration of authority to families (Raywid, 1987). This was a case for changing school governance to render it more democratic by readjusting the power balance. A more recent governance-driven choice proposal, in contrast, identifies democratic governance as the problem rather than the solution. This is the conclusion of John Chubb and Terry Moe (1990), who have argued that school governance must change radically because (a) democracy makes bureaucracy inevitable and (b) the democratic governance of public education means the external imposition of values on schools—values that have been negotiated and compromised. Thus Chubb and Moe call for a radically redefined "public education" in which many schools, not just publicly operated ones, can become public schools—and thus the recipients of public support. According to their proposal, each public school would be expected to meet only very minimal, largely non-instruction-related requirements (e.g., information requirements, nondiscrimination laws), and each would be governed according to its own, self-chosen structure.

The Chubb and Moe (1990) book, *Politics, Markets, and America's Schools,* has brought high visibility to the governance-oriented discussion of choice. Although the authors' proposal probably has little chance, it seems to have paved the way for a number of other suggestions now also being discussed. Most prominent, and perhaps most politically viable among them, is the proposal that the power to create and operate public schools be extended and multiplied. Instead of limiting public schools to those operated by school districts, boards would be encouraged, perhaps required, to authorize public schools they do not directly operate.

A still more far-reaching version of this proposal would seek not only to proliferate the types of public schools but also the ways in which they are authorized and created. In most locales, the power to create public schools belongs exclusively to the board of education governing the local school district. What is now proposed is the simultaneous empowerment of multiple levels of government (town or city, county, state, and federal as well as district) plus multiple public agencies (legislatures and city councils, social welfare departments, courts, and so on) to sanction public schools. The consequence would be that, within a given locale, families could select among public schools operated by the board of education, schools enfranchised as public by the board of education but not operated by it, and public schools established by the county, state, and/or federal government.

Both of these proposals would change the face of public education and in fact redefine it. The predictions offered in the final section of this chapter elaborate their change potential. Although the governance-driven argument for choice does not seem to have gained much prominence or much influence until recently, that concern seems currently to be figuring quite heavily in the choice discussion.

Selected Logical and Sociological Features of the Discussion

The choice discussion—or discussions—have now been going on fairly steadily for almost 25 years. A broad look at these four rather distinct sets of dialogues yields some interesting conclusions. In the first place, they continue to occur in considerable isolation from one another. It seems fairly common for choice advocates and analysts to combine two thrusts—for example, recall Charles Glenn's education- and policy-driven concerns—but more than two are rare and many seem to come to the choice discussion inspired by a single concern, whether it is to improve schools, desegregate them, force them to compete, or revise the way they are governed.

Predictably, the four main positions from which choice is argued disagree extensively as to what kind of choice is desirable, enough so as to prevent collaboration or even compromise among at least some advocates—such as between those who urge choice in the interests of equity and those who do so in the interests of privatization, or between the educator advocates who hold that the deliberate cultivation of diversity is essential to making a choice system work and the economics-driven advocates who hold that open enrollment yields competition and that's all that is necessary. Accordingly, choice is clearly not one policy or proposal, it is far more like a dozen proposals, among which the differences are no trivial matter but often indicative of the crux of what is sought.

Indeed, one of the logically interesting things about choice is that it is espoused for contradictory sorts of reasons. Some have urged it in the interests of establishing selective schools that would eliminate indifferent or poor or minority students, while others insist that choice is the best hope for exactly these neediest students. Some espouse choice in the interests of saving public education while others espouse different applications of the idea in the interests of subverting it.

The question of who espouses choice reveals some interesting contrasts, pitting educators against the public and dividing educators among themselves. The backing of the business community and of many political figures for choice is well known. It is interesting that, at the national level, choice has been a Republican party proposal, while, at the state level, choice initiatives have at least as often been successfully spearheaded by Democratic governors. General public support for the choice idea seems extensive. A 1989 poll found more agreement about the desirability of choice than about any other educational feature (Elam & Gallup, 1989). The following year (Elam, 1990), 62% of those interviewed supported the right of people to select the public school their children attend. Support among the parents of public school children was even higher: 65%. Educators who have experienced the choice arrangement often exhibit high degrees of support for it—sometimes near-unanimous affirmation (Raywid, 1989). But those who have not experienced the arrangement may be almost as unanimous in their opposition to it. Administrators too seem generally cool to the choice idea, although there appear some slight differences among them, with principals somewhat more receptive to choice than superintendents (Feistritzer, 1989).

One of the most interesting features of the choice debate involves the position of researchers on the matter. The question arises in connection with the issue of the research base for choice. A recent publication of the Association for Supervision and Curriculum Development (1990) argues that there is virtually no research base. At the 1991 American Educational Research Association (AERA) meeting, it appeared striking how many presenters in the several sessions on choice began their presentations with a statement similar to this one: "Of course, there is very little empirical research in support of choice." Now, whether one agrees with that claim or not, the frequency with which it was asserted was both marked and unusual. The AERA meeting included even more sessions devoted to school-based management than to choice—but there were no parallel introductory statements about the lack of evidence related to school-based management. The difference seems noteworthy, because there is considerably less evidence about this newer, parallel restructuring strategy than about choice. Furthermore, the evidence that is available on school-based management seems largely negative (Malen, Ogawa, & Kranz, 1990).

Coming Next for Choice

It seems likely that the choice movement will remain a prominent part of the educational policy scene: 29 states now have some sort of choice provision (Consortium for Policy Research in Education, 1991). Some are permitting cross-district choice, some are encouraging within-district choice, and some have specified choice only for specific populations (e.g., high school students desiring to attend classes in colleges and universities, students who have not succeeded in the schools to which they have been assigned). Even without the substantial support emanating from the White House, it is doubtful that the idea would die. Support sources appear too broad and substantial and, even should they dwindle, it could prove politically difficult to remove such a widely discussed prerogative after it has been claimed and exercised.

The education-oriented case for choice is likely to be strengthened and expanded. As the emergence of an increasing number and variety of choice systems permits the amassing of systematic evidence regarding them, the objection about a lack of evidence may be met. The continuing demand for adequate programs for the most challenging students is likely to continue to stimulate the number and variety of choice programs. And the continuing preoccupation of the business community with education is likely to sustain pressures for choice, particularly in the cities.

New sponsorship and espousal patterns for the choice arrangement may also emerge. As has been suggested, for political groups and figures to oppose something that 72% of the people under 30, 70% of the people of color, and 68% of the people in big cities favor is not very wise politics (Olson, 1991). Particularly because these are populations to which the Democratic party has sought to appeal, it may be rethinking the choice question. It is early yet to tell just what sort of difference the Democratic Leadership Council's decision to back choice ("Across the Nation," 1991) may make in the idea's political fortunes. Up to this point, the appeal of choice to the libertarian minded and to more substantively oriented conservatives has sometimes seemed stronger. At least nationally, choice has been more closely linked to the Republican than to the Democratic party, and advocates within the Republican party have appeared to be interested primarily in either an economics-driven or a governance-driven form of choice rather than in types more educationally oriented or calculated to serve other particular policy interests. Democratic espousal could bring more choice proposals with an equity orientation or more that are specifically designed to improve the quality of urban or other weak schools. Thus Democratic party acceptance of the choice idea could lead to new policy initiatives linking some sort of choice arrangement with purposes both equity oriented and excellence oriented.

Otherwise, probably what mainly lies immediately ahead in the choice movement is an increasing prominence for the governance-oriented position. Indeed, the current preoccupation of education reformers and restructurers with school governance may make the choice idea considerably more prominent than it has been to date. But it may also mean a new sort of choice with a new focus. The choice idea is certainly emerging now under new aegis, with an emphasis on "supply-side choice" rather than on the "demand-side choice" that has dominated the discussion to date. The latter refers to the options available from the consumer's perspective, the former to the options from the producer's perspective.

As applied a couple of years ago, the term *supply-side choice* referred to diversified schools and programs among which *teachers* could choose. The context in which it arose seemed to suggest that supply-side choice had to be considered in order to make a choice system work: If consumers are to have a range of options to select among, then options—or the permission to create them—must be encouraged by those controlling suppliers (Elmore, 1986) Today, the referent of the term *supply-side choice* has shifted. The term appears to address the matter of which institutions or agencies shall provide public education and to what governing bodies they shall report. In the course of this metamorphosis, an idea initially introduced in the context of how to make a choice system function adequately is now an idea about how to end run the Establishment—or, in other words, an idea about redesigning the governance and control of education.

It is happening this way. Open-enrollment arrangements that now exist in a number of states have not led to the diversification among schools that market loyalists predicted, and that their case requires. This led to the question of what would be necessary to produce such diversity. The answer proposed by analyst Ted Kolderie —and that Education Secretary Alexander, among others, has adopted—is that "the exclusive franchise" must be broken (Kolderie, 1990). To date, this has led to two kinds of thinking and developments. The first has to do with breaking the hitherto "exclusive franchise" held by teachers and building administrators hired by a school district. To break this sort of "exclusive franchise" is, then, to let people operate public schools and educational programs otherwise than through having been hired by the district.

The second sort of "exclusive franchise" that might be revoked is that held by school district officials—that is, school boards and superintendents. Thus other institutions and agencies might also be enfranchised to authorize, operate, and supervise public schools within a district, side by side with those the district administers.

Currently, under the banner of "breaking the exclusive franchise," two types of situations are occurring: (a) School districts are increasingly sponsoring the operation of schools and educational services supplied by multiple sources, and (b) states are beginning to talk about the sponsorship of public schools by entities other than school districts.

Actually, the first idea is not so radical, because there are numerous examples now where boards have made a variety of contractual arrangements for purchasing services from groups outside their employ. This has long been the case with respect to the provision of auxiliary services such as school buses and custodial and cafeteria services. But it is also the case with respect to the provision of education for special groups and in relation to particular sorts of instruction. For instance, New York City has long contracted with private providers for programs for particular severely handicapped populations and, in Washington State, some districts have for several years been sending their most challenging students to privately owned "education clinics." Elsewhere, commercial firms are supplying special reading and study skills instruction in public high schools and foreign language instruction in elementary schools (Walsh, 1989). In Dade County, Florida, a Minnesota-based, commercial corporation is running a school, having won a district-sponsored competition to launch an innovative new program (Holmes, 1990). And in Chelsea, Massachusetts, the school board signed a 10-year contract with Boston University to operate its schools (Foster, 1991). The widely publicized Chelsea agreement, like the other arrangements identified, are generally not linked to choice—that is, they do not create simultaneous *multiple* suppliers among which families may choose. But they have substantially broadened the precedent and the base for privatization—through school board contracting with private suppliers for educational services for public schools.

There is, then, little strikingly new about the prospect of public schools contracting for services or about obtaining some instructional services from outside suppliers while providing others through system employees. What is now being proposed, however, is that we ought to end the monopoly, or "exclusive franchise" enjoyed by school district officials and their employees, and deliberately cultivate the provision of multiple sets of services existing side by side and open to selection.

The second move to "break the exclusive franchise" might well prove considerably more far reaching in its revision of educational governance. Policy analyst Ted Kolderie (1990, p. 1), who has pioneered the "ending the exclusive" notion, summarizes it this way: "In order to create new public schools, and ultimately a new system of public education, the states would simply withdraw the local districts' exclusive franchise to own and operate public schools."

This would mean that school districts would no longer be in a position to control all public schools within their boundaries or even to decide what public schools may operate there. They could control their own schools, but other public schools could be franchised by other authorities to operate side by side with the district's schools. Such a change could happen in a number of ways. The simplest is through direct state chartering of schools with varied sponsors—for example, the state itself might operate some schools, or it might give charters to do so to colleges and universities, to educator groups and associations, or to commercial organizations. If so, local district officials could no longer control or limit the number and variety of public school programs offered within a particular area. The intent is to end exclusive control by any single body. The method is extending the franchise to operate schools to new groups or extending the *right* to enfranchise public schools to multiple groups.

Actually, even this idea is not as remote from current practice as it may first appear. The so-called Governor's Schools introduced several years ago represent state-run schools operating in a number of states. These are typically magnet schools offering special programs to a highly selective group of students, but they have nonetheless introduced a new genre of state-operated schools. Kolderie's idea is that the state might open the opportunity to sponsor these or other types of programs to other organizations as well, including colleges and universities.

In effect, this is what Britain's Education Reform Act of 1988 provided, but it did so in ways somewhat different than what is being talked about in this country. The act sought to end the exclusive franchise held by local education authorities, equivalent to our districts, by enabling individual schools to "opt out" of control by the local authority. They were thus enabled to become autonomous while yet remaining publicly funded institutions. This has proved tantamount to an arrangement in which private schools are publicly funded, because the "opting out" schools become, in effect, independent, self-governing institutions (Adler, Petch, & Tweedie, 1989). Kolderie's plan differs in leaving a district's set of existing schools intact, affecting only the auspices for launching new schools. It also keeps the newly enfranchised public schools more squarely in the public sector by requiring them to remain accountable to the franchising body for the educational outcomes they produce.

Thus the possibilities of Kolderie's ideas for drastically altering the face of school governance are considerable. To date, attempts to implement them have consisted primarily of proposals that the state (as well as districts) "charter" individual public schools as independent organizations to be held publicly accountable only through outcomes rather than by public operation and regulation. Such a bill was passed by the Minnesota legislature in 1991, but only after modifications limiting the number of schools that can be chartered and limiting the chartering agency to school districts. But the broader version discussed here will doubtless be introduced again, both in Minnesota and elsewhere. Meanwhile, although it is early to tell, President Bush's proposal that Congress fund the creation of 535 "New American Schools"—one in each congressional district—looks as though it could be intended at least in part to accomplish similar purposes. It would certainly increase and diversify the sponsorship, authorization, and control of public schooling, with highly visible and much touted schools having been chartered not in school districts but in congressional districts, and possibly not by school districts but by states, or even perhaps by the federal government.

The widespread determination to restructure school governance means that the governance-inspired branch of the choice movement is likely to be attracting a lot of attention in years to come. Not all governance-refashioning proposals involve choice, of course—school-based management makes choice an afterthought when it is included at all. And a proposal by Philip Schlechty (1991) that communities should periodically decide whether to leave their schools in the hands of district officials, or to competitively award extended contracts for school operation, makes no provisions for choice at all. But, as Kolderie's proposal suggests, the idea of choice can be brought to bear in enormously altering current control structures and balances in American public education. I suspect that over the next decade we are likely to be hearing more of plans for harnessing it to do so. Such possibilities are likely to dominate the choice discussion, even though they will not totally monopolize it.

References

Across the nation. (1991, May 22). Democratic group backs parental choice in school-reform plan. *Education Week*, p. 2.

Adler, M., Petch, A., & Tweedie, J. (1989). *Parental choice and educational policy*. Edinburgh: Edinburgh University Press.

Arons, S. (1982). Educational choice: Unanswered question in the American experience. In M. E. Manley-Casimir (Ed.), *Family choice in schooling* (pp. 23-31). Lexington, MA: Lexington.

Association for Supervision and Curriculum Development. (1990). *Public schools of choice*. Alexandria, VA: Author.

Bloom, V. (1958). *Freedom of choice in education*. New York: Macmillan.

Callahan, R. E. (1962). *Education and the cult of efficiency*. Chicago: University of Chicago Press.

Chubb, J. E., & Moe, T. M. (1990). *Politics, markets, and America's schools*. Washington, DC: Brookings Institution.

Clune, W. H., & Witte, J. F. (1990). *Choice and control in American education: Vol. 1. The theory of choice and control in American education*. London: Falmer.

Consortium for Policy Research in Education. (1991). *School choice legislation: A survey of the states*. Cambridge, MA: Harvard Graduate School of Education.

Coons, J. E., Clune, W. H., & Sugarman, S. D. (1970). *Private wealth and public education*. Cambridge, MA: Harvard University Press.

Coons, J. E., & Sugarman, S. D. (1978). *Education by choice: The case for family control*. Berkeley: University of California Press.

Elam, S. M. (1990, September). The 22nd Gallup poll of the public's attitudes toward the public schools. *Phi Delta Kappan, 72*(1), 41-53.

Elam, S. M., & Gallup, A. (1989, September). The 21st annual Gallup poll of the public's attitudes toward the public schools. *Phi Delta Kappan, 71*(1), 41-54.

Elmore, R. F. (1986, December). *Choice in public education*. Center for Policy Research in Education, Rutgers University, New Brunswick, NJ.

Etzioni, A. (1988). *The moral dimension: Toward a new economics*. New York: Free Press.

Fantini, M. (1973). *Public schools of choice*. New York: Simon & Schuster.

Feistritzer, E. (1989). *Profile of school board presidents in the United States*. Washington, DC: National Center for Education Information.

Foster, C. (1991, May 6). Boston University's attempt to rescue a city's schools falters. *Christian Science Monitor*, p. 9.

Friedman, M. (1962). *Capitalism and freedom*. Chicago: University of Chicago Press.

Garner, W. T., & Hannaway, J. (1982). Private schools: The client connection. In M. E. Manley-Casimir (Ed.), *Family choice in schooling* (pp. 119-133). Lexington, MA: Lexington.

Glenn, C. L. (1985, December 16). [Testimony to the National Governors' Association hearings on choice, Denver].

Glenn, C. L. (1990). *Perestroika* for American education. In W. Firestone & C. Richards (Eds.), *Rethinking effective schools* (pp. 154-168). Englewood Cliffs, NJ: Prentice-Hall.

Graubard, A. (1972). *Free the children: Radical reform and the free school movement.* New York: Random House.

Holmes, S. (1990, December 7). In Florida, a private company will operate a public school. *New York Times*, pp. A1 ff.

Kearns, D. T., & Doyle, D. P. (1988). *Winning the brain race: A bold plan to make our schools competitive.* San Francisco: Institute for Contemporary Studies.

Kolderie, T. (1985a, March). *Competition as a strategy for public school improvement.* Unpublished memo, Humphrey Institute, University of Minnesota.

Kolderie, T. (1985b, July). *School improvement and the dynamics of choice.* Unpublished memo, Humphrey Institute, University of Minnesota.

Kolderie, T. (1990). *Beyond choice to new public schools: Withdrawing the exclusive franchise in public education.* Washington, DC: Progressive Policy Institute.

Malen, B., Ogawa, R. T., & Kranz, J. (1990). What do we know about school-based management? A case study of the literature—a call for research. In W. H. Clune & J. Witte (Eds.), *Choice and control in American education: Vol. 2. The practice of choice, decentralization and school restructuring* (pp. 289-342). London: Falmer.

Middleton, L. (1977, July S). Mary F. Berry of HEW on education. *Washington Star.*

Mill, J. S. (1859). *On liberty.* London: J. W. Parker.

Nathan, J. (1984). *Free to teach: Achieving equity and excellence in schools.* Minneapolis: Harper & Row-Winston.

National Commission on Excellence in Education. (1983). *A nation at risk: The imperative for educational reform.* Washington, DC: Government Printing Office.

Olson, L. (1991, April). Voucher volcano. *Church & State*, pp. 7-16.

Raywid, M. A. (1987). Public choice, yes; vouchers, no! *Phi Delta Kappan*, 68(10), 762-769.

Raywid, M. A. (1989). The mounting case for schools of choice. In J. Nathan (Ed.), *Public schools by choice: Expanding opportunities for parents, students, and teachers* (pp. 13-40). Minneapolis: Free Spirit.

Schlechty, P. C. (1991, April 10). Education services as a "regulated monopoly." *Education Week,* pp. 36 ff.

Select Committee on Educational Reform. (1990, November). *Better schools for Arizona.* Phoenix: Arizona Business Leadership for Education.

Tyack, D. B. (1974). *The one best system: A history of American urban education.* Cambridge, MA: Harvard University Press.

U.S. Chamber of Commerce. (1991, January). Choice in education. *Media Sheet.*

Walsh, M. (1989, June 7). Private education firms discovering a lucrative market in public schools. *Education Week,* p. 7.

2

Minerva and the Market: The Sources of the Movement for School Choice

KEVIN J. DOUGHERTY

LIZABETH SOSTRE

The now decade-long surge of reform in education has recently taken a new direction. The first and second waves of reforms, which concentrated on imposing higher standards on students and teachers and giving teachers greater professional autonomy, have been joined by a third wave, which centers on expanding the power of parents to choose which schools their children attend. The most visible

AUTHORS' NOTE: This chapter previously appeared in *Educational Policy* (in June 1992); copyright © 1992 by Corwin Press. We share equally in the creation of this chapter. We wish to thank Amy Stuart Wells, Beth Stevens, and the editors and referees of *Educational Policy* for their comments.

manifestation of this new wave has been President Bush's April 1991 call for a "revolution" in schooling in which parents would be allowed to choose among "all schools that serve the public and are accountable to public authority, regardless of who runs them" (Miller, 1991a, p. 24). But the movement for school choice has not been just a call to arms. It has begun to be implemented nationwide. A host of cities now allow students to move more or less freely across the school districts, regardless of attendance zones (Clune & Witte, 1990, chaps. 1, 6; Snider, 1987, pp. C6, 9, 16, 1988a). At least 10 states have passed legislation allowing parents to choose among public schools (Schmidt, 1991; Snider, 1990d, pp. 26, 33). And Wisconsin has enacted state aid for students to attend private schools (Olson, 1990d; Snider, 1990a, 1990b, 1990c).

The rapid success of the movement for school choice is surprising because this is not the first time the idea of parental choice has been raised. It was first proposed by Milton Friedman (1955), and it attracted some attention in the late 1960s and early 1970s but failed to ignite any major interest until recently.

This chapter examines why the idea of school choice has been resurrected in the 1980s and 1990s. We will argue that this new effort owes its strength both to renewed interest among conservatives beginning in the late 1970s and to unexpected changes in sentiments toward public schooling among liberal policy scholars, urban educators, black and white parents, and state governors. We will also argue that this wide political base has also made the movement for school choice vulnerable to reverse. The movement may be shattered by the deep fissures it carries within it, especially the division between those who favor government support for private school choice and those for whom only public school choice is acceptable.

In analyzing the sources of the movement for school choice, we will draw on the "state relative autonomy" approach that has arisen to challenge the pluralist and instrumentalist Marxist theories of political power. Despite their differences, both theories base public policy in the demands of private interest groups and view government as a neutral register of the weight and direction of interest group pressure. State relative autonomy theory, however, demonstrates that government officials act on the basis not just of pressure from society but also of the autonomous interests and values of government officials themselves (Block, 1987; Dougherty, 1988, 1991, 1992; Evans, Rueschemeyer, & Skocpol, 1985).[1]

But, to reach its full promise, state relative autonomy theory needs to be coupled with a more sophisticated theory of decision making than it currently uses. Like most other theories of political influence, it implicitly assumes the classical model of rational choice in which problems are clearly understood, potential solutions are carefully researched, and the final solution is chosen on the basis of the optimum balance of benefits and costs. But, as James March and his colleagues have been demonstrating over the last 30 years, many decision-making processes do not adhere to such a tidy model. Instead, decisions often arise out of a "garbage can" process in which problems are not clearly understood, solutions are chosen less because they are optimal than because they are readily at hand, and the same policy might appeal to various actors for very different, and even conflicting, reasons (Cohen, March, & Olsen, 1972; March & Olsen, 1989). Hence, to make the best use of state relative autonomy theory, we will couple it with the insights provided by the theory of "garbage can" decision making.

The Rebirth of the Movement for School Choice

The current idea of school choice can be traced at least as far back as 1955, when Milton Friedman, the well-known conservative economist, broached the idea of vouchers for schooling. Portraying public schooling as a nationalized industry, Friedman (1955, p. 127, 1962, 1975) argued that government should disestablish it by giving parents vouchers redeemable for educational services at private educational institutions. Friedman's idea enjoyed a brief flurry of interest in the late 1960s and early 1970s (Jencks, 1970), but it died without any significant action.

Beginning in the late 1970s, however, several factors came together to revive interest in school choice. First, school choice became a major demand of several conservative foundations and policy groups rather than the isolated proposal of one intellectual. With the conservative flood tide of the 1980s, this assured that choice would attract attention. But, if it were to become a serious policy contender, choice had to escape the conservative ideological ghetto, and it did. Many liberal policy scholars came to view school choice as an antidote to hidebound, bureaucratized schools. Local educators introduced choice plans to keep white children in urban public schools and later to spur those schools to improve. White, middle-class parents

—and, surprisingly, many black parents—demanded choice either to get access to the islands of excellence within the public school system or to escape the system entirely. Meanwhile, driven by the desperate finances of the parochial system, the Catholic church leaped into the movement, hoping choice would bring its schools more refugees from the public schools. Finally, state governors took up the banner of school choice, not just because it was being demanded by many parents but also because it accorded with the governors' own values and interests. Although arising for different reasons, these separate factors have combined to powerfully propel the movement for school choice.

Business-Oriented Conservatives Rediscover School Choice

School choice became a favorite concern among conservatives in the late 1970s and early 1980s under the rubric of tuition tax credits. To encourage more use of private schooling, conservative policy organizations such as the Heritage Foundation called for legislation allowing private school tuition to be credited against federal income taxes. Conservatives hoped expanded private schooling would help dismantle government and unleash economic growth. Cheered on by business, conservatives increasingly argued during the 1970s that the growth of government over the last few decades fundamentally undercut economic growth. Rising expenditures meant higher taxes on corporations and the upper class, leaving less money for investment. Rising expenditures for social programs also weakened, they argued, workers' incentive to work hard, especially at low wages. The solution was to "privatize" the state by having the private sector take over government services.[2] Because public schools are one of the central agencies of government, conservatives particularly targeted them for retrenchment (Gardner, 1985; Heatherly, 1991; Sowell, 1981). In the case of the religiously oriented New Right, distaste for public schooling was also motivated by cultural animus. New Right conservatives believed that public schools undermined moral values by failing to have prayer in the schools and by promoting "value free" education. They also failed to prepare children adequately by offering curricular "frills" that detract from the "basics" of mathematics, science, English, and U.S. history (Gardner, 1985, pp. 79-83).

Influenced by these conservative ideas, various business organizations have advocated school choice in Minnesota, Indiana,

Louisiana, and California (Mazzoni & Sullivan, 1986; Olson, 1987, 1991b; Weisman, 1991). For example, the Minnesota Business Partnership in 1984 unveiled an influential plan for reforming education that, among other planks, called for state vouchers that would allow students to choose among public and private schools (Mazzoni & Sullivan, 1986, pp. 190-191).[3]

But it is at the national level that conservatives have made their most dramatic push for school choice. Between 1982 and 1984, the Reagan administration repeatedly submitted legislation to Congress providing for federal tax credits to parents paying private school tuition (Toch, 1991, p. 247). Unfortunately for conservatives, this legislation aroused passionate opposition and failed to pass. Conservatives found that their new fervor for school choice was enough to put it on the political agenda but not enough to get it passed. If it was to be made into law, school choice had to find a wider circle of advocates.

Realizing this, conservatives decided to repackage school choice in a form that its opponents might find more palatable or at least harder to oppose. In the first installment of this new campaign, the Reagan administration introduced a bill to provide *vouchers* to low-income youth to purchase remedial education at whatever school, public or private, they would like (Cooper, 1988, pp. 176-178; Crawford, 1986; Hertling, 1985; Toch, 1991, p. 246). This proposal neatly neutralized one of the most frequent objections to tuition tax credits: that they only really served the interests of those wealthy enough to have substantial income tax bills. As a result, conservative proposals for school choice began to lose the elitist hue they had in many liberals' eyes.

George Bush has also contributed to this effort to refashion parental choice by soft-pedaling private school choice and instead concentrating initially on public school choice. According to then White House Chief of Staff John Sununu, Bush deliberately framed his initial call for parental choice in terms of public school choice in order to make the general idea of choice palatable first before coming out in favor of his ultimate goal: private school choice (Olson, 1991a, p. 10; Walsh, 1991b, p. 1).

This effort to reclothe school choice, so that its conservative parentage might be less obvious, has been successful. By the mid-1980s, school choice began to enjoy unprecedented support by such unlikely groups as liberal policy scholars, urban educators, black parents, and state governors. Furthermore, the teacher associations, while adamantly opposed to private school choice, have had kind things to say about its public school counterpart. But, before we discuss these other supporters of school choice, we should explore in greater detail the reasons the Reagan and Bush administrations advocated it.

Certainly, old-fashioned political pressure played a role. As pluralist and instrumentalist Marxist theory would predict, Reagan and Bush supported parental choice because it was being demanded by key members of their political coalition: namely, business and its conservative ideologues. But state relative autonomy theory warns us that government officials also act on the basis of political ideology and self-interested political calculation. Both Reagan and Bush supported school choice out of a passionate belief that the market is the best regulatory device not only for the economy but also for areas such as education. In addition, personal electoral considerations have motivated Bush's enthusiasm for school choice. This issue has allowed him to make a dramatic proposal in favor of education that redeems his promise to be the "education president" even as he has been unwilling to countenance any great increase in school spending. For an administration that has run on the platform of no new taxes, school choice has the great virtue of revolutionizing education seemingly without requiring any great commitment of additional money. Furthermore, school choice, particularly if it includes private schools, draws a clear political line between the Republican party on the one hand and the Democratic party and its strong supporters among the educational associations on the other. Because liberal Democrats and the educational associations are opposed to private school choice (see below), this issue allows the Republicans to tag the Democrats as vassals of the "education establishment" and its "special interests." Finally, parental choice cuts across ideological boundaries in a way that fundamentally undermines the Democrats' New Deal coalition. Bush staffers have noted with great interest how supportive liberal policy scholars, black parents, and Catholic prelates have been of school choice (Olson, 1991a, p. 10).

Liberal Policy Scholars

One of the greatest coups for the conservative advocates of school choice has been the conversion of several liberal policy scholars to the faith that choice is the perfect panacea for the ills of public schooling.[4] John Chubb and Terry Moe have been perhaps the most notable converts. Located at the moderately liberal Brookings Institution, long a fountainhead for Democratic party policy proposals, they have made school choice the core of their program for reforming public schooling. In *Politics, Markets, and America's Schools* (1990), they advocate a shift in school governance from "democratic politics" to "the marketplace," arguing that the "most important prerequuisite for the emergence of effective school characteristics is school autonomy, especially from bureaucratic influence" (Chubb & Moe, 1990, pp. 23, 27). But, while the most noted, Chubb and Moe have been only two of several liberal policy analysts who have lost faith in government's ability to deliver quality education. Other liberal advocates of school choice include John Coons and Stephen Sugarman (Coons, 1979, 1985; Coons & Sugarman, 1983, 1990-1991), Joe Nathan (1983, 1987, 1989), and Mary Anne Raywid (1987, 1990). Although differing and even conflicting in their vision of parental choice, they are united in arguing that it can be a mighty engine for saving the American school system.[5]

It was in local and state school politics, however, rather than the airy reaches of the national ideological superstructure, that the choice movement attracted its most surprising disciples, ones who would allow it to decisively shed its conservative husk.

Urban Educators

School choice has a long lineage at the local level. In the 1960s, under pressure from white, middle-class parents, urban educators began to create "alternative" schools that stood in opposition to the "mass production, factory system" of conventional public schooling (Fantini, 1973, p. 14; Raywid, 1985, p. 454; Toch, 1991, p. 255). In the 1970s, alternative schools appeared in a new guise, as "magnet" schools. Districts that had become overwhelmingly peopled by minority students began to use magnet schools to hold, or attract back, the white middle class. Magnet schools resembled alternative schools in that they offered programs that were not part of the standard curriculum, and their catchment areas were districtwide rather than restricted to one attendance zone (Blank, 1990, pp. 78-81; Toch, 1991, pp. 253-255).

By the 1980s, districts began to use alternative schools not just to further racial and class integration but also to improve schools that would remain overwhelmingly working class and minority in student composition (Raywid, 1985, p. 449). Perhaps the most famous has been Community School District Four in the East Harlem section of Manhattan. Beginning in 1982-1983, its junior high schools were broken up into "schools within schools," and students and parents were allowed to choose which ones to attend (Domanico, 1989; Snider, 1987, pp. C10, 15; Toch, 1991, pp. 249-250, 256). Often following the lead of District Four, other school districts began to experiment with districtwide choice for purposes other than just desegregation (Snider, 1987). In New York City itself, Community School Districts Two, Three, and Five launched open-enrollment programs (Sostre, 1991; Toch, 1991, pp. 249, 257). Meanwhile, several other cities have moved to broadly conceived intradistrict choice, including Montclair (New Jersey); Rochester (New York); Boston, Cambridge, and Fall River (Massachusetts); Minneapolis; and Seattle (Snider, 1987, pp. C6, 9, 16, 1988b; Toch, 1991, pp. 249-250, 257; Wells, 1990).

White Parents

For many years, middle-class white parents have been leaving the public schools, but this hemorrhage has accelerated in recent years. It has prompted urban educators to create magnet schools to keep white children in the public schools, but it has also led to demands for even broader school choice. Many parents who want to opt out of the public schools entirely want vouchers that would allow them to more easily pay private school tuition, which has been rising rapidly in recent years. Increasingly, these advocates of private school choice are being joined by other parents who are more loyal to public education but have come to despair about its quality. To resolve this dilemma, they want their children to be able to attend the best school in the district, regardless of attendance zones, rather than being forced to go to an inadequate neighborhood school.

The Black Community

One of the most surprising features of the current choice movement is that many black parents have joined white parents in deserting the public schools. In fact, despite their long-standing loyalty to public schooling, blacks are now even *more* sympathetic to the idea of both public and private choice than are whites.[6]

This sentiment in favor of choice has vented itself politically in dramatic ways. In Detroit, community pressure prompted the black-led city board of education to explore bringing private schools into the public system (Olson, 1991a, p. 10). Meanwhile, in Wisconsin, Annette (Polly) Williams, a black state representative who served as state chair of Jesse Jackson's 1984 and 1988 presidential campaigns, secured the passage of a state law in 1990 that allows up to 1,000 low-income Milwaukee public school students to enroll in private, non-sectarian schools (Snider, 1990a, 1990b, 1990c; Olson, 1990c, 1990d). While a striking departure from blacks' traditionally strong support for the public schools, her bill had solid support among all the black Milwaukee aldermen, one of three black school board members, and all the black county supervisors (Olson, 1990c, p. 15).

This interest in school choice reflects in part conservatives' successful repackaging of school choice so that it does not carry the elitist hue of tuition tax credits. But the shift in black sentiment also reflects the changing political thinking of the black community. Black advocates of school choice know how important effective schooling is to black children's future, but they have become pessimistic about the prospects for reforming the public schools using conventional devices (Olson, 1990a, 1990c, pp. 15, 1991a, p. 10). Increasingly, they feel that extraordinary measures have to be used. And one of these is the market. Lawrence Patrick, president of the Detroit School Board, argues: "If we stiffen the competition by offering an opportunity where private schools are able to compete for students who are now attending public schools, it means that our existing schools are going to have to do a much better job" (Olson, 1991a, p. 10).

An element of angry populism also enters into the picture. Arguing that "white parents have been setting up elitist schools anyway," Polly Williams wants to give poor black parents the same freedom white parents now have to choose private schooling (Olson, 1990a, p. 5). This desire is closely tied to a preference for all-black institutions, a theme long associated with the powerful current of cultural nationalism that has alternated with the integrationist stream in black politics and culture. That cultural nationalism is rising in the black community is evidenced by the growing demand today for all-black and often Afro-centric schools, especially for males, whom many blacks view as an "endangered species."[7] Nationally, it is estimated that there are at least 284 "independent neighborhood schools" in which the enrollment is almost entirely African American. In fact, several such academies are participating in the Milwaukee private school voucher program (Walsh, 1991a).

The Catholic Church

Black and white parents seeking to opt out of the public schools have found an eager ally in the Catholic church. After remaining silent on the idea in the 1950s and 1960s, the church has emerged as a very strong supporter of school choice. In the late 1970s and early 1980s, the church strongly lobbied for tuition tax credits. In June 1989 and November 1991, Catholic educators met with President Bush to urge that private schools be included in any discussions about choice (Olson, 1991a, p. 10; Walsh, 1991b, p. 1, 1991c). And, in November 1990, the Catholic bishops voted to set up a national office to guide state and diocesan Catholic groups on the issue of choice and to establish a national Catholic parents' organization to lobby on the issue (Walsh, 1991b, p. 16).

The Catholic church's enthusiasm for school choice stems from the dire financial straits of the parochial school system. Many parochial schools have closed and many more are threatened with extinction (Olson, 1991a, p. 10; Sullivan, 1991). Government vouchers that would cut the price for public school students to go to Catholic schools would be a blessing. The fact that this might bring Catholic schools many low-income or minority children does not daunt Catholic educators because many parochial schools already serve disadvantaged populations (Walsh, 1991b, p. 16).

State Governors

In 1986, in its first major pronouncement ever on education, the National Governors' Association announced that governors were very interested in public school choice: "America is a land of choices . . . . Thus, it is ironic that . . . there is so little choice in the public school system. . . . [We recommend permitting] families to select from among . . . public schools in their state . . . with tax funds following the students" (National Governors' Association, 1986, pp. 12-13). This gubernatorial support has been no mere lip service. Governors have actively pursued school choice legislation in states such as Minnesota, Wisconsin, Washington, and Colorado. In Minnesota, Democratic Governor Rudy Perpich, a member of the NGA's Task Force on Parental Involvement and Choice, in January 1985 called for allowing elementary and secondary students to go to any public school statewide and high school juniors and seniors to take college courses at public expense. Despite great controversy, Perpich succeeded in getting choice legislation passed in 1985 and 1988 (Mazzoni & Sullivan, 1986, pp. 190-192; Nathan, 1987, pp. 750-751, 1989, p. 306; Toch, 1991, pp. 250-252). In Wisconsin, Republican Governor Tommy Thompson strongly supported Polly Williams's bill providing private school vouchers for low-income Milwaukee children (Donnelly, 1990, p. 1; Schmidt, 1990, p. 1; Viadero, 1988). In Washington, Booth Gardiner, a Democrat, made public school choice his "number one" education proposal in 1990 (Viadero, 1990, p. 12). And, in Colorado, Democratic Governor Richard Lamm in 1985 secured the legislature's approval for a "second-chance" voucher pro- gram to allow students who failed in traditional education settings to go to other kinds of public or private schools of their choice (Currence, 1985).

What factors have made governors so supportive of school choice? Certainly, interest group pressure has played a role. Governors are well aware that school choice is politically popular with voters. According to the National Governors' Association (1986, p. 71), "It is clear that many families would like to have more choice among schools. A Gallup Poll found more support than opposition to a program providing choice among public and private schools." Moreover, governors have been mindful of business's interest in school reform, including school choice (Mazzoni & Sullivan, 1986; Wills, 1991).

Still, governors no doubt would have been led to advocate school choice, even in the absence of interest group demands. As elected politicians, governors always seek a good issue on which to run, and education is invariably an attractive issue. As Governor Thomas Kean of New Jersey noted in 1986, "Education is good politics. Nobody is able to run for governor this year without an education agenda in either party" (quoted in Olson, 1986, p. 36). Governors have also been interested in school choice out of an interest in economic growth. The general state of the economy has a major impact on governors' reelection chances, and education is always seen as a means of fostering economic growth. As Lamar Alexander, formerly head of the National Governors' Association and now secretary of education, has noted,

> It's something every family understands at the dinner table. "Is Daddy or is Mommy or will I when I grow up have a good salary, or will the Japanese have all the money?" Now that's pretty basic. The only solution anybody can think of to that right now is better schools. (Olson, 1986, p. 36)

But if governors have their own powerful reasons for being interested in educational reform, why has school choice in particular been so attractive to them? One reason is that it is a dramatic proposal that resonates nicely with the American belief in the market. It is also cheap. Its costs are much less evident than, for example, raising teacher pay or extending the school year, which is a major attraction for governors facing huge deficits and taxpayer anger in the late 1980s and early 1990s (Donnelly, 1990, p. 16; Harp, 1990; Snider, 1987, p. C23). Furthermore, governors have come to believe that school choice may be a more effective way to improve the schools than imposing additional requirements or creating new programs here and there, which was their preferred method in the early 1980s (National Governors' Association, 1986, p. 12; Raywid, 1990, p. 141). As Republican Governor Terry Branstad of Iowa puts it, "Most of the recent reforms have not significantly altered the fundamentals of how students are taught. We need dramatic and fundamental changes in the way we design and structure education if we are to compete globally and achieve economic success" (Olson, 1990b, p. 7). Finally, there is reason to believe that governors seized on school choice as a means to make "dramatic and fundamental changes" not because it was the best among several carefully considered proposals but because it was in the air when they were ready to announce a new program for educational reform. When the National Governors' Association looked in 1986 for striking proposals that it might make for reforming education, it found school choice readily at hand. The Reagan administration and various state business organizations were strongly promoting it. And a well-known advocate of school choice, Joe Nathan, was a major figure on the staff that put together the governors' 1986 report (National Governors' Association, 1986,

p. 169; Snider, 1987, p. C2; Wills, 1991). As theorists of "garbage can" decision making point out, particular solutions are often picked not so much because they are optimal but because they are being promoted by some actor in the decision arena at the very moment a decision is being made. That is, the conjunction of problems and solutions is due not just to problems seeking solutions but also to would-be solutions searching for problems that they can plausibly claim to solve (Cohen et al., 1972; March & Olsen, 1989, pp. 11-14, 80-94, 118-130).

Doubts About School Choice

The fact that school choice has had wide support does not mean that it has not been seriously questioned. The principal skeptics have been teachers and school administrators, joined by their allies in the Democratic party. The national Forum of Education Organization Leaders has strongly urged the rejection of private voucher plans (Pitsch, 1990), and this stance has been echoed by educational associations in various states (Snider, 1990a, pp. 1, 14, 1990b, p. 18; Toch, 1991, p. 251; Wehrwein, 1985).[8]

Despite their hostility toward private school choice, the educational associations have been less opposed to, and even supportive of, *public school* choice. In 1986, the AFT indicated that it "remains open to the discussion of choice options within the public schools . . . . Our openness is a cautious one, for we recognize the pitfalls of the choice issue, even within the public school system" (American Federation of Teachers, 1986, p. 13; Snider, 1987, p. C14). The National Education Association, meanwhile, has also indicated support for parental choice in public schooling while making clear that it still remains opposed to private school choice (Geiger, 1990, p. 12; Pitsch, 1990).

The teaching associations' shift toward skeptical support for public school choice is in part tactical. Teachers feel that they cannot simply refuse in toto to deal with school choice for fear of seeming entirely reactionary and being left on the sidelines of the policy game (personal communication with B. Rosenberg, 1990). At the same time, there are also more positive reasons. The head of the Rochester AFT chapter, Adam Urbanski, believes that public school choice empowers teachers by reducing bureaucratic control. In fact, the school choice program in Rochester is closely allied with a program of shared governance involving teachers, school administrators, parents, and students (Urbanski, 1990, pp. 301-302, 304).

Several influential congressional Democrats—most notably Senator Edward Kennedy—have taken a position close to that of the educational associations. They have flatly declared their opposition to President Bush's call for private school choice (Miller, 1991b, p. 24). But, while rejecting private school choice, congressional Democrats have also come out in favor of public school choice. Senator Kennedy has introduced a bill that would provide incentives for state and local school districts to develop and implement public choice plans (Miller & Pitsch, 1991, p. 22).

Forecasting the Future of School Choice

The unusual coalition between conservatives, liberal policy analysts, urban educators, black and white parents, and the Catholic church has put school choice on the national policy agenda, but it also makes the movement very fragile. Until now, the advocates of public and private school choice have tended to mute their differences with each other in the interest of attacking a common enemy, the current public school system. This tactic may allow the advocates of private school choice to keep the champions of public school choice on board long enough to ensure that choice is irreversibly established and the movement's momentum sweeps into private school choice. On the other hand, if the proponents of public choice decide that the movement for parental choice may not stop at public school choice, they may take up arms not just against private school choice but even against the very idea of parental choice itself. In fact, as President Bush has become more candid about his preference for private choice (Pitsch, 1991), the American Federation of Teachers has become more and more muted about, and may even have abandoned, its previous support for public school choice (Chira, 1991; Miller, 1991c; Shanker, 1991).

Summary and Conclusions

In contrast to efforts in the 1950s and 1960s, the school choice movement of the 1980s has had unparalleled success, installing parental choice in several states and a host of localities. At the root of this popularity has been the fact that the same proposal has proved attractive not just to conservatives but also to other groups with a wide variety of concerns. Liberal policy scholars have been converted to a belief in choice as they have lost faith in bureaucratized public schooling. Urban educators have championed school choice to further integration and revive moribund public schools. White middle-class parents have demanded choice to avoid public education entirely or at least to get access to the best schools within it. More surprising, black parents have increasingly abandoned their steadfast loyalty to public schooling both to escape its troubles and to foster an Afro-centric culture. Meanwhile, driven by the financial decline of the parochial system, the Catholic church has eagerly embraced school choice. And the teachers' associations, even as they have condemned private school choice, have been willing to countenance public school choice, at least until recently. Finally, state governors have dramatically joined the movement, driven not just by public demand but also by their own values and political calculations.

The surprising support parental choice has received from outside the conservative camp has allowed the choice movement to achieve a success it never enjoyed in the 1950s and 1960s. As Jeanne Allen, an educational specialist for the Heritage Foundation, a New Right think tank, has noted, "Because of Polly Williams and people like John Chubb at Brookings, the American people have seen that choice is not just a conservative, lunatic idea. It's a safer message, because it's coming from a better messenger" (Olson, 1991a, p. 10).

The choice movement clearly illustrates the limitations of the pluralist and Marxist instrumentalist theories of politics. To be sure, these theories are partially correct. Demands from various interest groups—ranging from business-oriented conservatives to black parents—have certainly spurred government to pursue school choice. Yet, contrary to pluralist and instrumentalist theory, government action has by no means been a simple reflex of this pressure from civil society. Government officials also have been motivated by values and interests of their own, such as a belief in the redemptive power of the market and a desire for a political issue that can be turned to electoral advantage. That is, as state relative autonomy theory argues, government officials act with considerable, though not total, independence from the interests and actions of groups in civil society.[9] Furthermore, the choice movement has exhibited many of the features that James March and his colleagues ascribe to "garbage can" decision making: Policies are often chosen more because they are readily at hand than because they have been determined to be the best solution to the problem in question, and the same policy may appeal to various actors for very different, and even conflicting, reasons (Cohen et al., 1972; March & Olsen, 1989).

The fact that school choice has appealed to many different actors for often quite varied reasons may be a bane as much as a boon to the movement. The movement's wide support may fracture as the advocates of public school choice refuse to continue cooperating with those pursuing private school choice. The result might be that the choice movement may prove no more influential and lasting than the many previous efforts to reform the nearly century-old "one best system" of the bureaucratized public school.

Notes

1. The state relative autonomy perspective draws on both the structuralist Marxist and the Weberian political theories. For an exegesis and critique of the pluralist, Marxist, and Weberian theories, see Alford and Friedland (1985) and Carnoy (1984).

2. For analysis of the business-led New Right attack on the welfare state and on public schooling, see Aronowitz and Giroux (1985), Block, Cloward, Ehrenreich, and Piven (1982), and Offe (1984).

3. Business has not been uniformly in favor of school choice, however. The Business Roundtable and the National Alliance of Business have not endorsed school choice (Business Roundtable, 1991; Chira, 1991). And the Committee for Economic Development (1985) has only come out in favor of public school choice.

4. This disenchantment with public provision of services among many of its erstwhile advocates has occurred across all the major advanced industrial societies. It has been stimulated not only by the conservative counterattack on the welfare state but also by an autonomous critique of the increasing expense and unwieldiness of the bureaucratized state (March & Olsen, 1989; Offe, 1984).

5. Except for Coons and Sugarman, these other liberal advocates of school choice do not join Chubb and Moe in calling for private school choice, preferring public school choice instead.

6. When asked by the 1989 Gallup Poll on Education, "Do you favor or oppose allowing students and their parents to choose which public schools in this community the students attend, regardless of where they live?" 67% of nonwhites answered yes as opposed to 59% of whites

(Elam & Gallup, 1989, p. 43). And, in the case of private school choice, 54% of nonwhites answered yes, as opposed to 45% of whites, when asked in 1986, "In some nations, the government allots a certain amount of money for each child for his or her education. The parents can then send the child to any public, parochial, or private school they choose. This is called the 'voucher system.' Would you like to see such an idea adopted in this country?" (Gallup, 1986, p. 58).

7. It is noteworthy that, prior to her school voucher bill, Williams had proposed creating an all-black school district in Milwaukee and had opposed busing for racial balance (Olson, 1990d).

8. The teachers' associations argue that private school choice is unconstitutional, will increase racial and class segregation, will drain public schools of revenue and the best students, will lead parents to choose inappropriate schools for their children, and will threaten the jobs of public school teachers (American Federation of Teachers, 1986, p. 13; Olson, 1990d; Pitsch, 1990; Rosenberg, 1989; Snider, 1987, pp. C4, 9, 1990c, p. 18; Viadero, 1990, p. 12). For evaluations of these criticisms, see Clune and Witte (1990).

9. This relative autonomy of the state is by no means incompatible with a powerful capitalist influence over government policy. In fact, because government officials often depend on the help of business to realize their own interests, business exerts a powerful, but usually ignored, passive power of constraint over government (Block, 1987). For examples pertaining to educational policymaking, see Dougherty (1988, 1991, 1992).

References

Alford, R. A., & Friedland, R. (1985). *Powers of theory.* New York: Cambridge University Press.

American Federation of Teachers. (1986). *The revolution that is overdue.* Washington, DC: Author.

Aronowitz, S., & Giroux, H. (1985). *Education under siege.* South Hadley, MA: Bergin & Garvey.

Blank, R. (1990). Educational effects of magnet high schools. In W. Clune & J. Witte (Eds.), *Choice and control in education* (Vol. 2, pp. 77-109). Bristol, PA: Falmer.

Block, F. (1987). *Revising state theory.* Philadelphia: Temple University Press.

Block, F., Cloward, R. A., Ehrenreich, B., & Piven, F. F. (1982). *The mean season.* New York: Pantheon.

Business Roundtable. (1991). *Essential components of a successful education system.* New York: Author.

Carnoy, M. (1984). *The state and political theory.* Princeton, NJ: Princeton University Press.

Chira, S. (1991, July 22). A sea of doubt swells around Bush's education plan. *New York Times,* p. A12.

Chubb, J. E., & Moe, T. M. (1990). *Politics, markets, and America's schools.* Washington, DC: Brookings Institution.

Clune, W. H., & Witte, J. F. (Eds.). (1990). *Choice and control in education* (2 vols.). Bristol, PA: Falmer.

Cohen, M. D., March, J. G., & Olsen, J. P. (1972). A garbage can model of organizational choice. *Administrative Science Quarterly, 17,* 1-25.

Committee for Economic Development. (1985). *Investing in our children.* New York: Author.

Coons, J. E. (1979). Of family choice and "public" education. *Phi Delta Kappan, 61*(1), 10-13.

Coons, J. E. (1985). A question of access. *Independent School, 44*(3), 9-20.

Coons, J. E., & Sugarman, S. (1983). *Education by choice.* Berkeley: University of California Press.

Coons, J. E., & Sugarman, S. (1990-1991, December/January). The private school option in systems of educational choice. *Educational Leadership,* pp. 54-56.

Cooper, B. S. (1988). The uncertain future of national education policy. In W. L. Boyd & C. T. Kerchner (Eds.), *The politics of excellence and choice in education* (pp. 165-181). London: Falmer.

Crawford, J. (1986, December 10). Chapter 1 bill to include vouchers, Bennett aides say. *Education Week, 6*(14), 12.

Currence, C. (1985, June 5). Colorado approves "second chance" voucher effort. *Education Week, 4*(37), 1, 18.

Domanico, R. (1989). *Model for choice: A report on Manhattan's District 4.* New York: Manhattan Institute for Policy Research.

Donnelly, H. (1990, October 31). Money is the educational issue in gubernatorial races. *Education Week, 10,* 1, 16-17.

Dougherty, K. J. (1988). The politics of community college expansion. *American Journal of Education, 96,* 351-393.

Dougherty, K. J. (1991). *The contradictory college: The conflicting origins, impacts, and futures of the community college.* Unpublished book manuscript, Manhattan College.

Dougherty, K. J. (1992). *Schools to the rescue: The politics of the educational excellence movement* (Report to the Spencer Foundation). New York: Manhattan College.

Elam, S. M., & Gallup, A. M. (1989, September). The 21st annual Gallup poll of the public's attitudes toward the public schools. *Phi Delta Kappan, 71,* 41-54.

Evans, P. B., Rueschemeyer, D., & Skocpol, T. (Eds.). (1985). *Bringing the state back in.* New York: Cambridge University Press.

Fantini, M. D. (1973, September). Education by choice. *NASSP Bulletin, 57*(374), 10-19.

Friedman, M. (1955). The role of government in education. In R. A. Solo (Ed.), *Economics and the public interest* (pp. 123-144). New Brunswick, NJ: Rutgers University Press.

Friedman, M. (1962). *Capitalism and freedom.* Chicago: University of Chicago Press.

Friedman, M. (1975). *There's no such thing as a free lunch.* LaSalle, IL: Open Court.

Gallup, A. M. (1986, September). The 18th annual Gallup poll of the public's attitudes toward the public schools. *Phi Delta Kappan, 68,* 55-59.

Gardner, E. (1985). *A new agenda for education.* Washington, DC: Heritage Foundation.

Geiger, K. (1990, October 13). Choice that works. *Education Week, 10,* 12.

Harp, L. (1990, September 5). Budget troubles overshadow schools as the chief issue in legislatures. *Education Week, 10,* 26, 33.

Heatherly, C. L. (Ed.). (1991). *Mandate for leadership.* Washington, DC: Heritage Foundation.

Hertling, J. (1985, November 13). E.D. voucher bill in shift, offers parents choices. *Education Week, 5*(11), 1, 13.

Jencks, C. (1970). Giving parents money for schooling: Education vouchers. *Phi Delta Kappan, 52*(1), 49-52.

March, J. G., & Olsen, J. P. (1989). *Rediscovering institutions.* New York: Free Press.

Mazzoni, T., & Sullivan, B. (1986). State government and educational reform in Minnesota. In V. D. Mueller & M. P. McKeown (Eds.), *The fiscal, legal, and political aspects of state reform of elementary and secondary education* (pp. 169-202). Cambridge, MA: Ballinger.

Miller, J. A. (1991a, April 24). Bush strategy launches "crusade" for education. *Education Week, 10*(31), 1, 26.

Miller, J. A. (1991b, June 5). Bush's school plan is "Lamar's baby," participants agree. *Education Week, 10,* 1, 26.

Miller, J. A. (1991c, July 31). Wielding new NAEP data, Shanker assails choice. *Education Week, 10,* 36.

Miller, J. A., & Pitsch, M. (1991, May 29). Bush and Kennedy bills set stage for federal debate. *Education Week, 10,* 1, 22.

Nathan, J. (1983). Shouldn't we give vouchers a try? *Learning, 12,* 74-79.

Nathan, J. (1987, June). Results and future prospects of state efforts to increase choice among schools. *Phi Delta Kappan, 68,* 746-752.

Nathan, J. (1989, December). Helping all children, empowering all educators: Another view of school choice. *Phi Delta Kappan, 71,* 304-307.

National Governors' Association. (1986). *A time for results.* Washington, DC: Author.

Offe, C. (1984). *Contradictions of the welfare state.* Cambridge: MIT Press.

Olson, L. (1986, September 10). Governors draft 5-year blueprint to press reforms. *Education Week, 6,* 1, 36.

Olson, L. (1987, March 25). Louisiana businesses urge vouchers. *Education Week, 6,* 7.

Olson, L. (1990a, June 20). Forum suggests choice is gaining bipartisan tinge. *Education Week, 9,* 5.

Olson, L. (1990b, August 1). N.G.A. lists strategies for achieving national goals. *Education Week, 9,* 7.

Olson, L. (1990c, September 12). Milwaukee's choice program enlists 391 volunteers. *Education Week, 10,* 1, 14-15.

Olson, L. (1990d, September 12). Choice plan's architect relishes her role as state legislature's "lone independent." *Education Week, 10,* 14-15.

Olson, L. (1991a, February 20). Proposals for private-school choice reviving at all levels of government. *Education Week, 10,* 1, 10-11.

Olson, L. (1991b, September 18). California businessman's drive for choice sparking battle. *Education Week, 11,* 1, 19.

Pitsch, M. (1990, December 12). Coalition assails private school vouchers as "unwise public policy." *Education Week, 10,* 30.

Pitsch, M. (1991, February 13). Bush seeks to reward district plans that include private-school choice. *Education Week, 10,* 1, 29.

Raywid, M. A. (1985). Family choice arrangements in public schools: A review of the literature. *Review of Educational Research, 55*(4), 435-467.

Raywid, M. A. (1987, June). Public choice, yes; vouchers, no! *Phi Delta Kappan, 68,* 762-769.

Raywid, M. A. (1990, October). The evolving effort to improve schools: Pseudoreform, incremental reform, and restructuring. *Phi Delta Kappan, 72,* 139-143.

Rosenberg, B. (1989, Summer). Public school choice: Can we find the right balance? *American Educator,* pp. 1-12.

Rosenberg, B. (1990). Interview by K. Dougherty with the assistant to the president, American Federation of Teachers. Washington, DC.

Schmidt, P. (1990, October 31). Controversial education proposal gives Wisconsin governor extra edge. *Education Week, 10*, 1, 18.

Schmidt, P. (1991, September 11). Massachusetts districts turn thumbs down on state's hastily passed choice program. *Education Week, 11*, 1, 17.

Shanker, A. (1991, December 1). Private is public. *The New York Times*, p. E7.

Snider, W. (1987, June 24). The call for choice: Competition in the educational marketplace. *Education Week, 6*, C6-24.

Snider, W. (1988a, June 15). Seattle happy with "choice" plan. *Education Week, 7*, 4.

Snider, W. (1988b, December 7). Parental choice bill readied in Massachusetts. *Education Week, 8*, 10.

Snider, W. (1990a, March 28). Voucher system for 1,000 pupils adopted in Wisconsin. *Education Week, 9*, 1, 14.

Snider, W. (1990b, April 11). Washington lawmakers adopt school-choice package. *Education Week, 9*(29), 14.

Snider, W. (1990c, June 20). Group files suit to block Milwaukee's voucher plan. *Education Week, 9*, 18.

Snider, W. (1990d, September 5). "Choice" proposals make headway in statehouses in 1990. *Education Week, 10*, 26, 33.

Sostre, L. (1991). *Community School District Three middle school directory.* New York: Community School District Three.

Sowell, T. (1981, Spring). Tuition tax credits: A social revolution. [Heritage Foundation] *Policy Review, 4*, 79-89.

Sullivan, J. F. (1991, December 1). Catholic schools face financial strain. *The New York Times*, sec. 12, pp. 1, 16.

Toch, T. (1991). *In the name of excellence.* New York: Oxford University Press.

Urbanski, A. (1990). Restructuring schools for greater choice: The Rochester initiative. In S. Bachrach (Ed.), *Educational reform: Making sense of it all* (pp. 298-308). Reading, MA: Allyn & Bacon.

Viadero, D. (1988, February 3). Wisconsin governor seeks pilot voucher-style plan. *Education Week, 7*, 8.

Viadero, D. (1990, March 21). Gardner's once dead choice proposal revived in Washington legislature. *Education Week, 9*, 12.

Walsh, M. (1991a, March 13). Black private academies are held up as filling void. *Education Week, 10*, 1, 28-29.

Walsh, M. (1991b, April 17). Building on success, Catholic educators press their case for private-school choice. *Education Week, 10*, 1, 16.

Walsh, M. (1991c, November 13). Bush urges Catholic educators to back reform package. *Education Week, 11*, 20.

Wehrwein, A. (1985, October 23). Critics assailing Minnesota choice plan. *Education Week, 5,* 1, 13.

Weisman, J. (1991, September 18). In Indiana, business groups not talking as one on reform. *Education Week, 11,* 1, 18.

Wells, A. S. (1990, March 14). Quest for improving schools finds role for free market. *The New York Times,* pp. A1, B8.

Wills, J. (1991). Interview by K. Dougherty with the director, Center for Policy Research, National Governors' Association, 1976-1988. Washington, DC.

3

Choice:
The Fundamentals Revisited

JEFFREY KANE

With each passing year, the literature on educational choice is more extensive and sophisticated. Economic models and arguments for and against choice are detailed; demographic analyses are refined and enhanced; the problems and potential of the free market are elaborated. Yet beneath these considerations lies a profound, often unrecognized philosophical tension between the rights and interests of the individual and those of the state.

Much of the modern educational reform movement and the literature on educational choice has assumed a one-dimensional model of the individual, a model that resigns to obscurity the concept of the autonomous person whose developing mind and spirit are largely reserved from the authority of the body politic. This attenuated concept of the individual—so long assumed as to be self-evident, so basic as to be an axiomatic foundation for policy development—has largely "misframed" the question of choice. It is therefore necessary to consider the theoretical presuppositions of the discourse.

It is the intention of this chapter to explore a few assumptions implicit in both American democracy and educational choice and to suggest a reconstructed philosophical framework for the analysis and development of policy on educational choice.

Philosophical Foundations of Choice

Schools are a product of choice. They embody, in their function, organization and content; judgments regarding the nature and purpose of education; assertions about human intelligence, knowledge, and being as well as the suppositions regarding the respective rights and responsibilities of the individual and the state. Where such judgments have not been made, either explicitly or tacitly, there are no schools.

In our discourse regarding schools, we often refer to derivatives of the fundamental choices we make. We speak of curriculum, instructional methods, educational objectives, or organizational structures; we analyze and review subject matter and skill development. In addressing these questions, however, we apply varied philosophical, psychological, social, and political assumptions. Inevitably, we are forced to address fundamental questions. What is knowledge? What is intelligence and how may it be best developed? What is learning and how can it be measured? What is the nature of the world? How shall it be studied and interpreted? Is truth to be found through revelation or the scientific process, or is it knowable at all? What is it to be human? Is the very foundation of human identity to be found in the divine or are we social animals? What values or "valuing" processes would we teach? Are there responsibilities incumbent upon us by virtue of humanity or are our relations with ourselves, one another, and the larger world circumscribed by questions of the "common good"?

Despite the discomfort these questions are likely to cause, despite the desire to brush them aside as questions for philosophers, we nonetheless must answer them. The choices we make and the resulting schools we create are grounded in the assumptions and commitments we make concerning the foundations of the human spirit and intellect.

We cannot dismiss considerations of the human spirit—matters relating to our ultimate conceptions of ourselves, the world, and our moral responsibilities—from educational questions relating to the development of the intellect. Human intelligence does not exist in a vacuum but is defined and developed relative to cultural beliefs and values. These articles of faith, whether theistic or antitheistic, whether metaphysical or positivistic, give the intelligence its distinctive form and reflective capacity. Consequently, they form the foundations of one's understanding of the world, how it may be studied and interpreted and how one ought to conduct oneself. As we give shape to the intellect, we provide the context for the mind to understand the self and the world. Hence, in education, the questions of human intellect and of human spirit constitute an indivisible unity.

John Dewey suggests that our schools, with common faith in his conceptions of scientific method, could provide a universal foundation for the development of the spiritual and intellectual life. He states,

> We have mastered the elements of physical well-being, we can make light and heat to order, and can command the means of transportation. Let us now put a similar energy, good will, and thoughtfulness into control of the things of the spiritual life. Having got so far as to search for proper machinery, the next step is easy. Education is the modern universal purveyor, and upon the schools shall rest the responsibility for seeing to it that we recover our threatened religious heritage. (Ratner, 1970, pp. 504-505)

While the success of the schools as a purveyor of Dewey's conception of the intellectual and spiritual life is debatable, the nation's schools do, indeed, constitute the primary formal institution for shaping the emerging human mind. The shaping process is determined by our responses to the fundamental questions of human existence as they are conveyed in the pedagogical judgments we make. The nature and significance of testing, the organization of classrooms, the levels of engagement required of students, the role of art and music in the curriculum, and virtually every other aspect of the educational experience implicitly transmit the answers that we have found for ourselves.

One may argue that, because public schools are controlled democratically, incorporating numerous, diverse sources of judgment, the education they offer does not offer any discernable intellectual/

spiritual agenda. Such a position, however, (a) mistakes the operations of governmental bureaucracy for the nature of democracy and (b) fails to recognize that repeatedly compromised educational choices purvey a weighty, albeit virtually incoherent, set of intellectual/spiritual assumptions and aims. In the words of Stephen Arons (1984, pp. 6-7),

> The orthodoxy which prevails in public schools today is not secular humanism or socialism, not capitalism, protestantism or militarism, but a characterless bureaucratic order bent on denying values, and overly tolerant of emptiness. Driven perhaps by a fear of value conflict, the schools have created a confused and confusing consensus.

Although we have made great efforts to eliminate theological and religious ideas and practices from public schools, the education they provide is woven throughout with a vast array of presuppositions, values, beliefs, and objectives that affect the evolution of the way children learn to think, feel, and act. Philip Phenix (1961, p. 18) observes,

> The essence of the curriculum—whether considered formally in schools or informally in other agencies of education—consists not of objective lessons to be learned and courses to be passed, but of the scheme of values, ideals, or life goals which are mediated through the materials of instruction. The really significant outcome of education is the set of governing commitments, the aims for living that the learner develops. The various subjects of study are simple means for the communication and appropriation of these values.

In a similar vein, the Supreme Court's decision in *Wisconsin v. Yoder* (1971) recognizes the vital role of the implicit substructure of schools in shaping children's minds and spirits. Writing for the majority, Justice Burger explains,

> [The public] high schools tend to emphasize intellectual and scientific accomplishment, self-distinction, competitiveness, worldly success, and social life with other students. Amish society emphasizes informal learning through doing, a life of "goodness" rather

than a life of intellect, wisdom rather than technical knowledge, community welfare rather than competition, and separation from rather than integration with contemporary worldly society.

Given this perspective, the question of educational choice is relative to the preferability not only of one set of pedagogical judgments over another but of one set of intellectual/spiritual assumptions (however vague or confused) over another. Consequently, the question of choice relates less to pedagogy per se than to the proper political investiture of authority to make such fundamental judgments for the development of individual children.

Who is to determine what individual children will know, how they should view the world, how they shall govern their actions with others and understand themselves? Who has the right, through the schools, to guide the emerging intellect and spirit of individual children?

The Individual and the State

These questions, in that they regard ultimately the relationship between the individual and the state, require that we explore some broad yet fundamental tenets of American democratic theory. What is the status of intellectual/spiritual matters in democratic traditions? Despite the daunting challenge of interpreting the complexities of liberal democratic tradition, for the current purposes, it is possible to restrict ourselves to a relatively discrete, albeit broad, discussion of the relative rights and responsibilities of the individual and the state.

John Stuart Mill (1963, p. 131) cuts to the heart of the matter in his renowned essay "On Liberty"; he observes, "There is a limit to the legitimate interference of collective opinion with individual independence; and to find that limit, and maintain it against encroachment, is as indispensable to a good condition of human affairs, as protection against political despotism."

Mill maintains that the individual is answerable to the state only in so far as his or her actions affect others, and that the state may exercise authority over the individual only to prevent him or her from doing harm to others collectively or individually. Refining his position further, Mill identifies "the appropriate region of human liberty." He states,

> It comprises, first, the inward domain of consciousness; demanding liberty of conscience, in the most comprehensive sense; liberty of thought and feeling; absolute freedom of opinion and sentiment on all subjects, practical or speculative, scientific, moral, or theological. (1963, pp. 137-138)[1]

In matters of conscience, of the ultimate questions that we address in the course of life, the state is first and foremost a guardian of individual liberty.

This commitment to liberal democracy unfolds into the twin ideals that *citizens* have the right to rule themselves collectively and that *persons* have the right to rule themselves individually. With regard to the former, we recognize the body politic; with regard to the latter, we recognize both the protective role of the state and the sovereignty of the individual in matters within "the appropriate region of human liberty." Consequently, both the individual and the state are twofold. The individual is an autonomous agent, a person, a single and sovereign voice; the individual is also a member of a collective, a citizen, a single vote subject to the rule of the majority. The state, which derives authority from the consent of the governed, is accountable to the governed for its actions and is responsible to secure the natural rights of the individual.

This conception of liberal democracy begins, in the modern era, with Hobbes. He asserts that the most reasonable manner in which to organize political and social life and to ensure individual liberty is to ask individuals to surrender their rights to thereby create "one will" sovereign and unified. David Held (1987, p. 49) summarizes Hobbes's argument as follows: "If individuals surrender their rights by transferring them to an authority which can force them to keep their promises and covenants, then an effective and legitimate private and public sphere, society and state, can be formed."

John Locke, following Hobbes, accepts his notion of the establishment of political authority through consent but rejects the Hobbesian concept of the legitimacy of such political authority in all domains. He maintains that the function of political authority is to ensure the capacity of individuals to exercise their natural rights, to guide their individual destinies, and seek happiness in natural law. Locke explains,

> To understand political power right, and derive it from its origin, we must consider what state men are naturally in, and that is, a state of perfect freedom to order their actions and dispose of their possessions and persons, as they think fit, within the bounds of the law of nature; without asking leave, or depending upon the will of any other man. (cited in Russell, 1945, p. 625)

James Madison and Thomas Jefferson, deeply influenced by Hobbes and Locke, incorporated liberal and democratic ideals into the American Constitution. The concept of natural liberties, of a domain of individual conscience and authority, secured by and existing beyond the powers of the state, is particularly evident in the First Amendment in which the individual is granted rights with respect to the basic convictions that guide his or her life.[2]

Justice Jackson contends, in *West Virginia State Board of Education v. Barnette* (1943), that these rights constitute "the sphere of intellect and spirit which it is the purpose of the First Amendment to our Constitution to reserve from all official control."

This sphere, consistent with liberal democratic traditions, encompasses the entire domain of the individual consciousness and is not limited to specific rights of expression or religious judgment. Stephen Arons (1976, p. 96) explains that

> the freedoms or powers guaranteed by the First Amendment would be meaningless if government had within its legal power to dictate the desires, values, aspirations, world views, or ethics of individuals seeking to exercise these freedoms or powers. The specifics of the amendment in any period must, therefore, be interpreted as a right to individual consciousness.

The "right to individual consciousness" undergirds the freedom to engage in artistic pursuit, scientific inquiry, and other cultural activities. Justice Jackson, in his concurrence on *Thomas v. Collins* (1944), concluded, "The very purpose of the First Amendment is to foreclose public authority from assuming guardianship of the public mind." This is not to suggest that the individual is free to think and act as he will but that the state's primary responsibility is to protect the individual's sovereignty—with respect to the ultimate choices he or she makes. The authority of the state in this regard is first to guarantee liberty; the exercise of its managerial powers in the sphere of intellect and spirit is reserved for only the most profound of circumstances in which the state identifies possible harm to either individuals or the state—where the state demonstrates a "compelling justification" for doing so (Arons, 1984, p. 123).

Choice and Authority

When we apply these considerations to the question of proper authority in the matter of educational choice, the state's obligation is to defend the liberty of the individual rather than to exercise pedagogical judgment. The concept of liberty here is political, not personal. It refers to freedom from governmental control. Accordingly, the issue of educational choice is relative to the political sanctity of the sphere of intellect and spirit rather than to specific assumptions or aims. In this context, it is entirely possible that an individual's choice within this sphere may, in some measure, diminish one's *intellectual/spiritual autonomy* (however we define the terms). The possibility that one might define the term and pursue the goal in a way inconsistent with a given community is a necessary risk of democracy. The ideal of "liberty" within this sphere, whether in terms of psychology or theology, or personal satisfaction or eternal salvation, is to be defined by the individual, not the body politic (except, of course, in cases of "compelling justification").

The Supreme Court, in its ruling on *Pierce v. Society of Sisters* (1925), regarding the constitutional legitimacy of independent schools, argues that, "The child is not a mere creature of the state." Stephen Arons (1984, p. 40) explains: "The Court saw that schooling concerned socialization and the development of the individual mind, and refused to make this influence the sole possession of the political majority." The Court recognized that the individual, in the matter of his or her growth as an intelligent being, is not simply a citizen—a member of a group and subject to its will—but an autonomous person.

While it might be argued that the current dual system of public and independent schools provides the necessary balance of state interest and individual liberty, the constitutionality of independent schools does not ensure the liberty of the developing minds of those children who, due to family economic condition, cannot avail themselves of an alternative to the public system. For such individuals, the formal educational experience that will "shape and form" their minds is set by the state. Thus, for a significant part of the American population, their intellectual/spiritual development is subject to, rather than protected from, the authority of the state.

The level of governmental authority, whether federal, state, or local, is insignificant: Matters of intellect and spirit are properly reserved from governmental authority no matter how big or small the body politic. While "local control," school boards, and various community organizations such as parent-teacher associations provide parents with a reasonable degree of political engagement, if not clout, in the shaping of the schools, the fact remains that the rights of the individual are subsumed by the judgments of the majority. This is not to suggest that individuals must be guaranteed schools that meet their demands but that each individual, singularly, has the right to choose from available alternatives the school (or educational program, such as home schooling) that is most consistent with his or her values and beliefs.

Insofar as education affects the development of an individual's mind, with all that such a concept entails for his or her values, beliefs, and claims to knowledge, government must assume the defense of individual liberty. Education is a matter of public concern only to the extent that there is a clear and specific danger either to an individual or to the political structure itself. Education in the former sense relates to matters of curricula, educational psychology, educational philosophy, academic standards and assessment, pedagogical technique, and so on; education in the latter sense relates to matters such as funding patterns, child welfare laws, and civil rights.

The distinction between these conflicting concepts and contexts of education has long been blurred by our national commitment to governmentally controlled public school systems—systems that do not recognize the dual nature of democratic citizenship, democratic institutions, and education itself. Whether we consider Horace Mann's (1948, p. 84) central argument for the creation of the common school —that it would create "a more far-seeing intelligence and pure morality than has ever existed among communities of men"—or the National Commission on Excellence in Education report's (1983, p. 5) case for the educational reform—that it is necessary to stem the "rising tide of mediocrity that threatens our very future as a Nation and a people"—the fundamental conflict remains. Whether we fear the possible dissolution of American way of life due to its "alienating competitions" (1938, p. 84), as did Mann, or the competitions of modern international commerce, the fundamental conflict remains.

With the first step of the first child over the threshold of the common schoolhouse door, the idea was institutionalized that the state had the right to shape the individual's intellect and spirit. Whether the intention is to ensure that the child learns to think according to "proper" religious precepts or the logical requirements of information processing, we are met with the dilemma that, even as we fear for the needs of the state, the state has a more primary responsibility to secure the liberty of the individual.

While scholars may argue about the relative efficiencies of a free market or may debate demographic statistics, the issue of educational choice is problematic precisely because it *calls into question the primary definitions and respective rights and authorities of the individual and the state.* In nations that do not share the American commitment to the protection of the liberty of the individual (as obscure as it might be now in the field of education), the state assumes responsibility for educational judgments with reference to its priorities and objectives alone. The needs, interests, values, beliefs, aspirations, and ultimate commitments of the individual do not counterbalance or in any way contravene the prerogatives of the state.

Within this context, various communistic states restrict questions of educational choice to a consideration of the merits of various educational alternatives with respect to the state's objective of creating a classless society. Theocratic states largely confine their consideration of various educational alternatives to their utility in promulgating particular values, beliefs, and codes of action. Totalitarian regimes limit consideration of questions of education to the maintenance of political and social order.

While it is obvious that the above statements are general and that others may define the objectives of the various kinds of governments in different terms, the point remains that the state's educational judgments, the educational choices it makes, are relative to a circumscribed set of factors that do not include the right of individuals who may wish to select contrasting educational objectives, priorities, or models.

Conversely, the creation of educational policy in a democracy is a far more complex affair in that it requires judgments that recognize both the needs and the limited authority of the state with respect to the individual. As Israel Scheffler (1976, p. 311) reminds us, "To choose the democratic ideal for society is wholly to reject the conception of education as an *instrument* of rule; it is to surrender the idea of shaping or molding the mind of the pupil." This is not, of course, to say that the state has no proper interest in education—for democracy cannot long endure ignorance—but, instead, that it must achieve a carefully balanced policy that at once assures the development of the citizen and respects the independent development of the individual qua individual.

Choice: The Recent Context

The current choice debate began with the shifting political sentiments and strategies of the early Reagan years. Two distinct policy agendas generated the language and political assumptions of the current discourse.

During his initial presidential campaign and first two years in office, Ronald Reagan appealed to a nation victimized by petropolitics and humiliated by international terrorists. He championed a political ideology that promised to recapture the glories of the past. The call to America's past was political (emphasizing decreased government and increased military power), economic (focusing on deregulation and free markets), and cultural (promoting individual initiative and "traditional" American religious values).

The President's cultural ideological agenda consisted, in part, of attempts to establish educational vouchers and tuition tax credits as well as to reestablish school prayer. The "new federalism" also called for the disestablishment of the federal Department of Education. These initiatives proved politically untenable, however, and the President soon was in search of an educational policy.

Enter the report of Secretary Bell's National Commission on Excellence in Education, *A Nation at Risk: The Imperative for Educational Reform*. The report, in its language and content, melded the Reagan administration's political, economic, and educational ideological concerns through references to the cold war and the economic challenges posed by the Japanese, South Koreans, and Germans. The American people were told that "knowledge, learning, information and skilled intelligence [were] the new raw materials of international commerce" (National Commission on Excellence in Education, 1983, p. 7). The report, in its fusion of political, economic, and educational issues, set the political stage for the federal government to take a new leadership role in the creation of national educational policy. The report demonstrated that the federal Department of Education could be a valuable educational bully pulpit capable of promoting the new educational agenda. Talk of the disestablishment of the department faded into silence. Gone too were the boldly ideological arguments for vouchers and school prayer. In their place arose seemingly pragmatic declarations of the imperatives of a nation imperiled by an educational system that had "lost sight of the basic purposes of schooling, and of the high expectations and disciplined efforts needed to attain them" (1983, pp. 5-6). As noted previously, the commission explained that "the American foundations of our society are presently being eroded by a rising tide of mediocrity that threatens our very future as a nation and a people" (1983, p. 5).

With mediocrity identified as the "threat," the administration cited "excellence" as the road to deliverance. No longer could the nation suffer indulgence over rigor, technique over achievement, predilection over mandate. The commission, citing its concern for "*the intellectual, moral and spiritual strengths* of our people," argued that "*all children by virtue of their own efforts,* competently guided, can hope to attain the mature and informed judgment needed to secure gainful employment and to manage their own lives" (1983, pp. 7-8, italics added).

The ideological call was not now theological—specific to school prayer—but historical—relating to an idealized self-reliant conception of the American individual. A publicly appealing and seemingly reasonable pragmatic agenda was set—to renew education (as well as the political/economic stature of the nation) by calling upon the individualistic American spirit, which would respond with steely self-discipline and determination to the challenges posed. Implementing the agenda, the commission stated that excellence could be achieved only through heightened academic standards, an uncompromised focus on curricular content, and unfailing attention to "the new basics."

These shifts in the Reagan administration's educational policy, in their explicit emphasis on perceived political and economic risks, exacerbated the threat of governmental intrusion into the sphere of intellect and spirit. The commission not only assumed, but asserted, that education was properly a governmentally controlled enterprise to direct the development of the human intellect and spirit, of the human mind, just as it might create policies regulating the mining of coal or the drilling of oil. The commission further supposed that, like coal and oil, which had driven an industrial economy, the human mind could properly be considered a public resource to be developed to meet the political and economic requirements of a new age of information. The report explained that it was "essential—especially in a period of long-term decline in educational achievement—for government at all levels to affirm its responsibility for nurturing the *nation's intellectual capital*" (1983, p. 17, italics added). In so doing, it shifted the human mind from a position of constitutional sanctity to one of public servitude (Kane, 1989, p. 6).

With these assumptions as the basis for educational reform, the outstanding issues of policy and practice were limited to pragmatics, and the threat to democracy in terms of the diminution of the sphere of intellect and spirit grew without notice. In this context, the Commission's report posed perhaps a greater risk to the nation than the political and economic problems it cited.

In roughly the same time frame, James Coleman's (1982) study of the relative academic virtues of private over public schools (*High School Achievement: Public, Catholic and Private Schools Compared*) and Mary Metz's (1986) encouraging portrait of the alternative school movement (*Different by Design*) provided impetus for renewed review and debate regarding the relative advantages of competitive market and diverse educational models. These considerations, coupled with the "imperatives" for reform and excellence, created a dynamic national context for the question of choice. The concept of choice evolved during the 1980s less as a result of our national commitment to a democratic model of the individual—protected by and from public authority—and more as a by-product of the attempt to redesign the nation's educational organization and structure to make it more responsive to national political and economic priorities.

Consequently, much of the literature on educational choice has come to assume a social, political concept of the individual and that the human mind—the intellectual/spiritual core of the human being—is a public resource. This is not to say that the literature on choice is insensitive to the needs and interests of children; it is not to claim collusion; it is not to deny the human sensibilities that drive various arguments. Rather, it is to suggest that, in our attempts to improve public schools, in our efforts to ensure educational quality consistent with the needs of the nation, in our focus on the technical and practical, we have lost sight of our crucial democratic commitment to the "individual" beyond the "citizen".

Tacitly, much of the literature on choice has shared the presupposition of the commission that the child is indeed "a creature of the state." Much of the debate on choice has either incorporated or failed to account for the underlying assumption that the human mind is a source of energy for the "information age." In this regard, it is worthy to note the U.S. Department of Education's (1991, p. 5) presentation of the Bush administration's educational agenda, *America 2000: An Educational Strategy,* which asserts that "our country is idling its engines, not knowing enough nor being able to do enough to make America all it should be." As part of the strategy to get the nation's engines in gear, the plan includes an agenda for choice. The choice initiative is designed relative to the Bush administration's desire to set and achieve "world-class" standards and to ensure that federal monies are used to that effect. The concept of choice is limited to the selection of alternative educational means, to educational instrumentalities rather than to the selection of alternative educational ends—philosophical goals and objectives distinct from those of the state.

The underlying assumption here, as in the report of the National Commission on Excellence in Education (1983), is that government has the authority and responsibility to oversee the "nation's intellectual capital." Few seem to question the legitimacy of such governmental claims of proprietary interest in, euphemisms aside, human minds. The sphere of intellect and spirit continues silently to fade from our language and thought. In the words of David Purpel (1989, p. 16), "Our current administration values freedom of the marketplace more than freedom of ideas."

As Thomas Jefferson (cited in Koch & Peden, 1944, p. 447) once wrote, "The natural progress of things is for liberty to yield and for government to gain ground." This evolutionary process occurs in minute increments as the concept of the individual, an autonomous person, is increasingly eroded by the apparent needs of the state. With each argument regarding instrumentalities and statistical analyses for or against educational choice, we are led further away by the long-term trend that threatens our fundamental commitment to democracy as well as democracy itself.

The Dynamics of Choice

Schools are products of multiple choices—choices relative not only to content, technique, standards, organization, or objectives but to the often unspoken beliefs, values, and goals that constitute the intellectual/spiritual substance of the educational experience. Consequently, schools always and necessarily educate human minds —human beings who use their intelligence to define themselves, to understand the world, and to chart the course of their lives. Schools cannot and should never, so long as we are a democratic nation, simply develop publicly owned "intellectual capital."

The educational task is primarily intellectual and spiritual in nature and, as such, should be reserved from, rather than subject to, the authority of the state. If the state is not responsible for the intellectual/spiritual development of individual children, the question arises as to where such responsibility is properly vested. The answer, quite simply, is that the responsibility for educational choice should rest with those who have parallel obligations in virtually all other areas of children's lives: their parents or guardians. As we find in *Pierce* (1925), "those who nurture [the child] and direct his destiny have the right, coupled with the high duty, to recognize and prepare him for additional obligations."

The competence of parents (or guardians) in this regard has been a subject of much debate. We may ask whether they understand the alternatives available or the implications of the judgments they make. Such a question has little bearing on the legitimacy of their authority, however. Were expertise requisite for responsibility, the state would be justified in legislating diet, medical treatment, and child-rearing practices.

Consistent with the concept of "compelling justification," the state can and should intervene where parental action or inaction significantly endangers a child's health and safety. It should act as the child's guardian when, and only when, parents have not properly assumed their full responsibilities. Educational authority shifts to the public domain when the child is abused or neglected. Such a shift is a function of the state's obligation to defend the sanctity of the child's sphere of intellect and spirit rather than to exercise its managerial prerogatives.

This is not to suggest that the state is precluded from organizing and operating schools. Rather, it is to assert the right of parents and guardians to oversee the educational destiny of the children in their charge. Their judgments regarding educational philosophy, objective, and method should be free of the coercive political or economic power of the state.

Parental educational authority is limited, however; it does not extend into educational matters within the political/social domain. Just as *state* and *individual* are compound terms, so is *education*. Individual choice is limited by the "compelling justifications" of the state in the educational enterprise.

The democratic ideal of liberty in matters of individual consciousness is counterbalanced by the democratic ideal of equality in matters political and social. In political/social matters, individual voice amounts to but a single vote and individual action is subject to the rule of the majority. In such matters, the individual is without name or rank, without distinction by virtue of belief or history. Despite the injustices that mar our common past, the political/social ideal against which we measure justice itself is equality—the conviction that no one is above the requirements, or beneath the protections, of the law. In this context, educational institutions that present a danger to institutional ideals that underlie the fundamental stability of the political/social domain or the security of the realm of intellect and spirit should be denied public support or resource.

In this regard, the state has the responsibility and duty to ensure the rights of all citizens. These rights include equal access to educational funding (according to local, state, and federal resources) and equal access to educational institutions (respecting their academic requirements) that may, as a consequence of parental choice, receive public monies.[3]

As a consequence of the twofold nature of education, policy on choice may be split into two categories. Barry Bull (1984, p. 81), in his analysis of liberty and control, explains,

> There are in general two ways in which a state may ultimately treat matters affecting its inhabitants—it may decide them or not. In not deciding a matter, the state does not necessarily preclude a decision being made in that matter. Rather, it simply precludes the use

in the matter of the state's decision making apparatus and its coercive instrumentalities.

Given the state's "compelling justifications" within the political/ social aspects of education, government may decide the matter— government may take the responsibility for educational judgment. For example, the state is responsible for the creation of an equitable system of public funding for and public access to educational institutions. Given the democratic ideal of liberty in the sphere of intellect and spirit, however, government is obligated to reserve judgment relative to the pedagogical destiny of individual children or schools (except as may be necessary to ensure children's welfare). The intellectual/spiritual aspects of a child's educational experience and destiny are first and foremost in the hands of his or her parents. In this context, the state's role is to protect and defend the individual's sovereignty against the authority of the state itself. Neither is it justified in preferring one curriculum to another, one school to another (such as is the case with the preferential funding of governmentally operated as opposed to independent schools), one assessment mechanism to another, one academic standard to another, and so on.

Conclusion

In our attempts to reform our educational system, in our attempts to meet national problems perceived and/or real, we have turned our attention from democratic ideals to pragmatics; we have limited the definition of the individual and thereby diminished his or her rights in the name of supposed postindustrial exigencies.

While it may be true that risk is the constant companion of liberty, and that educational choice will complicate the already complex educational dilemmas we face, the concept of a democratic nation dedicated to liberty must assume the risk and sustain a complex balance of interests. In the end, if we are seduced by pragmatics, if we limit our considerations to the mechanics of choice rather than to its function in American democracy, we may well strike a Faustian bargain. In return for possible "revenues" in the form of well-developed "intellectual capital" to meet economic, domestic, and national needs, we may lose the soul of democracy. In the end, our educational polices and practices may slowly define out of existence the intellectual/spiritual core of the individual on whom our nation depends and for whom it exists. As John Stuart Mill (1963, p. 139) concludes,

> Apart from the peculiar tenets of individual thinkers, there is also in the world at large an increasing inclination to stretch unduly the powers of society over the individual, both by the force of opinion and even by that of legislation: and as the tendency of all the changes taking place in the world is to strengthen society, and diminish the power of the individual, this encroachment is not one of the evils which tend spontaneously to disappear, but, on the contrary, to grow more and more formidable.

Notes

1. Mill goes on to identify two other aspects of "the appropriate region of human liberty." These relate to the liberty of "tastes and pursuits; . . . of framing the plan of our life to suit our own character" and the "freedom to unite, for any purpose not involving harm to others."

2. The discussion of the First Amendment through reference to and interpretation of Supreme Court actions is not intended to constitute legal argument. Rather, its purpose is to elaborate several philosophical presuppositions regarding the nature of democracy undergirding our constitutional commitments.

3. The state also has other "compelling justifications," including the enforcement of health, safety, and fire laws as well as the development of an independent mechanism to assess the success of schools receiving public funds in achieving their own objectives. The creation of such a mechanism is highly complex and involves considerations beyond the scope of this chapter. Suffice to say that the intention here is to suggest an agency something on the order of the Middle States Association and other professional educational organizations of its type in other regions of the country.

References

Arons, S. (1976, February). The separation of school and state: Pierce reconsidered. *Harvard Educational Review*, pp. 39-58.

Arons, S. (1984). Pluralism, equal liberty, and public education. *A Blueprint for Educational Reform*, pp. 6-7, 40.

Bull, B. L. (1984). "Liberty and the new localism: Toward an evaluation of the trade-off between educational equity and local control of schools." *Educational Theory, 34*, 75-96.

Coleman, J. (1982). *High school achievement: Public, Catholic and private schools compared*. New York: Basic Books.

Held, D. (1987). *Models of democracy*. Stanford, CA: Stanford University Press.

Kane, J. (1989). Public policy and the erosion of democracy. *The Threefold Review, 1*, 6-7.

Koch, A., & Peden, W. (Eds.). (1944). *The life and selected writings of Thomas Jefferson*. New York: Modern Library.

Mann, H. (1938). *First annual report of the secretary of the board of education*. Boston: Dutton Westworth, State Printers.

Mann, H. (1948). *Twelfth annual report of the secretary of the board of education*. Boston: Dutton Westworth, State Printers.

Metz, M. (1986). *Different by design*. New York: Routledge & Kegan Paul.

Mill, J. S. (1963). *The six great humanistic essays of John Stuart Mill*. New York: Washington Square.

National Commission on Excellence in Education. (1983, April). *A nation at risk: The imperative for educational reform*. Washington, DC: Government Printing Office.

Phenix, P. N. (1961). *Education and the common good*. New York: Harper & Row.

Pierce v. Society of Sisters, 268 U.S. 510 (1925).

Purpel, D. E. (1989). *The moral and spiritual crisis in education*. New York: Bergin & Garvey.

Ratner, J. (Ed.). (1970). *Characters and events: Popular essays in social and political philosophy* (Vol. 2). New York: Octagon.

Russell, B. (1945). *A history of Western philosophy*. New York: Simon & Schuster.

Scheffler, I. (1976). The moral content of American public education. In *Educational research: Prospects and priorities*. Washington, DC: Government Printing Office.

Thomas v. Collins, 323 U.S. 545 (1944).

U.S. Department of Education. (1991). *America 2000: An educational strategy*. Washington, DC: Author.

West Virginia State Board of Education v. Barnette, 319 U.S. 642 (1943).

Wisconsin v. Yoder, 406 U.S. 210 (1971).

4

Do Parents Choose School Quality or School Status? A Sociological Theory of Free Market Education

AMY STUART WELLS

ROBERT L. CRAIN

Behind the latest political push for free market school choice programs that allow parents to spend public dollars at private schools lies a simplistic view of how families make educational decisions. For if we conjecture that public-private school choice programs will, as their proponents claim, lead to educational improvements through competitive market forces, then we must assume that the main criteria parents use when choosing schools are the quality of the academic program offered and the match between teaching styles and their child's individual needs. That is a rather large assumption.

Borrowing from economic rational choice theory of consumer behavior in the marketplace, advocates of deregulated educational choice argue that when families are given tuition vouchers to spend at public or private schools of their choice, they will act rationally, in a goal-oriented fashion, to maximize their educational utility by finding the "best" school for their children. This consumer demand for high-quality schools will, in turn, force all schools to compete for students in a marketplace where "bad" schools attract few customers and eventually go out of business. Hence tuition voucher programs should lead to better school organization and improved educational services for all children and, subsequently, greater overall academic achievement (see Chubb & Moe, 1990).

The aim of this chapter is to reevaluate rational choice theory as applied to school choice models by examining the impact of nonacademic factors, especially the race and class of the students in a given school, on parents' school preferences. In other words, we will argue that the use of economic supply-and-demand principles to describe parental behavior in the educational free market completely ignores the way in which racial and class bias can and will leave poor and minority children with few attractive educational options. We will explore, from a sociological perspective, ways in which families are constrained or "bounded" in their education choices by their lack of market resources and their perceptions of where they fit into the social hierarchy.

Rational Choice Theory Revisited

Riker and Ordeshook's (1973) positive political theory—a political science offshoot of economic rational choice theory—states that people form "bundles of opinions" by logically arranging their preferences before choosing among various alternatives. Once the preference bundles are formed, according to this theory, people are directed by a cost-benefit analysis in making goal-directed decisions. Riker and Ordeshook note that when people seek goals there is a rationale for behavior. The authors state, therefore, that goal-directed and highly purposeful behavior is the substance of rationality.

According to Becker (1986, p. 108), this rational decision-making theory is as applicable to understanding people's demand for "retail trade, films or education" as it is for "autos and meat." In fact, Becker states that, after long reflection on his own research applying this economic approach to "fertility, education, the uses of time, crime, marriage, social interactions, and other 'sociological,' 'legal,' and 'political' problems," he concludes that the goal-oriented, self-maximizing rational theory is applicable to all human behavior.

While other social scientists might enjoy disproving Becker's conclusions concerning the goal-oriented rationality of choosing a marriage partner or making childbearing decisions, we would like to point out the fundamental flaws in this economic theory as it has been applied to the argument that free market school choice leads to educational improvement. To do this, we must first examine the necessary assumptions concerning how parents and students create "preference bundles" when comparing complex social institutions such as schools. It is important to keep in mind that school choice policy will only force schools to improve if parents prefer "school quality"—in terms of the actual instruction going on in the classroom—over other school characteristics, such as location, extracurricular activities, or the status of the students who attend.

Unfortunately, in American society, "school quality" is often a misnomer for "student quality," which is measured by heavily biased principles. In fact, the true delineation between desirable and undesirable schools is frequently drawn along racial and social class lines. The whiter and wealthier a school, the better. In other words, the quality of a school is too often defined by the color and, less distinctly, the class of the students who attend rather than by any objective measure of the teaching and learning that goes on there. This is a deep-seated truism that nearly every parent and educator is aware of, although few will admit. It's a truism buttressed by two central themes:

(1) White and wealthy students, on the average, score higher on standardized tests and are more likely to go to college than nonwhite and low-income students. Hence the two most frequently applied measures of a "good" school—standardized test scores and college-going rates—are constantly employed to reinforce the belief that whiter, wealthier schools do a better job of teaching students than schools serving darker, lower-income students. Schools are rarely graded on yearly *improvements* in student test scores or other achievement indicators such as the number of students who are the first in their families to graduate from high school or go on to college. These would be better measures of how the schools, as opposed to family backgrounds, help students succeed.

(2) The social climate or "moral atmosphere" of a school—the achievement ideology of the students, their educational and occupational aspirations, their cultural capital, and so on—is yet another way in which the larger society defines good and bad schools (see Maddaus, 1988). Many of these social climate variables are shaped by the cultural mores of the students who attend—mores that vary radically between different racial and socioeconomic groups and are shaped by the perceived opportunity structure for members of each (see Fordham & Ogbu, 1986; Willis, 1977). "Good" schools are those that enroll students who are quiet in the hallways and able to stay awake in class, students who see a direct link between a high school diploma and their futures, and students who value a traditional Eurocentered curriculum. "Bad" schools, on the other hand, are those enrolling students who carry weapons, have little hope of going to college or getting a high-paying job, and know more about the life of Malcolm X and the origins of rap music than the history of Western civilization.

These two sets of standards are used in rating both private and public schools, which means that private schools are invariably considered "better" than public schools because they admit students on the basis of test scores, they can expel disruptive students, and they attract predominantly white families that are above average in terms of wealth, religious conviction, and the emphasis they place on "good" learning environments (see Coleman, Hoffer, & Kilgore, 1982; Cookson, 1991).

The fact that our society tends to measure school quality by factors that are inherently biased toward white and wealthy schools has been one of the major forces behind American suburbanization and the growing isolation of minority students in inner-city public schools—schools that are as much fraught by their low-status image as they are by the realities of their poor communities. These status-based differences in how people perceive school quality are evident in the Braddock, Crain, McPartland, and Dawkins (1986) study of the hiring practices of business owners and personnel managers. They found that the type of high school—all black, inner city versus predominantly white suburban—that a black graduate attended plays an important role in whether or not he or she will be hired by a white-owned business. In fact, all other factors being equal, a black graduate of a suburban school was, on the average, assigned to a job roughly three and two-thirds points higher in occupational prestige (based on a socioeconomic index) than a black male graduate of an inner-city school.

If such school-status factors influence, indeed delude, educational consumers' perception of "school quality," then the argument that free market school choice will force educational improvements becomes more tenuous. In fact, there is considerable evidence that educational choices based more on school-status factors than on school-quality factors have, for years, contributed to the extremely separate and unequal educational opportunities for poor and minority students. Since 1954, when the Supreme Court declared legally segregated schools unconstitutional, white parents have resisted enrolling their children in schools with black children even when those schools are closer to their homes and offer distinctive educational programs (Orfield, 1978).

There is a fair amount of research evidence that race- and class-based views of image and status affect parents' perceptions of "good" and "bad" schools. For instance, a study by Sobel and Beck (1980) found that black parents were more likely to rate their children's school favorably (on factors such as teaching methods, discipline, administration, and curriculum) if they thought it was a predominantly white school. This was true even for black parents whose children were actually enrolled in all-black schools. Similarly, black parents whose children were attending predominantly white schools but who thought that their children were in all-black schools were much more likely to rate the school poorly.

Obviously, such school-status perceptions affect parents' school choices. For instance, some poor and minority parents fear that their children cannot compete with whiter and wealthier students in high-status schools. Wells (1991) found clear evidence of such reactions to choice in her study of urban black students' willingness to participate in a voluntary transfer program that would enroll them in predominantly white, upper-middle- and middle-class high schools. She found that isolated poor and minority students often maximize on the comfort and familiarity of the neighborhood school when making a choice despite their stated beliefs that the far away suburban schools—the whiter and wealthier schools—are "better." The parents of these students, many of whom expressed feelings of powerlessness and alienation from their children's school, deferred to the wishes of their children and did not involve themselves in the school choice process at all. Some of these parents openly stated that they did not believe their children were "smart enough" to succeed in a suburban school.

In a comprehensive study of parental choices in a voucher demonstration project in Alum Rock, California, Bridge and Blackman (1978) found that providing the least educated parents with vouchers to spend at the school of their choice did not lower their high level of alienation. Instead, the researchers found that these parents were inhibited from gathering information that would allow them to make decisions based on school-quality factors as opposed to school location and convenience.

The problem, therefore, in discussing objective goal-oriented, economic behavior in the context of school choice is that people do not make choices in social and economic vacuums. Decisions about symbolic social institutions such as schools are strongly affected by where the choosers see themselves fitting into a highly stratified society.

Indeed, one could argue that maximizing on the social clout of a given school is highly rational, especially for an upwardly mobile family. Similarly, one could argue that maximizing on the comfort, familiarity, and convenience of a same-race school is an equally rational choice for an isolated and alienated black family. But will choices based on such nonacademic factors lead to any real and meaningful educational improvement? Will these "rational choosers" place pressure on schools to provide better services to all children?

The Bounded Rationality of School Choosers

Becker (1986, p. 110), in his contention that the economic approach is uniquely powerful because of its ability to integrate a wide range of human behavior, states that because "economists generally have had little to contribute" to the understanding of how people form preferences, they assume that preferences do not change substantially over time, nor are they "very different between wealthy and poor persons, or even between persons in different societies and cultures."

Yet, while it may satisfy economists to dismiss the issue of how preferences vary among people of different status groups simply because their discipline has contributed little to the topic, social scientists who study class and status group conflict are less inclined to believe that everyone—rich, poor, black, white, and so on—has similar preferences.

In fact, the tendency of policymakers and economists to ignore the social context of the chooser in "goal-directed" decision-making processes such as school choices makes the rational choice argument seem so inappropriate to the understanding of everyday life and the real world. Sociologists and psychologists, for example, are more likely to view rationality as a relative, norm-directed concept. In other words, what is a rational educational choice for a low-income student, who has no money for a college education and who perceives few opportunities for social mobility, is probably not a rational educational choice for an upper-class student, whose parents can afford the most expensive colleges and whose primary responsibility is to secure the necessary educational credential to maintain his social status. In choosing schools, both of these students have greater considerations than simply objective measure of "school quality" per se.

Paradoxically, those who tout the value of rational choice theory in predicting the actions of all people—despite race or class differences—in a competitive free market often point to Weber's writing on rationality and the function of the capitalist market to bolster their arguments (see Dex, 1985). Yet these writers often ignore some of Weber's most critical points concerning economic and social action. For instance, Weber (1979) wrote that goal-oriented rationality, tradition, and affect *all* shape actions. Weber defined *traditional action* as the expression of settled customs or a dull reaction to accustomed stimuli and *affective action* as a situation in which an agent is prompted by a simple, unreflective desire. Weber stated that, even in instances where there is a high degree of rationalization of action, the impact of traditional and affective orientations remain considerable. Indeed, he wrote that most actions are of mixed types—rational, traditional, and affective.

Furthermore, Weber divided rationality into two spheres:

(a) *formal rationality* of economic action, or the "quantitative calculation" by the technically most adequate available methods and accounting as applied to economic decisions, and

(b) *substantive rationality*, which is shaped by "economically oriented social action under some criterion (past, present or potential) of ultimate value," regardless of the nature of these ends.

According to Weber, substantive rationality, unlike formal rationality, is full of ambiguities because it includes one element common to all "substantive" analyses:

> to apply certain criteria of ultimate ends, whether they be ethical, political, utilitarian, hedonistic, feudal, egalitarian, or whatever, and measure the results of the economic action, however formally "rational" in the sense of correct calculation they may be, against these scales of "value rationality" or "substantive goal rationality." (Weber, 1979, p. 85)

Weber's emphasis on tradition or settled customs, affective or unreflective desire, and substantive rationality in describing social or economic action demonstrates his understanding of the role of cultural and economic dominance in human decision making. In fact, he wrote that the emergence of "rational association from amorphous social action" is often due to domination and the way in which it has been exercised. He writes that the structure of dominance can determine the form of social action and its orientation toward a goal (Weber, 1979, p. 941). Weber's writing on rationality and action therefore includes decision makers whose goal-directed, rational behavior is strongly influenced by and cannot be separated from his or her position in a complex and stratified society.

Contemporary social scientists have also looked for socially embedded meanings of rationality. Elster, for instance, writes that, while economists tend to explain all decision-making behavior in terms of maximized economic utility, sociologists attempt to explain human behavior in terms of social norms and are therefore more likely to emphasize the effect of habit, tradition, roles, or duty—either as a deliberate act to meet the expectations of other people and conform to a self-image or as an unthinking acting out of what one is—on decisions:

> Sociologists argue that the choice of a criminal career or of higher education really is no choice at all, but that the individual is propelled into certain channels by subculture-specific norms or values. The economist tends to assume that individuals are attracted by differential rewards associated with the available courses of action. (Elster, 1986, p. 23)

In a discussion of the difference between economists' and psychologists' viewpoints on rationality, Simon (1987, p. 39) states:

> In situations that are complex and in which information is very incomplete (i.e., virtually all real world situations), the behavior theories deny that there is any magic for producing behavior even approximating an objective maximization of profits or utilities. They therefore seek to determine what the actual frame of the decision is, how that frame arises from the decision situation, and how, within that frame, reason operates.

In an attempt to determine "the frame of the decision," Simon created the concept of subjective or "bounded rationality," which he contrasts to objective rationality by delineating "objective characteristics of the environment external to the choosing organism" and "perceived characteristics" or "characteristics of the organism itself" that are thought to be fixed and out of its control. Objective rationality, therefore, concerns a cost-benefit analysis of what is available for the choosing (i.e., Is a better school worth a longer bus ride?) whereas bounded rationality is strongly tied to the self-perception of the decision maker (Simon, 1983, p. 401). Simon describes this psychological view of bounded rationality as procedural, a view that attempts to take into account the decision maker's *perception* of the real world.

Constraints on the decision-making process—that is, incomplete information, a lack of self-confidence, or low expectations—lead to what Simon calls "satisficing" as opposed to maximizing. According to Simon's (1987) satisficing theory, settling for less than the maximum or most desired preference given a set of constraints is sensible even though it might not be sensible if the constraints were removed.

Of course, Becker and other laissez-faire economic advocates (see Arrow, 1987) do admit a certain degree of constraint upon most decision makers. But, as far as these economists are concerned, constraints come only in the form of limited resources—limits that seemingly have nothing to do with the chooser's perception of his or her social status. According to Becker, prices and "other market instruments" allocate scarce resources and thereby "constrain the desires of participants," performing most, if not all, of the functions assigned to "structure" in sociological theories.

Both Becker and Arrow state that rational consumers maximize utility "under budget constraints," which include a limited amount of knowledge (concerning prices and the behavior of others) that a consumer is able to acquire before choosing and the limited amount of time that consumers have to spend in acquiring that knowledge. Arrow (1987, p. 208) states that "all knowledge is costly, even the knowledge of prices" and that optimizing under limited knowledge is certainly more difficult. Arrow even acknowledges that decisions often depend on the individual decision maker's expectations of the future, which are in turn conditional on the information available to him or her. He doubts the "most prevalent" of all macroeconomic assumptions: that all individuals have the same utility function—or at least that they differ only in broad categories. "This postulate leads to curious and, to my mind, serious difficulties in the interpretation of evidence," writes Arrow. He cites research on the relationship between years of education and increased wages, interpreting the latter as a return on investment in the former. "But if all individuals are alike, why do they not make the same choice?" Arrow (1987, p. 205) asks. Yet he fails to take this analysis one step further to ask how an individual's rank in the social hierarchy can affect his or her expectations and the amount of knowledge that he or she has ready access to or can afford to acquire.

Becker (1986, p. 111), on the other hand, denies the usefulness of anything but a straightforward economic approach to assessing constraints:

> The economic approach does not assume that all participants in any market necessarily have complete information or engage in costless transactions . . . [but it] has developed a theory of the optimal or rational accumulation of costly information that implies, for example, greater investment in information when undertaking major than minor decisions.

Furthermore, Becker states that the assumptions of incomplete or costly information are the economist's answer to the same kind of behavior that theorists of other disciplines label "irrational," "traditional," or "nonrational" behavior. Yet, he, like Arrow, refuses to link class or cultural status to the distribution of costly information in a highly stratified society. Nor does he go as far as Arrow does even to mention differences in individual preferences that could easily discredit the notion that choice will inevitably lead to greater demand for school "quality": "I do not mean to suggest that concepts like the ego and the id, or social norms, are without scientific content. Only that they are tempting materials . . . for ad hoc and useless explanations of behavior" (Becker, 1986, p. 117).

Becker and Arrow's failure to acknowledge how racial and class-based differences leave some people more constrained than others is certainly bothersome when applied to a model of a competitive, free market educational system. Furthermore, it does not take a very sophisticated analysis of racial and class-based stratification and segregation in America to figure out that those students who could benefit most from a quality education will be burdened with the most market constraints.

And, despite Becker's accusation that theorists of other disciplines consider people with incomplete information to be acting "irrationally," one could certainly argue that a careful application of sociological and psychological principles of dominance and stratification to an analysis of the social context of the decision maker will discredit the concept of "irrationality." For, if sociological conflict theory demonstrates ways in which "choices" are not actually what they appear to be, then sociologists have done far more to explain the rationality of a seemingly irrational action than an economic explanation of maximized utility within "informational constraints" that are unrelated to class, culture, or the social structure. The sociological "deterministic" view, as Elster (1979) states it, of people being propelled into choices by norms, values, tradition, expectations of others, or self-image places decision making into a social framework, whereas the economic assumption of identical preference functions, in which more is usually better, presumes that all people make decisions within a social void.

Class, Status, and the Educational Market

We predict, therefore, that a deregulated, free market system in which the government gives all parents a set dollar amount to spend in public or private schools of choice—a system in which every family fends for itself—will lead to greater racial, ethnic, and economic segregation and stratification through two forms of bounded rationality.

(1) Members of dominant status groups—that is, the white and wealthy —will have greater market resources, including time, money, information, educational background, political clout, and personal connections and far fewer market constraints (see Elmore, 1986). This will give them a definite advantage in the competition against members of subordinate status groups for seats in the most demanded schools. These market resources include even the less obtrusive aspects of privileged backgrounds—that is, Bourdieu and Passeron's (1979) "cultural capital." For, when parents of the dominant class are able to transmit high-status culture that is greatly valued and generously rewarded in the educational system to their children, the children of lower-status groups are at an extreme disadvantage in a competitive educational market.

In his comparison of "formal" versus "substantive" rationality, Weber (1979, p. 107) describes "substantive conditions of formal rationality" in a money economy as affected by the distribution of wealth and the structure of marginal utilities in income groups with the resources and inclination to purchase a given utility. Weber states that formal rationality itself does not tell us anything about the satisfaction of real wants unless it is combined with an analysis of the distribution of income.

He wrote that the mode of distribution, in accord with the law of marginal utility, excludes the nonwealthy from competing for highly valued goods; it favors the owners and, in fact, gives them a monopoly to acquire such goods (Weber, 1979, pp. 926-927). Weber also notes that class situation is ultimately a market situation—although he added that culturally based status groups can hinder the strict carrying through of the sheer market principle (1979, p. 930).

Weber portrays the culturally based status groups as being in constant competition either to maintain their privileged status or to gain a more privileged status, and that struggle—for wealth, power, and prestige—is carried out primarily through social institutions, such as schools. Because educational attainment is a crucial element for status and economic maintenance and achievement, there is great demand for high-status education credentials. Thus high-status parents will use whatever means available to enroll their children in the highest-status schools. This investment in high-status education will pay off in the form of easy access to high-status postsecondary education, which will lead to high-status employment:

As to the general effect of the status order, only one consequence can be stated, but it is a very important one: the hindrance of the free development of the market. This occurs first for those goods that status groups directly withhold from free exchange by monopolization, which may be effected either legally or conventionally. (Weber, 1979, p. 937)

Meanwhile, as the work of neo-Weberians has demonstrated, there are several different ways in which upper-class and high-status groups can monopolize wealth, power, and prestige. For instance, according to Collins (1979), members of various status groups distinguish themselves from people outside of the group through "moral evaluation" such as "honor, taste, breeding, respectability, propriety, cultivation," and so on. Participation in these "associational groups" gives each individual a fundamental sense of identity as well as legitimate cause to exclude those who lack the in-group culture. "The 'parvenu' is never accepted, personally and without reservation, by the privileged status groups, no matter how completely his style of life has been adjusted to theirs." Status groups often use a common culture as a mark of group membership, writes Collins, and therefore status group education tends to include much ceremony to demonstrate group solidarity and to publicly distinguish members from nonmembers (1971, pp. 1010-1011). Cookson and Persell's (1985, p. 30) study of the socialization process that takes place within America's elite boarding schools provides clear evidence of such ceremony and solidarity: "The cultural capital that prep school students accumulate in boarding schools is a treasure trove of skills and status symbols that can be used in later life."

Such in-group and out-group demarkation and solidarity causes students and parents to prefer cultural homogeneity in choosing among various schools. For lower-status students, such choices could obviously work to their disadvantage in terms of their chances of ever entering higher-status groups.

(2) The second form of bounded rationality in school choice emanates from the worldview, or what Bourdieu and Passeron (1977) call "habitus," of a large number of the subordinate status group members. This lower-status viewpoint is such that these group members are either intimidated by, distrustful of, or resistant to members of the dominant group and therefore will often remove themselves from the

competition for seats in the "best" schools. Bourdieu and Passeron describe habitus as "a system of durably acquired schemes of perception, thought and action," usually generated by objective conditions, that tends to persist even after alteration of those conditions. Therefore they see habitus as a crucial element in the reproduction of the existing social order:

> [If] the school and "society" take as much account of the relation to culture as of culture, then it is clear how much remains unintelligible until one goes to the principle underlying the production of the most durable academic and social differences, the habitus—the generative, unifying principle of conducts and opinions which is also their explanatory principle . . . it tends to reproduce the system of objective conditions of which it is the product. (Bourdieu & Passeron, 1977, p. 161)

In their research on the educational decisions of French college students, Bourdieu and Passeron found that the habitus of the more rural and lower-class students led them to eliminate themselves from competition for places in high-status educational institutions.

One of the key elements of Bourdieu and Passeron's theory of reproductive process is this self-elimination of "culturally unfavored" students from the competition for high-status education. This comes in three forms: "self-depreciation," "devaluation of the school and its sanctions" (resistance), or a resigned attitude to failure and exclusions. All of these self-eliminating practices involve choices made by lower-status or "culturally unfavored" students based upon an evaluation of their chances of succeeding in an educational system that rewards high-status students for their "cultural capital" and other market resources mentioned above. This could also mean that the alienation and powerlessness that results from being a member of a lower-status group—a racial or ethnic minority or a lower-income, less educated person—in a highly structured society will sometimes cause parents to feel that they are incapable of making a high- versus low-status school choice for their children. As was noted earlier, powerlessness and alienation were prevalent findings in Wells's (1991) study of black students and parents who "chose" to stay in inner-city high schools instead of transferring to suburban ones.

In a study of working-class school boys in England, Willis (1977) analyzed the role of cultural background in influencing students' educational aspirations and job choice. He found that "cultural forms" are powerful determinants of an individual's outlook and that working-class boys' career decisions are based on what they view to be a realistic assessment of their opportunities and life chances. The work of other sociologists and anthropologists, including Kohn (1969) and Fordham and Ogbu (1986), support the theory that members of subordinate races or classes have less optimistic outlooks on their life chances, which affect important decisions and actions.

Hence "rational" educational consumers can be expected to choose schools based on several factors other than academic quality and could quite possibly, given their view of their access routes to high-status and high-paying jobs, choose a school of inferior academic quality but with a superior athletic program. It is also highly feasible that the most alienated educational consumers will choose not to choose—that they will be overwhelmed by the race for seats in high-status schools and will therefore withdraw themselves from that competition.

Conclusions

To the extent that status group conflict and the social context of the decision makers complicate the school choice process, the possibility that parental choice policies will force most schools to improve through parents' demands for high-quality instruction appears less likely. The definition of a "rational," self-maximizing choice between various social institutions such as schools, which is somewhat easy to explain from an economic rational choice perspective, becomes blurred when viewed through a sociological lens. If parents and students cannot remove themselves from their social context and choose "good" academic institutions over "bad" ones—regardless of the social status of the students in either—then the pressure placed on educators is to supply high-status schools to educational consumers as opposed to high-quality ones. Should the two overlap, those who maximize on status should get higher quality as well—provided they have the market resources to access high-status schools. Meanwhile, those who remove themselves from the competition for higher-status schools—because they lack information and access, because they feel incompetent, or because they feel it won't pay off in the long run—will be left behind in schools drained of valuable resources and students from more upwardly mobile families.

All parents—rich and poor, black and white—want what is best for their children. But some parents are faced with more difficult choices than others—choices that are mired in the reality of discrimination and domination. Black parents who have sent their children to desegregated schools often tell of the trade-off between the pain of exposing their sons or daughters to racism and thereby possibly crushing their self-esteem and the desire to enroll them in a higher-status school. White parents, in their search for whiter, wealthier schools, do not have to make such trade-offs. In a society steeped in status group conflict and stratified according to race and class, a decision to keep a black child in a low-status all-black school to spare him the pain of racism is a perfectly rational choice. But it is not maximizing—it is satisficing.

Unfortunately, exploring these various social science perspectives of how parents and students choose schools is politically unpopular. Those who raise such issues are accused of calling poor and minority parents too stupid to choose schools. Yet we argue that to examine the social context of decision makers and consider the different ways in which they are bounded by a view of where they fit into the larger social structure is not an attempt to judge the rationality or irrationality—and certainly not the intelligence—of their decisions. Rather, it is a way of looking more carefully at the social framework of those decisions and asking what variables may cause people to make educational choices in which academic quality plays a role secondary to issues of dominance and resistance.

Answers to such questions can lead to the creation and implementation of equitable and inclusive (as opposed to competitive and exclusive) school choice programs in which all families are guaranteed access to high-quality schools, and school "status" as a reflection of student enrollment is deemphasized (see Alves & Willie, 1990). Such programs do exist in public-school-only choice programs within single school districts in Massachusetts and New Jersey. In these more controlled choice settings, every parent has a choice of several elementary schools, each of which offers a different curricular emphasis or educational philosophy and each of which is racially balanced to reflect the makeup of the district as a whole. Only through inclusive, regulated programs such as these can we achieve anything close to equal educational opportunity through parental choice in education.

References

Alves, M. J., & Willie, C. V. (1990). Choice, decentralization and desegregation: The Boston Controlled Choice Plan. In W. H. Clune & J. F. Witte (Eds.), *Choice and control in American education: Vol. 2. The practice of choice, decentralization and school restructuring* (pp. 17-75). London: Falmer.

Arrow, K. J. (1987). Rationality of self and others in an economic system. In R. M. Hogarth & M. W. Reder (Eds.), *Rational choice: The contrast between economics and psychology* (pp. 201-216). Chicago: University of Chicago Press.

Becker, G. (1986). The economic approach to human behavior. In J. Elster (Ed.), *Rational choice* (pp. 108-122). Oxford: Basil Blackwell.

Bourdieu, P., & Passeron, J. (1977). *Reproduction in education, society, and culture* (R. Nice, Trans.). London: Sage. (Original work published in 1970)

Bourdieu, P., & Passeron, J. (1979). *The inheritors: French students and their relation to culture* (R. Nice, Trans.). Chicago: University of Chicago Press. (Original work published in 1964)

Braddock, J. H., Crain, R. L., McPartland, J. D., & Dawkins, R. L. (1986). Applicant race and job placement decisions: A national survey experiment. *International Journal of Sociology and Social Policy, 6,* 3-24.

Bridge, R. G., & Blackman, J. (1978). *A study of alternatives in American education: Vol. 4. Family choice in schooling* (Report No. R-217014-NIE). Santa Monica, CA: Rand Corporation.

Chubb, J. E., & Moe, T. M. (1990). *Politics, markets, and America's schools.* Washington, DC: Brookings Institution.

Coleman, J. S., Hoffer, T., & Kilgore, S. (1982). *High school achievement: Public, Catholic and private schools compared.* New York: Basic Books.

Collins, R. (1971). Functional and conflict theories of educational stratification. *American Sociological Review, 36,* 1002-1019.

Collins, R. (1979). *The credential society.* Orlando, FL: Academic Press.

Cookson, P. W., Jr. (1991). Politics, markets, and America's schools: A review. *Teachers College Record, 93,* 156-160.

Cookson, P. W., Jr., & Persell, C. H. (1985). *Preparing for power: America's elite boarding schools.* New York: Basic Books.

Dex, S. (1985). The use of economists' models in sociology. *Ethnic and Racial Studies, 8,* 516-533.

Elmore, R. F. (1986). *Choice in public education* (Report No. JNE-01). Santa Monica, CA: Rand Corporation.

Elster, J. (1979). *Ulysses and the sirens: Studies in rationality and irrationality.* Cambridge: Cambridge University Press.

Elster, J. (1986). Introduction. In J. Elster (Ed.), *Rational choice.* Oxford: Basil Blackwell.

Fordham, S., & Ogbu, J. (1986). Black students' school success: Coping with the burden of acting white. *Urban Review, 18*(3), 176-206.

Kohn, M. L. (1969). *Class and conformity: A study of values.* Homewood, IL: Dorsey.

Maddaus, J. (1988). *Parents' perceptions of the moral environment in choosing their children's elementary schools.* Paper presented at the annual meeting of the Association for Moral Education, Pittsburgh, PA.

Orfield, G. (1978). *Must we bus? Segregated schools and national policy.* Washington, DC: Brookings Institution.

Riker, W. H., & Ordeshook, P. C. (1973). *An introduction to positive political theory.* Englewood Cliffs, NJ: Prentice-Hall.

Simon, H. (1983). *Models of bounded rationality: Behavioral economics and business organizations.* Cambridge: MIT Press.

Simon, H. (1987). Rationality in psychology and economics. In R. M. Hogarth & M. W. Reder (Eds.), *Rational choice: The contrast between economics and psychology* (pp. 25-40). Chicago: University of Chicago Press.

Sobel, M. G., & Beck, W. W. (1980). Phenomenological influences in minority attitudes toward school desegregation. *The Urban Review, 12*, 31-40.

Weber, M. (1979). *Economy and society* (G. Roth & C. Wittich, Trans.). Berkeley: University of California Press.

Wells, A. S. (1991). *The sociology of school choice: A study of black students' participation in a voluntary transfer plan.* Unpublished doctoral dissertation, Teachers College, Columbia University.

Willis, P. (1977). *Learning to labor: How working class kids get working class jobs.* New York: Columbia University Press.

5

The Ideology of Consumership and the Coming Deregulation of the Public School System

PETER W. COOKSON, JR.

The Crisis in Citizenship

The American belief in the efficacy of education to reform and re-shape the economy and society is almost cosmological. A day hardly passes without politicians, educators, and pundits at large reiterating the social catechism that good schools lead to a strong economy and a harmonious society. If our civil religion were to have ten social commandments, certainly "thou shall honor education" would be among the top five. Americans tend see schools as redemptive institutions (Popkewitz, 1991, p. 148). President Bush's *America 2000: An*

AUTHOR'S NOTE: The material quoted from *The New York Times*, copyright © 1991 by The New York Times Company, are reprinted by permission

Education Strategy epitomizes this reverence for this idea of education in rhetoric meant to stir the heart, if not to engage the head (U.S. Department of Education, 1991). Only the bravest heretics question the assumption that there is an intimate relationship between what goes on in schools and what goes on in society (Averch, Carroll, Donaldson, Kiesling, & Pincus, 1972; Jencks et al., 1972). Usually, these heretics are found in university settings, in good part because it is in the university that assertions are expected to be supported by empirical evidence. Traditionally, the relationship between facts and faith has been uneasy because, while the former requires a suspension of unexamined beliefs, the latter requires the suspension of skepticism. Thus the American faith in education is largely undiminished by the fact that there is convincing evidence that the connection between academic achievement and economic productivity is weak at best (Berg, 1971; Jencks et al., 1972). Celebrated multimillionaires do not often become notorious because of their erudition and subtlety of mind.

If, then, the facts only weakly support the American faith in education to improve the economy, from where does this faith draw its undeniable power? Obviously, one could fill volumes answering this question, because faith is no less complex than reason; it is common in American educational reform movements to overlook the complex issues of history and power and to "reinvent" reforms on a cyclical basis (Cuban, 1990; Popkewitz, 1988). It could be argued that, in its simplest form, the essence of the American faith in education springs, in part, from the need for a national identity (Cremin, 1977). As a nation of immigrants, Americans have self-consciously tried to create a national identity from a variety of European, South American, African, and now Asian identities. One mechanism for creating the American identity has been through common schooling (Cremin, 1977). Children have gone to public schools to be initiated into citizenship. This belief in the social importance of good citizenship has given purpose to public education even when it has failed to produce literate and numerate students.

Ramirez and Boli-Bennett (1982) have traced the origins of citizenship to the ongoing dialectic between the ideologies of state expansion and individualism. In effect, years of education have become a proximate measure of a nation-state's capacity to create loyal citizens. The actual content of that experience is of secondary importance (Collins, 1971, 1975; Kamens, 1974; Meyer, 1970, 1977). The credentializing function of education not only sorts and selects students by class background but establishes a unifying ideology of group cohesion (Collins, 1979). Perhaps the "genius" of American education has been its ability to maintain the class structure, while at the same time creating a sense of national cohesion (Bowles & Gintis, 1976).

In the 1980s, however, the value of educational credentials suffered through a period of deflation. A diploma from a public high school did not prepare students for the world of economic competition in good part because the economy was rapidly changing. Even a college degree did not guarantee employment. The belief in education faltered (Center for Education Statistics, 1987, p. 82). Perhaps this explains why so many conservative groups focused on reforming education, which by implication the liberals (and radicals) had left in shambles. The sense that public education had lost its luster could not but tarnish its image as the all-American molder of citizens. The decline of the public school was accompanied by the rise of the private school (Coleman & Hoffer, 1987; Coleman, Hoffer, & Kilgore, 1982). Various explanations have been offered as to why private schools seem to be more effective learning environments than public schools. Chubb and Moe (1990) have argued strongly that private sector schools are more effective than public sector schools because they are market driven and thus more competitive than public sector schools. To this date, however, it is still unclear whether or not private schools are more academically effective than public schools, once the family backgrounds of students are taken into account. From a political point of view, the differences that distinguish public and private schools in terms of causing differences in student achievement are less significant than the fact that these differences exist and can be used effectively in the larger political struggle to break the public school "monopoly." In the eyes of some reformers, education should be treated as a consumer item like any other consumer item.

The marketplace (with its competitive social Darwinistic root metaphor) is hypothesized to be more powerful than democracy (with its cooperative root metaphor) for creating schools of excellence and equity (Chubb & Moe, 1990; Paulu, 1989). The ideal of commonality and citizenship has suddenly become old-fashioned and even vaguely unpatriotic in the eyes of some important educational policy planners. The ideology of consumership is flexible in that it attaches itself to almost any suitable cultural artifact, but, at its core, it is the belief that the good society—and the good school—is best created and maintained through the mechanisms of the marketplace (Friedman & Friedman, 1980). Simply put, individuals pursuing their own self-interest create a common good because, viewed collectively, self-interest is a better arbiter of human affairs than "social engineering." Many market-driven educational reforms have already been enacted in Great Britain. As these reforms only began in 1988, it is too early to evaluate their effects on schools and students. We already know, however, that predicting the impact of markets on school organization is extremely complex, and there can be unintended consequences when public sector schools are removed from state control through deregulation (Walford, in press).

Clearly, this belief in the power of the marketplace to create the good society has been with us from at least the time of Adam Smith. Its most recent incarnation, however, has been fueled by the conservative "revolution" of the 1980s, which has given the marketplace the central place in its pantheon of virtues. Curiously, the world according to Adam Smith has found new advocates at the very time when marketplace mechanisms have proven to be extremely vulnerable to manipulation and at a time when the art of buying has surpassed the art of saving to such a degree that Americans are now a nation of debtors. Ambiguity and paradox, however, are not the long suits of the new proponents of consumership. On the contrary, they are close to being true believers in Adam Smith's market morality. The body politic is being transformed into the body economic.

This chapter examines the origins and implications of the ideology of consumership as it relates to the educational reform movement known generically as "school choice." Few school reform proposals have attracted as much attention as choice. It is difficult to determine whether this attention reflects a deeply felt need by the American public to change the way elementary and secondary schools are governed or whether it is simply a response to a well-financed, slickly orchestrated publicity blitz. One might wonder whether American families, if left to their own thinking, would decide that what really ails American education is state control. Most parents, according to the Gallup Poll, are more disturbed by the lack of discipline in the schools and what they perceive to be poor teaching than they are by governance issues (Cookson, 1987).

The essential argument of this chapter is that, if consumership does replace citizenship as the basic ethos and driving force of American education, the public school system will cease to exist as we have known it. The logic of consumership leads to deregulation because, if market mechanisms are superior to democratic governance, then inhibitions of market mechanisms are counterproductive and destructive (Chubb & Moe, 1990). If we are able to select our schools the way we select our laundry detergents, then state regulation must be minimal, unobtrusive, and probably insignificant. Not all school choice plans are fundamentally antistate but, by their very nature, free market school choice plans are designed to limit the power of the state in determining where students will attend school. An examination of the ideology of consumership is timely, one might say past due.

Investigations of educational policy can be approached at many levels. In this chapter, I examine the ideology of consumership as a form of public discourse. As we will see, the advocates of free market school choice have been very successful in developing a public rhetoric that, in effect, sets the parameters for the debate on whether or not the current form of school governance in the United States is responsible for many of the educational problems the nation faces. Ideology and rhetoric can be very significant in swaying public as well as professional opinion. The relationship between public discourse and policy is intimate; before a policy can be successfully implemented, its rationale must be seen as credible. Rhetoric often precedes and influences reality.

I begin this examination of the ideology of consumership by distinguishing free market school choice policies from school choice policies that are based on empirical observations of how schools work. School choice advocates who base their arguments on empirical observations will be referred to in this chapter as "pragmatists." Below, the difference between pragmatists and what I call "true believers" in free market school choice will be articulated. The differences between these two groups are significant. In the public mind, the distinction between school choice pragmatists and school choice true believers may be blurred, but the distinction is important, because the pragmatists and the true believers are suggesting significantly different types of reforms in educational governance. I also examine the "gospel" of free market school choice in some depth and finish by speculating on how the emerging ideology of consumership might affect public education in the coming decade.

The School Choice Movement:
Pragmatists and True Believers

In politics and in policy formation, the distinction between substance and illusion can be ephemeral. The idea of school choice has captured the public's imagination but there is little genuine understanding of what the term means or how school choice policies could affect the operations of schools. This confusion may be in part due to the fact that the school choice coalition is itself a loose confederation of educational interest groups rather than one unified movement. Generally, there is little consistency on how to characterize this coalition. Who are the major actors and what are their agendas? As mentioned above, I would suggest that a distinction ought to be made between the pragmatists and the true believers. Essentially, the pragmatists are educators and scholars who have studied alternative schools and, through their research, have come to believe that diversity in education provides a healthy leaven to the weight of the public school bureaucracy (Alves & Willie, 1990; Glenn, 1990; Raywid, 1987). Many of these educators and scholars were doing research and writing long before the school choice movement was invented. The true believers are essentially not school reformers at all; they simply have faith in the virtues of the free market and apply those beliefs to educational governance. Usually they come from outside the traditional educational community and have little previous experience as practicing elementary and secondary school educators. This lack of training and experience is seen as an asset by many of the true believers, however, because they are able to portray themselves as being without vested interests or loyalties to the old way of thinking (Chubb & Moe, 1990). Very often, the findings of the pragmatic empiricists have been used by the true believers as evidence that school choice works (Domanico, 1990). In some cases, the evidence has been somewhat loosely interpreted to suit the argument (see, for instance, Paulu, 1989, p. 15, for examples of how free market choice advocates use empirical studies to support their conclusions). Contrary to the claims of many school choice advocates, however, there is a growing body of research that seems to indicate that innovation precedes choice, not the other way around (Harrington & Cookson, in press).

Lest one think that the distinction between pragmatists and true believers is somewhat arch or artificial, Anthony Alvarado, who was superintendent of schools in Manhattan District Four in the early 1970s and the architect of the educational reforms that made District Four so famous, recently wrote,

> Much of the literature on school choice cites the experience of New York City's Community School District 4, where I was superintendent for 10 years, as evidence that choice can improve schools. But I espoused choice in District 4, as I have in District 2, where I have served since 1987, out of pragmatism, not ideology.

He continued, "Promoting choice as the primary method of educational change is like rearranging the deck chairs on the Titanic" (Alvarado, 1991, p. 19A). The free market school choice reformers approach the problem of finding supporting evidence of the effectiveness of school choice differently than do the pragmatists. The true believers begin with the premise that the marketplace is even-handed and an efficient sorter and selector of students and then search for evidence, while the pragmatists examine alternative schools and recognize choice as one element in creating productive learning environments.

Clearly, the driving political force of the consumership coalition is the Republican party and the various research institutes, centers, and individuals who provide intellectual support for conservative causes. In the last five years, the U.S. Department of Education has been consistently pro-school choice and the Roman Catholic church supports school choice for financial, if not ideological, reasons. The president himself makes the connection between school reform and the marketplace regularly. He recently asserted, "There's a special place in inventing the New American School for the corporate community, for business and labor" (Bush, 1991). A 1989 White House workshop on school choice unabashedly connected school choice with the marketplace. Dennis Doyle, a senior research fellow at the Hudson Institute in Washington, DC, and a workshop participant, summarized,

There is in the popular mind a vision of cut-throat competition, of profit-taking buccaneers swashbuckling across the State, people who are . . . merciless, kind of Atlas Shrugged/Ayn Rand types. Well, there certainly is that type of competition, but there is competition which is closer to home . . . and that is the competition which emphasizes the supremacy of the consumer, consumer sovereignty, and that, in fact, is what competition is all about. (Paulu, 1989, p. 14)

This position was echoed throughout the workshop, which, in turn, echoed the National Governors' Association 1986 report, *Time for Results*, in which the governors said, "If we first implement choice, true choice among public schools, we unlock the values of competition in the marketplace. Schools that compete for students, teachers, and dollars, will by virtue of the environment, make those changes that will allow them to succeed" (Paulu, 1989, p. 14). Apparently, this deep faith in the marketplace was substantiated for those attending the workshop by 14-year-old Andre Lawrence of New York City, who testified that "I was very happy to decide which school I wanted to attend. It was like shopping, buying a pair of shoes, shopping around until you find something you like" (Paulu, 1989, p. 14).

Another important element of the ideological energy driving the free market school choice movement comes from a group of young White House conservatives who advocate a politics of self-help. The elements of this position include free markets, decentralization, and individual choice. They are strong advocates of government vouchers that will allow parents to choose their children's schools. Sometimes, this position is referred to as the "new paradigm." Representative of this new paradigm is Chester E. Finn, Jr., who is credited as being the current administration's "true education philosopher— and the chief architect of Bush's master plan for fixing schools" (Toch, 1991, pp. 4-6). He argues that the "race is to the swift" and he backs public funding of private schools. He believes that competition with private schools will improve public schools. He goes so far as to imply that there is something unpatriotic about the opposition to private school vouchers when he says, "It's un-American to force students to go to schools they don't want to attend" (Toch, 1991, pp. 4-6).

What has made the consumership coalition so powerful is that it has institutionalized itself, both inside and outside of the government. Such seemingly independent organizations as the Manhattan Institute Center for Educational Innovation in New York City, for instance, have been advocating school choice for a number of years. Its advisory board reads like a mini-*Who's Who* of the education and business elites that constitute the inner circle of the market-oriented school choice movement. The advisers include Peter Flanigan (Managing Director, Dillon Read & Co.), Raymond Chambers (Chairman, Wesray Capital Corp.), Linda Chavez (Senior Fellow, Manhattan Institute), John Chubb (Senior Fellow, Brookings Institution), James Coleman (Professor of Sociology, University of Chicago), A. Wright Elliott (Executive Vice President, The Chase Manhattan Bank), Chester E. Finn, Jr. (Professor of Education and Public Policy, Vanderbilt University), Seymour Fliegal (Former Deputy Superintendent, N.Y.C. District Four), Colman Genn (Superintendent, N.Y.C. District 27), Richard Gilder, Jr. (Partner, Gilder, Gagnon, & Co.), Nathan Glazer (Professor of Education, Harvard University), the Honorable Thomas Kean (President, Drew University), Joe Nathan (Senior Fellow, Humphrey Institute), Robert S. Peterkin (Superintendent, Milwaukee Public Schools), Mary Anne Raywid (Professor of Education, Hofstra University), and Adam Urbanski (President, Rochester Teachers Association) (Domanico, 1991).

As this list indicates, the market-oriented school choice movement represents a working coalition of major banking and corporate interests, university professors, Republican politicians, and a sprinkling of public school administrators and labor leaders. This select group is highly influential. Their resources are considerable and they are able to enlist a number of intellectuals and researchers in their cause, thus giving their conclusions an aura of objectivity and authenticity. Yet, a close examination of the data that these interest groups use to substantiate the argument for greater free market school choice shows they are empirically weak. In fact, one could say that there is almost no convincing evidence that there is a relationship between school choice policies and student achievement (Cookson, 1991a). Strictly speaking, however, many school choice advocates are not interested in scholarly studies of choice; they are interested in promoting their beliefs. Identifying these beliefs is important because, to understand the ideology of consumership, we need a clear sense of its core assumptions.

The Gospel of Free Market Choice

Beliefs and ideologies, if they are to have power, must resonate with individuals' needs, hopes, anxieties, passions, and even fantasies. It is not surprising, therefore, that there is almost an inverse relationship between ideology and reason. Because free market school choice is deeply ideological, discussions of school choice that coolly dissect the possibilities and problems of "rational choice" or eloquently examine the theory of individual liberty are intellectually rewarding but politically unrevealing. To arouse the public to support a cause, the cause's intellectual and political leaders need to define social issues in language and symbols that will arouse in the public a visceral response. The free market school choice advocates have been remarkably successful in this regard. The very word *choice* itself has a patriotic all-American ring to it; the fact that President Bush has linked his educational reforms to the "victory" over Iraq indicates how politicized education reform has become. In this section, we examine the "gospel of choice." I use the word *gospel* with care. An examination of the rhetoric of free market schooling reveals that its advocates begin with a priori assumptions about the social world that are closer to religious beliefs than they are to reasoned arguments. Moreover, the gospel of choice is infused with a sense of social mission that transcends the details related to school governance. For instance, Secretary of Education Lamar Alexander, at the 1989 White House workshop on school choice, summarized the efforts of the group as follows:

> The fact that so many people have come together . . . shows that this movement is kind of beyond all of us. It's bigger than all of us. It will keep going on after us, but perhaps we can do something to nurture it, and that's what we are all here for today. (Paulu, 1989, p. 25)

President Bush (Paulu, 1989, pp. 25-26) also speaks of choice in near-religious terms:

> The evidence is striking and abundant. Almost without exception, wherever choice has been attempted—Minnesota, East Harlem, San Francisco, Los Angeles, and a hundred other places in between—choice has worked. . . . Bad schools get better. Good ones

get better still, and entire school systems have been restored to public confidence by the implementation of these choice plans. Disaffected families have been brought from private schools back into public education. Any school reform that can boast such success deserves our attention, our emphases, and our effort.

For free marketers, school choice is fundamental. Perhaps that's why they insist on an extremely simple view of the American school system (see Witte, 1990, for a critique of how some choice advocates underestimate the diversity of American elementary and secondary education). The fact that we already do have a choice system—and most families choose their local public schools—matters little. The educational world according to the true believers is divided into good schools and bad schools; good schools are choice schools and bad schools are bureaucratic (Chubb & Moe, 1990; Paulu, 1989).

The gospel of free market school choice rests on two main pillars of faith. The first declares that choice is a panacea for virtually all our educational problems and, the second, that only free market mechanisms can unleash human ingenuity, individuality, and creativity. The work of Chubb and Moe (1990) is significant in this light, because they assert that they have solid empirical evidence that market-driven schools are superior to schools that are governed through "direct democratic control." Whether or not these authors' data actually support their primary hypothesis is a matter of debate (Cookson, 1991b). What is of interest in this discussion are their assumptions about markets and their effects on schools.

Chubb and Moe (1990, p. 217) argue, "Without being too literal about it, we think reformers would do well to entertain the notion that choice *is* a panacea." In a world of compromise, such sweeping assertions are rare, and perhaps for good reason. True believers believe in panaceas; pragmatists believe in possibilities. Chubb and Moe (1990, p. 217, italics in original) continue:

> Choice is a self-contained reform with its own rationale and justification. It has the capacity *all by itself* to bring about the kind of transformation that, for years, reformers have been seeking to engineer in myriad other ways. Indeed, if choice is to work to greatest advantage, it must be adopted *without* these other reforms, since the latter are predicated on democratic control and are implemented by bureaucratic means.

But why is choice a panacea? Because, according to Chubb and Moe (1990, p. 189):

> A market system is not built to enable the imposition of higher-order values on the schools, nor is it driven by a democratic struggle to exercise public authority. Instead, the authority to make educational choices is radically decentralized to those most immediately involved. Schools compete for the support of parents and students, and parents and students are free to choose among schools. The system is built around decentralization, competition and choice.

Curiously, despite all the accolades devoted to market mechanisms in the work of Chubb and Moe, their conception of how markets work in contemporary society is simplistic to say the least. They seem to have almost no sense of the history of markets or of the sociology of markets. Their somewhat sanitized, idealized, naive conception of how markets actually operate romanticizes markets and to that degree distorts reality. From what we do know about markets, we can say with some assurance that (a) markets are not benign but are usually indifferent to the needs of the disadvantaged and can be manipulated through fraud and false advertising and (b) markets do not operate naturally but are socially constructed. The relationship between supply and demand is influenced by culture, class, and consumption.

This same lack of historical grounding and sociological sophistication can be found throughout the free market school choice literature. President Bush's *America 2000: The President's Educational Strategy* speaks of reforming education as a "crusade" but tells us little about why a crusade is necessary or how complex the issues are. There are several provisions for school choice within the strategy, including a $200 million Education Certificate Program Support Fund and a $30 million fund for the creation of "National School Choice Demonstration Projects." There is virtually no rationale within the strategy to justify such expenses or any rationale that would allow us to expect that choice would lead to better student outcomes.

Perhaps the president views the issue as settled. At the 1989 White House Workshop on school choice, the participants concluded that there was virtually no educational problem that could not be solved by choice. According to workshop participants, choice does at least eight things for education. These are (Paulu, 1989):

1. Choice can bring basic structural change to our schools.
2. Schools of choice recognize individuality.
3. Choice fosters competition and accountability.
4. Choice can improve educational outcomes.
5. Schools of choice can keep potential dropouts in school and draw back those who have already left.
6. Schools of choice increase parents' freedom.
7. Choice plans increase parent satisfaction and involvement in the schools.
8. Schools of choice can enhance educational opportunities, particularly for disadvantaged parents. (pp. 11-24)

As this litany indicates, the free market gospel of school choice is a complex mixture of faith and fact, of subjective belief and objective reality. The power of a gospel, however, does not spring from its scientific plausibility but from its emotional intensity. As was discussed earlier, rhetoric is powerful when it is backed by powerful people and institutions. Thus the faith of a few can be acquired by the many through the power of suggestion. The fact that there is no genuine empirical evidence to support the eight choice postulates above is not critically important in the political struggle for the core values in American education. The ideology of consumership promises us a painless, inexpensive, and total reformation of public education, and what matters is that people believe it, not that it is true (Chira, 1991).

Public Education at the Crossroads

The connection between business and education in the United States is long-standing (Bowles & Gintis, 1976; Callahan, 1962; Spring, 1972). In a society as commercially oriented as American society, this is not entirely surprising; the belief that education and the economy are tightly linked is virtually unshakable, despite evidence to the contrary. To some degree then, the free market advocates of school choice are simply the latest expression of the American civil religion that holds that cognition best serves commerce.

Yet, the current free market school choice coalition goes one—or two—steps beyond the traditional rhetoric about economy, efficiency, and education. The new paradigm advocates argue that public education should not simply implement certain business practices, they argue that public schools are businesses. They have gone beyond calls for efficiency in public education to arguing that schools should join the ranks of other small businesses that rely on the market for survival. How ironic it is that, in the age of huge conglomerates and multinationals, schools should be asked to become mom-and-pop educational stores, struggling along from year to year entirely dependent on the whims of the marketplace. At the very time when big business is consolidating its holdings and becoming increasingly international, it is suggested that schools be run according to business principles that were discarded and discredited more than 50 years ago.

What would be the consequences to American education if the consumership coalition were to triumph? What would the world of designer schools be like? Would we experience an educational renaissance or an educational collapse? Based on what we know about other privatized institutions, such as the health industry, we can safely say that cost to the consumer would go up, not down. We would also find public dollars following all manner of private schools. Some of these schools might be laudable, others might be horrible. As the work of Wells (1991) has shown, families do not always choose schools on the basis of academic excellence but sometimes on the basis of racial affiliation. There is the real risk that free market school choice plans would lead to a further stratification of the American school system and of American society. Will we be asked to support all-white schools with public dollars? Will the architects of the new paradigm be content to watch public dollars support a series of schools funded by latter-day Leninists? Who will monitor these new schools of choice and hold them accountable? Who will financially insure parents and students when they are swindled, as has happened to so many students when they have enrolled in bogus trade schools and other diploma mills? Will the idea of a common national bond simply drop out of the public ethos?

These and other questions quickly come to mind. Not all school choice policies imply the deregulation of the American school system. Controlled choice, for instance, does not rely on deregulating assumptions or on arguments against democratic control and state regulations (Alves & Willie, 1990). Free market school choice, however, if it is to succeed as an educational reform, must lead to the deregulation of the public school system, because state control is antithetical to the operations of a free market. If public schools are deregulated, a chapter in American history will be closed. Despite all of the criticisms directed at them—and the criticisms are legion—public schools have survived because they fulfill a basic requirement of democracy. In principle, free public education promises every child an equal educational opportunity. This promise has been violated repeatedly, but not because the idea is flawed. It has been violated because, in a highly stratified society, schools have limited capacities to bring about greater social equity. If the public school system was to lose its authority and mission, it would wither and collapse, leaving in its wake an educational wasteland, not an educational wonderland as the free market advocates claim.

In sum, the next several years are critical for public education. Its very organizational raison d'être is under attack. If the consumership coalition succeeds, then we will have entered a new era of American education, an era in which self-interest and competition will pit student against student, and family against family, in the struggle for educational survival.

References

Alvarado, A. J. (1991, April 30). Beyond buzzwords in education. *The New York Times*, p. 19A.

Alves, M. J., & Willie, C. V. (1990). Choice, decentralization and desegregation: The Boston "controlled choice" plan. In W. H. Clune & J. F. Witte (Eds.), *Choice and control in American education: Vol. 2. The practice of choice, decentralization and school restructuring* (pp. 17-75). New York: Falmer.

Averch, H. A., Carroll, S. J., Donaldson, T. S., Kiesling, H. J., & Pincus, J. (1972). *How effective is schooling? A critical review and synthesis of research findings.* Santa Monica, CA: Rand Corporation.

Berg, I. (1971). *Education and jobs: The great training robbery.* Boston: Beacon.

Bowles, S., & Gintis, H. (1976). *Schooling in capitalist America: Educational reform and the contradictions of economic life.* New York: Basic Books.

Bush, G. (1991, April 18). [Remarks by the president at the presentation of the National Education Strategy, the White House].

Callahan, R. E. (1962). *Education and the cult of efficiency.* Chicago: University of Chicago Press.

Center for Education Statistics. (1987). *The condition of education: A statistical report.* Washington, DC: U.S. Department of Education.

Chira, S. (1991, June 12). The rules of the market place are applied to the classroom. *The New York Times,* pp. 1, B9.

Chubb, J. E., & Moe, T. M. (1990). *Politics, markets, and America's schools.* Washington, DC: Brookings Institution.

Coleman, J. S., & Hoffer, T. (1987). *Public and private high schools: The impact of communities.* New York: Basic Books.

Coleman, J. S., Hoffer, T., & Kilgore, S. (1982). *High school achievement: Public, Catholic and private schools compared.* New York: Basic Books.

Collins, R. (1971). Functional and conflict theories of educational stratification. *American Sociological Review, 36,* 1002-1019.

Collins, R. (1975). *Conflict sociology: Toward an explanatory science.* New York: Academic Press.

Collins, R. (1979). *The credential society.* New York: Academic Press.

Cookson, P. W., Jr. (1987). More, different, or better? Strategies for the study of private education. *Educational Policy, 1,* 289-294.

Cookson, P. (1991a). A review: "Politics, markets, and America's schools." *Teachers College Record, 93,* 156-160.

Cookson, P. (1991b). *When is a little a lot? Student achievement, school choice and the politics of educational research.* Unpublished paper.

Cremin, L. A. (1977). *Traditions of American education.* New York: Basic Books.

Cuban, L. (1990). Reforming again, again and again. *Educational Researcher, 19,* 3-13.

Domanico, R. J. (1990). *Restructuring New York City's public schools: The case for public school choice.* New York: Manhattan Institute Center for Educational Innovation.

Domanico, R. J. (1991). *A model public school choice plan for New York City school districts.* New York: Manhattan Institute Center for Educational Innovation.

Friedman, M., & Friedman, R. (1980). *Free to choose.* New York: Harcourt Brace Jovanovich.

Glenn, C. L. (1990). Parent choice: A state perspective. In W. H. Clune & J. F. Witte (Eds.), *Choice and control in American education: Vol. 1. The theory of choice and control in American education* (pp. 327-331). New York: Falmer.

Harrington, D., & Cookson, P. W., Jr. (in press). School reform in East Harlem: Alternative schools vs. "schools of choice." *Empowering teachers and parents: School restructuring through the eyes of anthropologists.*

Jencks, C., et al. (1972). *Inequality.* New York: Basic Books.

Kamens, D. (1974). Colleges and elite formation: The case of prestigious American colleges. *Sociology of Education, 47,* 354-378.

Meyer, J. (1970). The charter: Conditions of diffuse socialization in school. In W. R. Scott (Ed.), *Social processes and social structure.* New York: Holt, Rinehart & Winston.

Meyer, J. (1977, July). Education as an institution. *American Journal of Sociology, 83,* 55-77.

Paulu, N. (1989, October). *Improving schools and empowering parents: Choice in American education.* Washington, DC: Government Printing Office.

Popkewitz, T. S. (1988). Educational reform: Rhetoric, ritual and social interests. *Educational Theory, 38,* 77-93.

Popkewitz, T. S. (1991). *A political sociology of educational reform.* New York: Teachers College Press.

Ramirez, F. O., & Boli-Bennett, J. (1982). Global patterns of educational institutionalization. In P. G. Altbach, R. F. Arnove, & G. P. Kelly (Eds.), *Comparative education* (pp. 15-36). New York: Macmillan.

Raywid, M. A. (1987, June). Public choice, yes; vouchers, no! *Phi Delta Kappan, 68*(10), 762-769.

Spring, J. H. (1972). *Education and the rise of the corporate state.* Boston: Beacon.

Toch, T. (1991, July 15). The wizard of education. *U.S. News and World Report,* pp. 4-6.

U.S. Department of Education. (1991, April 18). *America 2000: An education strategy.* Washington, DC: Author.

Walford, G. (in press). Educational choice and equity in Great Britain. *Educational Policy.*

Wells, A. S. (1991). *The sociology of school choice: A study of black students' participation in a voluntary transfer plan.* Unpublished doctoral dissertation, Teachers College, Columbia University, New York.

Witte, J. F. (1990). Choice and control in American education: An analytical overview. In W. Clune & J. Witte (Eds.), *Choice and control in American education: Vol. 1. The theory of choice and control in education* (pp. 11-46). New York: Falmer.

PART II

Private and Public School Choice

6

Public Subsidies for Private Schools: What Do We Know and How Do We Proceed?

JOHN F. WITTE

Choice in American education, whether it deserves it or not, is the most visible reform idea of the 1990s. The idea of using public revenue to support private school options is 35 years old and its advocates believe its time has come (Friedman, 1955). Those advocates include the president, a number of governors and state legislators, and numerous interest groups throughout the country. The idea has also attracted the attention of scholars and education policy experts. A recent book by John Chubb and Terry Moe (1990b), which makes an unequivocal argument for a largely unregulated public-private

AUTHOR'S NOTE: This chapter previously appeared in *Educational Policy* (in June 1992); copyright © 1992 by Corwin Press. I gratefully acknowledge financial support from the Spencer Foundation and the University of Wisconsin Robert La Follette Institute of Public Affairs.

scholarship system, has stimulated wide discussion and placed choice on the national agenda (Chubb & Moe, 1990a).

This chapter deals only with the issue of public-private school choice. I will not review programs that are restricted to educational choice in the public schools. Although those programs, which include interdistrict open-enrollment plans, magnet schools, and intradistrict choice plans, are more prevalent than programs involving private schools, they do not evoke the degree of controversy or the specter of radical change that private school choice plans do. Public school choice programs are reviewed elsewhere (Witte, 1991a).

As several scholars have noted, it is difficult to discuss public-private school choice (hereafter simply *choice* or *educational choice*) in the abstract. Rather than concentrate on a single, detailed choice plan, however, I define educational choice in general terms to include programs that provide substantial public subsidy of private education.[1] Payment could either go to families who select schools or directly to the schools. Tuition in private schools could vary but could also be capped. It is assumed that private schools in the program would generally operate within existing state statutes regulating private schools (which means much less regulation than for existing public schools). Students could not be rejected for admission based on race. Curriculum, teacher certification, testing, and so on would not be regulated. These are minimal conditions; other requirements could be imposed.[2]

This chapter will review three ways of discussing and analyzing this general form of educational choice. The first is theoretical, the second is evaluation of existing choice programs, and the third is to infer from differences between public and private schools as they now exist. The basic argument is that, currently, we know very little about the potential impacts of choice and that we should therefore move carefully, experimenting with constrained programs along with other nonchoice options.

Theoretical Issues in Educational Choice

Opposing sides in the debate over educational choice come to radically different conclusions on what would result from a choice system. The arguments are quite familiar so I merely summarize them in Table 6.1. The arguments outlined in the table are empirical in

TABLE 6.1 Pro- and Antichoice Arguments

Prochoice Arguments:

1. Choice would require less bureaucracy and more school-level autonomy.
2. Staff motivation, leadership, and morale would improve with educational choice.
3. Parental involvement will be greater under choice.
4. Schools will be more diverse, innovative, and flexible.
5. As a result of 1 through 4, student achievement will increase under choice.
6. Competition and market forces will reduce costs and increase efficiency under choice.

Antichoice Arguments:

1. Selectivity of students will increase inequality between schools.
2. Geographic distribution of students by race and class will produce inequitable choices and increase school segregation.
3. Special needs of students with learning disabilities and handicaps will not be met as well under a choice system.
4. Accountability will be considerably reduced and minimum standards will not be maintained under choice.
5. Information on schools will be costly, inadequate, and more readily available to families of higher socioeconomic status.
6. The common school tradition will be lost as educational diversity increases.

nature; that is, they emphasize what theorists believe would result from an educational choice system. Theorists, however, also differ greatly in the values they place on different outcomes. Advocates stress liberty and diversity. They speak of choice as a primary value that would also further educational opportunity and our pluralistic tradition. Opponents emphasize equality of result, integration, and a common school tradition.

As these positions illustrate, the choice debate evokes deep-rooted values and raises controversial issues that education policymakers have grappled with for generations. It is difficult to see a clear path through this web of claims and counterclaims. Indeed, some of the empirical propositions seem questionable on both sides of the debate. Henry Levin has argued, for example, that bureaucracy in a realistic choice system may be even more cumbersome than in the current system (Levin, 1988).

One could also challenge the assumption that morale and motivation would be higher under a choice system, particularly if that system encompasses some of the more difficult teaching environments such as those in our cities. Teachers and administrators might well be paid less, in addition to feeling the strains of competition. If effective private schools require strong principals, as argued by some choice advocates (Chubb & Moe, 1990a; Coleman & Hoffer, 1987), teacher autonomy could be less than in many current public schools. Teachers and administrators might also lack union protection. Finally, although parental involvement may be valuable in its own right, teachers may justifiably perceive excessive involvement as a hindrance.

That choice would greatly improve the diversity of schools and programs is also not obvious. If the economy is the relevant model, for every innovative, imaginative new industry and product (e.g., Apple Computers), we have other examples of successful companies that acquire enormous profits by delivering a highly uniform, assembly-line product (e.g., McDonalds, WalMart, or Toyota). Indeed, some existing private schools that now provide a unique service to a few families might even be tempted to provide a more common education to attract more clients and increase their market share.

Perhaps equally questionable is the claim by choice opponents that educational choice will destroy accountability. Most school districts in the United States are not forced to produce public records of educational achievement by school and grade level. As most parents would agree, even more rare are instances where systematic information is available on specific teachers. And even in those instances where information is available on school, district, grade, or teacher performance, there is little evidence that the levers of accountability are pulled when performance is inadequate. Thus proponents of choice question existing accountability concerns and stress that the exit option is a much more effective accountability mechanism.

Similar questions arise in considering the problems of adequate, equitable information under a choice arrangement. We currently know very little about the information that parents use to make decisions about where to live or where to send their children to school. There is some evidence that it is considerably differentiated by socioeconomic class. Whether or not more accurate information would be available under choice would probably be determined by truth-in-advertising regulations that would have to be part of any choice plan. It may well be that information would increase for all families, as has happened in the health industry, where HMOs have a significant market share.

The value arguments are also not pristine. They are inextricably linked to empirical claims, which means they are on as solid or shaky ground as the empirical evidence on choice. Even if any of these arguments is accepted at face value, however, it is unclear what to make of the debate. Proponents of choice stress the primary value of liberty, a more equitable dispersion of that liberty, and pluralistic diversity. Opponents of choice stress equality, an integrated society, and common school traditions. Philosophers have been debating these value differences for thousands of years. It is no wonder that these arguments divide well-intentioned parents, education providers, and policy experts.

Experiments With Educational Choice

As educational choice has been defined in this chapter, we have only one, very modest experiment in the United States. Before discussing the Milwaukee Parental Choice Program, I will briefly mention two additional programs that are often raised in discussions of public-private educational choice.

Alum Rock

In 1972, the Office of Equal Opportunity reluctantly began a voucher experiment in Alum Rock, California, after several years of trying to start voucher programs elsewhere. The program changed considerably over the years. By all accounts, however, it was very constrained and offered only limited choice. Although they were allowed after the first year, no private schools ever participated. After one year, enrollment limits were placed on all schools so that the only incentive was to maintain enrollment levels. This was easy for almost all schools because of the enrollment limits placed on the desirable schools (Bass, 1978; Cohen & Farrar, 1977; Puckett, 1983a). In essence, Alum Rock became a carefully limited open-enrollment school district. Approximately half the schools in the district chose not to participate at all. Since the Alum Rock experiment, other cities, including Milwaukee, St. Louis, and Louisville, have created choice systems using magnet schools that are more extensive than in the Alum Rock experiment.

Tuition Tax Credits

The most important program of government support for private school education is the tax deduction program in Minnesota that was ruled constitutional in *Mueller v. Allen* in 1983. Although this program is now serving as a model for other states, little is known about its effects, and no information is available on student achievement. Because the state allows a capped tax deduction on state taxes and not a credit (a factor affecting the court's judgment), the financial benefits for any family are quite limited. A survey of Minnesota parents found that private school parents were the most likely to use the deduction. The survey, however, revealed an even stronger correlation with income, which is to be expected because low-income families rarely itemize deductions. The survey authors concluded that the impact on altering educational choices was minimal and was surpassed by choice of residence as a factor in school selection, particularly for higher-income families (Darling-Hammond & Kirby, 1988; Kirby & Darling-Hammond, 1988).

The Milwaukee Parental Choice Program

The Milwaukee Parental Choice Program is the result of legislation enacted in 1990 as a part of the Wisconsin budget process. The program provides for state aid to nonsectarian private schools. The amount of state aid per student is the equivalent of the aid received in the Milwaukee Public Schools (MPS), approximately $2,500 per student in 1990-1991. The program is limited to 1% of the students in the MPS (about 1,000). Students must come from families with an annual income of no more than 1.75 times the poverty line. They cannot have been enrolled in a private school the previous year or come from outside the school district. Students will either not have been in school the previous year or have come from within the MPS. Parents apply directly to the schools for admission of their children.

Individual schools must be certified by the Department of Public Instruction. They have to agree to meet one of four standards of accountability: achievement test gains, grade completion, attendance and dropping out, or parental involvement. Schools may only enroll up to 49% of their students under the choice program. Receiving schools cannot discriminate against students based on race, ethnicity, or prior academic or behavioral record. If the number of applicants in a grade exceeds available space, schools have to select students randomly for the oversubscribed classes.

In July 1990, 10 private schools applied and were certified for participation in the Choice Program. Seven schools actually enrolled students in the first year. The only nonelementary school was a specialty job training program for at-risk students (with only 24 choice students). During the summer of 1990, 640 students applied for admission to the choice schools, 361 were admitted, and 341 enrolled in September 1990. Of those, 249 completed the first year, and 155 of those students enrolled in the second year along with 407 new choice students.[3]

Summary

Although policy debates over educational choice are numerous, experience with actual experiments in choice is very limited. Although the Milwaukee experiment will eventually yield useful results, the program is relatively small and carefully targeted in terms of eligible families and schools. Because of the lack of actual evidence emerging from choice programs, the empirical debate has instead centered on what can be gleaned from studies comparing differences between public and private schools under the existing, separate educational systems.

Inferences From Studies of Public/ Private School Differences

Fundamental Inferential Problems

The debate over what is likely to result under choice programs is often based on inferential evidence drawn from studies of differences in organization and outcomes between existing public and private schools. Given the hybrid system that no doubt would develop with a widespread choice system, it is unclear whether such information is very useful in making policy decisions. Under most proposed systems, including the amalgamated system proposed by Chubb and Moe, both types of schools would be operating in very different environments. If, however, the evidence was overwhelming that either current public or private schools produce far superior educational results, we might at least recommend what shape that hybrid system should take. The evidence, however, is not overwhelming.

An additional problem is that the information that has framed the debate in the 1980s is derived almost exclusively from the High School and Beyond (HSB) Study, a 1980-1984 study of 1,000 public and private high schools. The inferential problems are obvious. High schools enroll 40% of public school pupils but only 25% of private school students. High schools are very different than elementary or middle schools: They differ in size, attendance rates, organization, curriculum complexity, tracking, disciplinary problems, and the amount of learning per year that students acquire.

In addition, if Catholic schools are the modal private school comparison, which they are in the HSB, Catholic high schools differ substantially from Catholic elementary schools. The latter are almost all run by parishes with very simple organizations that give primary responsibility to the parish priest, the principal, and a school board. The students are mostly Catholic, and religious training is a major element of instruction. Catholic high schools, on the other hand, are run as independent schools (40%, often associated with religious orders), as diocesan schools (40%), or as parish schools (20%). The governing structures vary considerably, as do the student populations. Religious instruction is much less emphasized in most Catholic high schools.

To build the case for choice on research conducted almost exclusively at the high school level raises major questions both in terms of the comparison between public and private schools and even in terms of generalizing within each sector.[4]

Basic Research Designs

Because the HSB was a panel study that tracked sophomores from 1980 into their senior years, the primary research has analyzed two-

TABLE 6.2 Summary of Hypothesized Factors Affecting High
School Achievement

Individual Student Factors:

1. Prior achievement and educational experience (achievement tests, remedial courses, educational expectation, disciplinary record)
2. Family background characteristics (socioeconomic status, race, parent expectations, family education resources)

School/District Level Factors:

3. School/district resources (dollars spent, salaries, buildings, educational resources)
4. School context variables (size, aggregate student characteristics: percentage poor, percentage minorities)
5. School policies (tracking, course taking, discipline, homework, truancy)
6. School governance (principal leadership, teacher influence, teamwork, morale)
7. External authorities (influence of school boards, district administrators, state agencies; parental involvement and influence)

---

year changes in student scores on a battery of standardized tests. Several studies have also been done of the characteristics of those students who dropped out between their sophomore and senior years. For test scores, the research task was to try to explain the variation in achievement changes from 1980 to 1982 for the sophomore cohort (36 sophomores in each school). The primary method was to use multivariate regression models, which estimated achievement gains based on a large number of independent variables. Table 6.2 lists these variables and the level of the data.

Student family background characteristics and educational experiences were based primarily on student self-reports. Statistical controls were included for family background differences (family structure, income, parent education, and so on), student characteristics (prior achievement and academic records, race, education expectations), courses taken by the student, and whether the student was in an academic track. School variables were also included as explanatory variables. In studies using the full set of schools, school variables were limited to size, student composition (percentage poor, percentage minority), school location (city, suburbs, rural), and school resources. Several studies employing a subsample of approximately 400 schools also included extensive data on school organization and practices collected through follow-up surveys in 1984 with administrators and teachers (the Administrator and Teachers Survey). The 1984 data were applied backward in time to the change scores between 1980 and 1982.

Studies focusing on the differences between public and private schools (rather than, for example, simply trying to determine what predicts achievement gains in public schools), analyzed these differences in one of two ways. The first, used by Coleman, Hoffer, and Greeley (Coleman & Hoffer, 1987; Hoffer, Greeley, & Coleman, 1985), estimated separate multivariate models for students in public and private schools and then compared the different effects of independent variables and estimated achievement gains in each sector. Other researchers included all students together and then employed a simple binary variable (0 if public, 1 if private) to estimate the independent effect of school sector. This approach was recommended by most of the econometricians analyzing these data. The sector variable estimates the differences in achievement gains (or the probability of dropping out), controlling for the variance explained by the other variables. Both the statistical significance and the size of these estimated effects are important in answering the question of private school superiority. Because of sampling response problems, most researchers included only public and Catholic high schools, excluding other private and elite private schools from their analyses.[5]

Measuring Achievement

One of the problems with basing policy recommendations on HSB research is that student achievement has been almost exclusively boiled down to a set of six multiple-choice achievement tests given to 72 students in each school. Many education experts argue that such tests are a very poor measure of overall learning and achievement. Currently, test experts not only challenge standardized tests as the sole indicator of achievement but also single out this form of single-step, single-referent test item as particularly bad (Cohen, 1991; National Council of Teachers of Mathematics, 1989).

In addition to these general issues, the HSB tests themselves present specific problems. Reliability of tests is measured in two ways. The first measures the relationship of each item to the overall subject being measured. This is done by computing and aggregating the correlations between items. For all the subject tests except the civics test, the HSB tests were in this sense reliable by normal standards. A second measure of reliability, however, is to use a test-retest methodology to determine whether the same subjects have similar results on two or more trials of the same test. If not, the tests contain an inordinate degree of measurement error. A recent paper by Robert Meyer questions the reliability of the HSB tests on this basis. He finds the reliability of the tests are as follows: math = .30 (which means that it has a predicted measurement error of .7 or 70%); reading = .20; vocabulary = .16; writing = .35; science = .05; and civics = .16. There are ways to correct for this error statistically, but, to date, he is the only one who has employed the correct statistical model to do so (Meyer, 1988, table A-1).

How Much Is Learned in High School?

One of the findings from the HSB that seems not to trouble researchers as much as it might trouble policymakers is that very little learning occurs between the sophomore and senior years. The HSB test battery used in most analyses includes 115 items in math (38), reading (19), vocabulary (21), writing (17), and science (20). *Excluding dropouts*, on average, the sophomores answered 61.3 items correctly and the seniors (repeating the same tests) 67.5. That is a gain over two years of approximately 11% of the items they could have mastered (6.4/[115 − 61.3]). In statistical terms, they improved approximately 0.2 standard deviations. Although researchers have argued that these modest gains may be expected given that the last two years of high school are the accumulation of 12 years of school, another interpretation is that a considerable amount remains that could have been learned but was not.

This learning rate is even more problematic when compared with that of elementary schools. The learning rate in the first seven grades on standardized tests not unlike the HSB tests is, on average, 1 standard deviation per year (Glass, McGraw, & Smith, 1981). The high school rate based on the HSB is approximately 0.1 standard deviations per year. This not only reinforces the inferential problems discussed earlier but also suggests two conclusions. First, if we want to understand why students learn, we should focus on when they are learning, and that means studying elementary and not high schools. Second, with so little learning taking place, it is difficult to produce large enough effects that really seem to make a difference, especially a difference leading to strong policy conclusions.

What Explains Higher Achievement Gains?

Research based on HSB data covers 10 years and includes dozens of studies. The details involved in these research projects are complex; samples, variables, statistical techniques, and conclusions vary (see Witte, in press, for a summary). There is general agreement, however, on one set of variables; everyone agrees that these variables have consistent, systematic, and policy-relevant effects on educational achievement. They are also not surprising and they include the following:

- *Prior achievement,* as measured by sophomore tests and prior academic and behavioral records, always has a significant and strong effect on senior achievement.
- *Family and student background characteristics* (e.g., family socioeconomic status, parent education and expectations, race) are statistically significant and are consistently among the largest effects relative to other variables in predicting student achievement gains.
- Students in an *academic track,* students taking more *academic courses,* and students enrolled in *advanced or honors courses* consistently learn more, but the estimates vary depending on modeling specifications.

Other factors predict achievement gains in some studies but not in others that use different statistical models or techniques.

- For some studies, *school composition* (percentage low SES, percentage minority, and ethnic diversity) and the *percentage of students in an academic track* have significant effects. In other studies, when a student's academic track and course taking are controlled, school-level composition variables are no longer relevant. The substantive importance of these effects is also uncertain because they are measured as relative school effects.

- Several studies indicate that *school environment* (staff morale and attitudes toward education, personnel practices, strong leadership, high expectations, and the like) are related to improved achievement. The results are hard to interpret in substantive terms that apply to individual student learning. In addition, the effects appear to be marginal in terms of the amount of gain one can expect from significant changes in relative organizational effectiveness.

What Is the Effect of Private Schools on Student Achievement?

The simple answer is: "very little". In absolute terms, Catholic high school students do much better than public high school students both on the sophomore test and in how much more they master between the sophomore and senior years. The simple means are depicted in Table 6.3. For simplicity, I have combined reading, vocabulary, and writing tests into a verbal composite score and general and advanced math and science into a math/science composite score. Catholic school students do better in all areas—sophomore, senior, and gain scores in both subject areas. They do relatively better, however, on the verbal composite. Overall, they end up answering 10.4 more questions correctly (out of 115) than public school students. The real question is why, and is it a function of being in a private school?

To determine whether these differences are due to the private nature of these schools, we must take into account the difference in the student bodies, the courses students take, tracking practices, and other variables. Statistically, multivariate analyses can provide these types of controls. If these variables adequately model general student achievement, the effect of private schools can be measured by a sector variable that indicates whether a student is in a public school (coded 0) or a private school (coded 1).

Controlling for differences in relevant variables, the private school or sector variable remains statistically significant in most studies

TABLE 6.3 Mean Achievement Scores, Public and Catholic School Students, 1980 to 1982

| | Public | | | Catholic | | |
	Sophomore	Senior	Gain	Sophomore	Senior	Gain
Verbal composite (57 items)	30.6	34.6	4.0	35.6	40.3	4.7
Math/science composite (58 Items)	30.1	32.2	2.1	33.7	36.9	3.2

SOURCE: Computations derived from Willms (1985, table 1).
Dropout students are not included.

estimating achievement on standardized tests.[6] From a policy perspective, however, the *size of the effect* is even more important than is statistical significance. There are two reasons for this. First, with the very large samples used in these studies, it is much easier to attain a statistically significant result than in studies based on small samples that have much higher sampling error.[7] Second, the size of the effect indicates the size of the resulting gain in achievement that would be predicted if we could change the independent variables.

The modest size of the effect of private schools on achievement was adequately summarized by sociologist Christopher Jencks in an important article in 1985. Using estimates by those who claim Catholic school superiority (Hoffer et al., 1985), Jencks computed the estimated yearly average achievement gain by public and Catholic students measured in standard deviations of the sophomore test. This is his summary:

> Public school students' scores on the HS&B tests rise by an average of .15 standard deviations per year. Catholic-school students scores rise by an average of .18 standard deviations per year if they start at the Catholic-school mean and by .19 standard deviation per year if they start at the public-school mean. The annual increment attributable to Catholic schooling thus averages .03 or .04 standard deviation per year. By conventional standards this is a tiny effect, hardly worth study. But conventional standards may be misleading in this case. (Jencks, 1985, p. 133)

He then offers an explanation of the modesty in differences by speculating about the effects of prior years of Catholic schooling. He admits, however, that, based on the HSB alone, there is no realistic way to estimate these effects (Jencks, 1985, p. 134).

Karl Alexander and Aaron Pallas, reexamining the work of Greeley, Hoffer, and Coleman, put the magnitude of the Catholic school effect in substantive terms. They estimate that differences are so trivial that, if we could change public schools to look like Catholic schools on relevant factors, it would shift the public schools only from the 50th percentile ranking on standardized tests to the 53rd percentile. They conclude:

> What then of Coleman, Hoffer, and Kilgore's claim that Catholic schools are educationally superior to public schools? If trivial advantage is what they mean by such a claim, then we suppose we would have to agree. But judged against reasonable benchmarks, there is little basis for this conclusion. (Alexander & Pallas, 1985, p. 122)

Recent Research

Has research since 1985 changed the conclusion that private schools by themselves have little impact on student achievement? No. In one very thorough and complex study that focused on school composition and advanced course taking as the key variables in estimating math performance (the test with least measurement error), the sector variable was not even statistically significant. After controlling for individual student differences, the relevant differences in achievement gains were the result of racial and socioeconomic school composition, average numbers of advanced courses taken, amount of homework assigned, and staff problems in the school. Private school status meant nothing (see Lee & Bryk, 1989, table 5).

The highly publicized study by John Chubb and Terry Moe (1990b) argues, both directly and indirectly, that major differences between the public and private schools exist and that they explain the achievement superiority of private schools. Their conclusion is that a radical reform of all American education is needed and should take the form of an almost completely unregulated system centering on student scholarships that could be used for any schools. The public/private distinction would essentially vanish.

The Chubb and Moe study is anomalous in many regards. The empirical evidence they offer is drawn entirely from the HSB. They disregard much of the prior research that established cautions, limitations, and standard practices observed by prior researchers using HSB data.[8] Second, unlike other studies that base policy recommendations on inferences drawn from differences in achievement outcomes in public and private schools, *they never directly test the differential effect of public and private schools on achievement.* As noted above, prior studies either ran separate regressions for public and private school students or analyzed all students together but included a variable indicating whether the student was in a public or private school. They did neither.

They chose a circuitous research design and line of argument. They first estimated achievement gains for all students, controlling for school selectivity bias, prior student achievement, parent socioeconomic status, and school socioeconomic composition and effective school organization. Their emphasis was on the effective school organization variable, which is a very complex index, composed of numerous subindices. In the second stage of their analysis, they attempted to explain school-level variation in variables measuring administrative personnel constraints 'that interfere with school-level autonomy and what they judge to be effective school organization. It is in those regressions that they finally include, among other variables, a variable for the students' school (public or private—with "elite private" and "other private" included along with Catholics). Each of these steps is problematic.

The comprehensive measure of school organization includes 50 variables; the condensed measure, 27. Although they argue that such a broad measure is exactly what they want, with that many variables, it is almost impossible to isolate effects of specific organizational practices. That really does not matter much, however, because the predicted effect on achievement is minuscule anyway. Although there is a statistically relevant effect of this index, the size of the result is very small. And the result becomes even smaller when they include a variable controlling for a student being in an academic track, which prior studies consistently found relevant.

Direct estimates of substantive relevance are difficult given the uninterpretable dependent variable they use (see Note 8). By making several simple assumptions, however, I estimate that, if one could modify a school's organization enough to move it from the median school (200th best out of 400 in their study sample), to the 84th percentile (74th best), students in the school would, on average, get a fraction of 1 more item correct out of 115 items on the test. That is a small effect for an enormous change in organizational effectiveness.[9] In addition, in terms of a policy recommendation, given the complex nature of the index, how would one know which of the 50 variables to begin to alter first?

The second stage of their analysis (as well as other data), which includes the sector variable, does indicate that private schools have considerably less interference from outside actors (e.g., school boards) or central office staff in personnel and administrative decisions. Similarly, the effect of the sector variable on school organization is also very significant and not inconsequential in size. In part, these effects are no doubt due to a shift in analysis from the individual student level (in stage 1) to the school level.[10] These findings, however, and the extensive argument Chubb and Moe generate around these results, are among the major contributions of their book.

Whether the findings about school governance and organization matter much in the debate on educational choice is not as clear. No one who has set foot in a private school would argue, for example, that school district boards, superintendents, or central office staff have much influence on school-level decisions in private schools. That is simply because, in the vast majority of those schools, they do not even exist. The same is true of teacher and administrator unions and the rules, procedures, and constraints they invoke. Similarly, given the wide disparity in teacher salaries and benefits between the two sectors, not to mention the different student bodies they teach, one suspects that teacher motivation, cooperation, and morale are based on very different environments in the two worlds of public and private education.

Given these vastly different worlds, two questions are relevant. The first relates to how much of a direct effect the organizational differences have on achievement. In their recent "Response to Our Critics," Chubb and Moe fail to challenge the conclusion that these effects are minuscule (Chubb & Moe, 1991). The second question concerns whether a program with widespread educational choice could realistically be created that looks like the current private school world without state actors and regulations, school boards, district offices, and unions. In their last chapter, Chubb and Moe outline a hypothetical plan and imply that it is possible. Whether or not it is, experimentation should not be discouraged.

How to Proceed

A comprehensive discussion of the problems and solutions in American education requires much more space than is available here. It would first require a very careful delineation of where the problems exist and the historical and comparative magnitude of the failures. Instead of offering anything of that magnitude, I have compiled a set of general guidelines, expectations, and approaches to educational policy that I think are sensible. They are based not on a claim of systematic evidence or experimental success but on my experience and observation primarily of public school systems.

These ideas assume that the American education system is highly complex, diverse, and decentralized. The common elements in American education are overshadowed by differences in student populations, governance, organization of schools, resources, and the educational outcomes of students in different school systems (Witte, 1991b). This decentralized complexity is one of the reasons that education policymaking is often so frustrating.

What Not to Do

Do not assume that the problems of American education are similar across districts or that all American education is in crisis or failing. An obvious feature of American education is that educational achievement, however measured, varies widely among school districts. That may well be one of our major problems, but to begin from an assumption that all public education is producing similar results, and/or similar failures, is foolhardy. The problems vary in substance and gravity and the differences must be taken into account when looking for policy solutions. What might make sense in an inner-city system might well be a waste of resources and could have serious negative effects in affluent suburban districts.

Do not look for or expect single, simple solutions. There are no panaceas. The most serious problems in American education exist in the same place they have for several generations in our inner cities. The problems are multifaceted. They include, but are not limited to, a lack of basic skills, poor or nonexistent study habits and skills, low educational expectations, low self-esteem, poor language skills, dropping out (for many different reasons), and concentration on nonacademic distractions that range from athletics to the streets. These problems are not simple; they cannot even be catalogued easily. They certainly are not all captured, or even approximated, by standardized test results, contrary to what people in my profession seem to imply. And they will not be solved quickly or easily by implementing some single policy key—including choice. (See Chubb & Moe, 1990b, for an alternative view.)

Do not expect schools to solve all education problems by themselves. The most serious education problems are directly and immediately affected by problems of poverty, family structure, employment prospects, drug and alcohol abuse, crime and delinquency, and discrimination. The evidence from the studies cited in this chapter, along with more comprehensive literature reviews, indicates that student and family background characteristics are significant predictors of educational achievement. As much as this should trouble us, it also should tell us to be realistic about how much we can expect schools to do in isolation.

What to Do

Accept and adopt long-term strategies to improve education. School districts, particularly inner-city school districts, are under enormous pressure to show improvements quickly. Some of the worst abuses in public education, such as changing and manipulating tests, constantly shifting personnel, and erecting impenetrable bureaucratic fortresses, are due at least in part to pressures for short-range solutions. Some of the guidelines are as follows: (a) Do not institute programs, curriculum changes, and so on without at least a five- to ten-year commitment from decision makers and funding sources; (b) start in preschool and the early grades because expecting dramatic changes at the high school level is unreasonable; (c) provide support and aid for long-term solutions to nonschool problems. Finally, although difficult to imagine happening, I would argue it would be beneficial to leave troubled districts alone to try to work out problems without constant and intense political scrutiny. That pressure and scrutiny make it difficult to adhere to a long-range strategy of improvement. Alleviating pressure requires the development of longer-range systems of accountability and some forms of political insulation.

Target resources on a few programs and problems rather than responding in a shallow way to every constituency demand. This is also very difficult to achieve given the decentralization of and political pressures on American education. The number of demands on schools is a function of the number of problems and the number of constituency groups that exist. In large, diverse districts, these are almost infinite. Without mechanisms to protect against these demands, the natural response is to create yet another microprogram or hire another administrator to placate the constituency group. Resources are spread thinly, programs are viewed as short term, and the effects are unknown.

Experiment, but give experiments time to run, and provide adequate evaluation. Advice to experiment with educational practices, organization, pedagogy, and curriculum goes back at least to the early twentieth-century writings of John Dewey. But it may be even more applicable in today's complex educational environment. If the problems are complex and sticky, and the solutions not simple or singular, experimentation is an obvious course and one that is naturally and continuously accepted by school districts. The problem is that the experimentation must fit with long-term reform and targeted resources, which means longer-term commitment to selective experiments that can be adequately monitored.[11]

Does experimentation include experimentation with public-private school choice? Yes. This chapter has attempted to outline the arguments about whether educational choice would wreak havoc on our current education system, produce great improvement, or generate results somewhere in between. I have argued that there are no clear and definitive answers based on theory, practice, or inferences drawn from research undertaken in existing public and private schools. Because we know little, however, does not mean that we should not experiment with choice; indeed, that may be one of the strongest arguments for experimenting. Does experimentation mean that a state should contemplate completely overturning its existing systems and adopting an amalgamated, deregulated system of choice such as Chubb and Moe advocate? In a democracy, that is up to the citizens and officials of each state. Given the limited knowledge and evidence available to date, I would counsel great caution and prior assessment of educational problems throughout the state. Choice is not without risk or potential damage to education systems that may be functioning adequately.

Notes

1. The word *substantial* is intentionally vague. The range I have in mind is approximately the average amount of per pupil state aid going to a district, which is about half of the cost of educating a child in public schools (U.S. Department of Education, 1988, table 71, pp. 86-93). Because private school expenditures are substantially less on average than public school expenditures, this would represent significant marginal revenue for most private schools.

2. The model for these conditions is the Milwaukee Parental Choice Program, which is the only actual choice initiative we have to use as a model. All of these conditions fit within the Chubb and Moe proposal, although they stipulate many more, including only local school unions, elimination of tenure, and the reduction of district administration to little more than information centers. (See Chubb & Moe, 1990a, p. 211; for an excellent review of prior voucher models proposed by Friedman, Jencks, and Coons and Sugarman, see Puckett, 1983a, 1983b.)

3. The main source of attrition during the year, 63 students, came as the result of one school withdrawing from the program and then going out of existence. Of the 249 students in the program in June 1991, 86 did not return to the private schools and had not graduated from their schools.

4. A recently published study focusing on the importance of parental involvement and effective school characteristics on achievement in city and suburban public schools demonstrates that these factors have different effects, and quite different estimation models are applicable at the elementary, middle, and high school levels (see Witte & Walsh, 1990).

5. The response rate for Catholic high schools was 79% (68 of 86), and, for other private schools, only 50% (14 of 28 eligible). Substitutions had to be used for the schools that refused (Coleman, Hoffer, & Kilgore, 1982, table 1-1, p. 12). The elite private schools, because of their cost and selectivity, were anomalies from the beginning. Based on the bias implied in the non-Catholic sample, nearly all researchers heeded the early advice of Arthur Goldberger and Glen Cain to drop those schools (Goldberger & Cain, 1982). Exceptions are Coleman, Hoffer, and Greeley, who include them but perform separate analyses with notes of caution. Only Chubb and Moe lumped them together with Catholic schools. They repeat their analysis in an appendix using only public schools.

6. Exceptions are Willms (1985) and Lee and Bryk (1989).

7. Sampling error is the error that exists when generalizing from a study sample (HSB students) to the targeted population (all U.S. high school students). This depends primarily on sample size. This should not be confused with measurement error of individual variables, such as in the tests described above.

8. I have described these technical problems in considerable detail elsewhere. The problems include (a) sole reliance on a dependent variable that is a logged achievement change variable not used by anyone else, uninterpretable in terms of substantive effects, and one that greatly magnifies high and low achievement differences; (b) inclusion of schools in their sample that have enormous measurement error in key variables, and inclusion of elite and other private schools excluded or separately analyzed by all other researchers because of serious sampling bias (see Note 5); (c) use of a 1.64 standard error level of significance for results when all other researchers use a minimum of 3.0; (d) failure to include course-taking variables (number of academic or advanced courses) as predictor variables despite the repeated significance of these variables in dozens of prior studies; (e) reporting of tracking effects only in the appendix; and (f) the unclear inclusion of a complex control for selectivity bias. They also consistently report mean differences in high- and low-quartile schools, which is a comparison of roughly the 12.5th percentile school with the 87.5th percentile school. These already extreme comparisons are exaggerated by their choice of the dependent variable and their sample of schools (Witte, in press).

9. When they replicate their analysis using public schools only (reported in appendixes), the school organization variable remains significant but explains even less of the variance (40% less) than the small amount that is explained when private schools are included. The standardized coefficient drops from .065 to .039 (Chubb & Moe, 1990a, table D-1).

10. This is because, when variables are aggregated at the school level through averaging across responses, the within-school variance (say, on teachers' responses to questions) is ignored. One of the results of this is a great increase in the variance explained. In their individual student models, they only explain 4% to 5% of the variance; in their school models, they explain from 32% to 67%. This problem is one of the main reasons for using hierarchical linear modeling techniques, which first use individual-level estimates and, in a second stage, estimate effects at the school level.

11. A comparative guide in this area may be experimentation with job programs and welfare/work initiatives. Those types of long-term, carefully monitored studies (often with random assignment research designs) are very rare in public education. See Haveman (1987) for an overview and discussion.

References

Alexander, K. L., & Pallas, A. M. (1985). School sector and cognitive performance: When is a little a little? *Sociology of Education, 58,* 115-128.

Bass, G. (1978). *Alternatives in American education: Vol. 1. District policies and the implementation of change.* Santa Monica, CA: Rand Corporation.

Chubb, J. E., & Moe, T. M. (1990a). *Politics, markets, and America's schools.* Washington, DC: Brookings Institution.

Chubb, J. E., & Moe, T. M. (1990b). America's public schools: Choice is a panacea. *The Brookings Review, 3,* 4-12.

Chubb, J. E., & Moe, T. M. (1991, February 17). Response to our critics. *Education Week,* p. 1.

Cohen, D. K. (1991). Governance and instruction: The promise of decentralization and choice. In W. H. Clune & J. F. Witte (Eds.), *Choice and control in American education: Vol. 1. The theory of choice and control in education* (pp. 337-386). New York: Falmer.

Cohen, D. K., & Farrar, E. (1977). Power to the parents? The story of educational vouchers. *The Public Interest, 48,* 72-97.

Coleman, J. S., & Hoffer, T. (1987). *Public and private high schools.* New York: Basic Books.

Coleman, J. S., Hoffer, T., & Kilgore, S. (1982). *High school achievement.* New York: Basic Books.

Darling-Hammond, L., & Natarja Kirby, S. (1988). Public policy and private choice: The case of Minnesota. In T. James & H. M. Levin (Eds.), *Comparing public and private schools: Vol. 1. Institutions and organizations* (pp. 243-267). New York: Falmer.

Friedman, M. (1955). The role of government in education. In R. A. Solo (Ed.), *Economics and the public interest.* New Brunswick, NJ: Rutgers University Press.

Glass, G. V., McGraw, B., & Smith, M. L. (1981). *Meta-analysis in social research.* Beverly Hills, CA: Sage.

Goldberger, A., & Cain, G. (1982). The causal analysis of cognitive outcomes in the Coleman, Hoffer and Kilgore report. *Sociology of Education, 55,* 103-122.

Haveman, R. (1987). *Poverty policy and poverty research.* Madison: University of Wisconsin Press.

Hoffer, T., Greeley, A. M., & Coleman, J. S. (1985). Achievement growth in public and Catholic high schools. *Sociology of Education, 58,* 74-97.

Jencks, C. (1985). How much do high school students learn. *Sociology of Education, 58,* 128-135.

Kirby, S. N., & Darling-Hammond, L. (1988). Parental schooling choice: A case study of Minnesota. *Journal of Policy Analysis and Management, 7,* 506-517.

Lee, V. E., & Bryk, A. S. (1989). A multilevel model of the social distribution of high school achievement. *Sociology of Education, 62,* 172-192.

Levin, H. M. (1988). Education as a public and private good. *Journal of Policy Analysis and Management, 6,* 628-641.

Meyer, R. H. (1988). *Applied versus traditional mathematics: New econometric models of the contribution of high school courses to mathematics proficiency.* Washington, DC: National Assessment of Vocational Education.

Mueller v. Allen, 102 S.Ct. 3062 (1983).

National Council of Teachers of Mathematics. (1989). *Curriculum standards for school mathematics.* Reston, VA: Author.

Puckett, J. L. (1983a). Educational vouchers: Rhetoric or reality. *The Educational Forum, 47,* 467-492.

Puckett, J. L. (1983b). Educational vouchers: Rhetoric and reality. *The Educational Forum, 48,* 7-26.

Willms, J. D. (1985). Catholic school effects on academic achievement: New evidence from the High School and Beyond Follow-up Study. *Sociology of Education, 58,* 98-114.

Witte, J. F. (1991a). Choice in American education. *Educational Considerations, 19,* 12-19.

Witte, J. F. (1991b). Choice and control in American education: An analytical overview. In W. H. Clune & J. F. Witte (Eds.), *Choice and control in American education: Vol. 1. The theory of choice and control in education* (pp. 11-46). New York: Falmer.

Witte, J. F. (in press). Public school versus private school achievement: Are there findings that affect the educational choice debate? *Economics of Education Review.*

Witte, J. F., & Walsh, D. (1990). A systematic test of the effective schools model. *Educational Evaluation and Policy Analysis, 12,* 88-212.

7

Do Private Schools Outperform Public Schools?

ALBERT SHANKER

BELLA ROSENBERG

It is hard to pick up a newspaper or tune in to radio or television these days without coming across some story proclaiming that the salvation of American education lies in allowing public dollars to follow students to private and parochial schools. So-called private school choice has been at the heart of the Bush administration's education agenda. It has been the subject of an increasing number of education hearings, bills, and referendum initiatives in an increasing number of states. It has even been under consideration at the local level. And, in Milwaukee, Wisconsin, private school choice exists, that is, in the form of a state-initiated "experiment" that allows a small portion of

AUTHORS' NOTE: An earlier version of this chapter, by Albert Shanker, appeared under the title "Do Private Schools Outperform Public Schools?" in the Fall 1991 issue of the *American Educator*, the magazine of the American Federation of Teachers.

the district's low-income students to use state education dollars at nonsectarian private schools that have agreed to participate in the program.

This is, of course, not the first time that the public has been asked to subsidize the tuition costs of families who choose, and whose children are chosen by, private schools. Nor is Milwaukee the only place in the nation where public dollars support students in private schools. In fact, private and parochial schools enjoy a considerable amount of public assistance. But what distinguishes this movement for public aid to private education from all others is that this one is being marketed almost exclusively on the basis of education reform and improvement—indeed, as the education reform that would eradicate the need to make any other improvements.

The pitch goes something like this: "Students in private schools achieve at much higher levels than do public school students. Private schools, particularly Catholic schools, accept students just like the ones attending public schools and do a far better job of educating them. It should be no surprise that private schools do so much better. After all, they don't have bureaucracies, teacher unions, tenure, desegregation orders, affirmative action, bans on school prayer, or due process in student expulsion cases to contend with; they are subject only to the discipline of the market. Therefore, to overcome the crisis in education and for the sake of fairness, we should allow all parents, and especially poor parents, to use public funds to send their children to private schools."

Are the claims of private school choice supporters substantiated? Do private schools outperform public schools? Are they really working with the same kids but getting far better results? According to the 1990 National Assessment of Educational Progress math examinations, the answer is no on all counts (National Assessment of Educational Progress [NAEP], 1991).

Most news stories about the 1990 NAEP exams concentrated on the first-ever, state-by-state comparisons of math achievement among eighth graders: Which state came in first, which was second, and which was at the bottom. But there was another first that everyone ignored: the fact that the NAEP's simultaneously released *national* study of math achievement, which covered fourth, eighth, and twelfth graders, contained private school data and thus allowed us to compare public and private school performance to an extent never before possible. What these results tell us is that there is virtually no difference in the performance of public and parochial and other private schools; students in *all* our schools are achieving at disastrously low levels. And what this evidence means is that, under so-called private school choice, if half or even all of our public school students were to "choose" and be chosen by private schools tomorrow, we'd still be a nation at risk. We also would be a nation that had abandoned its common school ideals.

What, specifically, do the 1990 NAEP math results tell us about public and private school performance? The most logical place to start is with the 12th grade, the end of the elementary-secondary school road, where we can make some judgments about the value added by a public or private school education. The first thing to notice is that there is only a 6- or 7-point difference in average scores among seniors in public, Catholic, and other private schools. That's not much of a difference, and it is certainly not evidence of the superiority of private over public education (see Table 7.1).

It is true that a little more than half of seniors in private schools achieve at the 300 level, which means they can handle content that the NAEP says is typically introduced by the seventh grade: decimals, fractions, percents, elementary geometry, and simple algebra. This is a few percentage points better than the public school figure, but, again, it's hardly evidence for the excellence of private school education. The relevant fact is that both school sectors performed miserably: Approximately half of our graduating seniors, from both public and private schools, cannot handle math operations they should have mastered before they even entered high school.

For still worse news, let's look at the proportion of graduating seniors who achieved at or above level 350, which the NAEP terms an indicator of readiness to handle college-level math. It is 5% in the public schools and 4% in both the Catholic and other private schools: 5% is nothing to cheer about, but neither is 4%. It is of course plausible that this public school figure is higher than the private schools' only because public schools have a higher dropout rate; more of the kids who would score poorly are gone. That's probably true. But, if you adjust for that, and even if you ignore the private schools' dropout rate, the result is that 4% of students graduating from public school are prepared to do college math as are 4% of students graduating from Catholic and other private schools.

That's terrible. And the results are even more shocking when you compare them with the achievement of students in our competitor

TABLE 7.1 Average Proficiency and Percentage of Students at or Above Four Anchor Levels on the NAEP Mathematics Scale by Type of School

	Percent of Students	Average Proficiency	Percentage of Students at or Above			
			Level 200	Level 250	Level 300	Level 350
GRADE 4						
Public Schools	88(1.2)	214(0.9)	70(1.3)	10(0.8)	0(0.0)	0(0.0)
Catholic Schools	8(1.1)	224(2.0)	83(2.6)	16(2.2)	0(0.0)	0(0.0)
Other Private Schools	4(0.8)	231(2.8)	89(3.8)	22(3.4)	0(0.0)	0(0.0)
GRADE 8						
Public Schools	89(1.3)	264(1.2)	97(0.5)	66(1.3)	13(1.3)	0(0.1)
Catholic Schools	7(1.1)	278(2.6)	100(0.2)	84(2.6)	22(3.4)	0(0.2)
Other Private Schools	4(0.7)	274(2.4)	100(0.5)	80(3.8)	18(2.9)	0(0.0)
GRADE 12						
Public Schools	90(1.3)	295(1.1)	100(0.1)	90(0.7)	45(1.4)	5(0.6)
Catholic Schools	6(1.1)	302(3.0)	100(0.0)	96(1.2)	54(4.5)	4(1.0)
Other Private Schools	4(0.8)	301(3.1)	100(0.0)	97(1.1)	51(4.8)	4(1.8)

The standard errors of the estimated percentages and proficiencies appear in parentheses. It can be said with 95% certainty that for each population of interest, the value for the whole population is within plus or minus two standard errors of the estimate for the sample. When the proportion of students is 0%, the standard error is inestimable. Although percentages less than 0.5% are rounded to 0%, a few eighth-grade public school students (0.2%) and Catholic school students (0.1%) reached Level 350.

DESCRIPTION OF NAEP LEVELS:

Level 200: Simple additive reasoning and problem solving with whole numbers; content typically covered by 3rd grade.

Level 250: Simple multiplicative reasoning and two-step problem solving; typically covered by 5th grade.

Level 300: Reasoning and problem solving involving fractions, decimals, percentages, elementary geometry, and simple algebra; content introduced by 7th grade.

Level 350: Reasoning and problem solving involving geometry, algebra, and beginning statistics and probability; content generally covered in high school math courses in preparation for the study of advanced math.

SOURCE: The State of Mathematics Achievement: NAEP's 1990 Assessment of the Nation and the Trial Assessment of the States, U.S. Department of Education, National Center for Education Statistics, June 1991, Table 2.6 and Executive Summary, pp.6-7.

nations, where 20% to 30% of students meet standards that are at least as high as the NAEP's 350 level to get into college. Given those standards, 95% of our public and private high school graduates would not be admitted to college anywhere else in the industrialized world.

"OK, so there's not much difference between the performance of public and private schools in the 12th grade, and their students are in a dead heat at the NAEP's highest level," private school choice supporters might say. "But look at the fourth- and eighth-grade average scores. There's a 10-17 spread in points there, and a clear case of private school superiority."

Let's say, then, that it makes more sense to concentrate on results one third or two thirds of the way through the education process instead of on the end results. From this perspective, the NAEP results tell us that, the longer students stay in private schools, the worse they do, and the longer students stay in public schools, the better they do; private school children end up scoring like public school children, and public school children end up scoring like private school children. Rather than constituting proof of private school superiority, this seems more like evidence that public schools add more value to their students than do private schools.

This conclusion becomes more compelling—and the small differences between public and private school performance in all the grades become more shocking—when you look at how different public school students are than the youngsters who attend Catholic and other private schools. Contrary to what private school choice supporters claim, especially about Catholic schools, the students public and private schools educate are not alike, and not even remotely so. In fact, given the dramatic differences in their socioeconomic status and in the courses they take, to name just two, what's surprising is not that private school students, on average, performed slightly better than public school students but that they didn't leave public school students behind in the dust.

The basic difference is that private schools can and do select their students and turn away applicants who do not meet their standards. For example, 71% of Catholic high schools require an entrance exam, as do 43% of other religious schools and 66% of independent schools. Moreover, 71% of Catholic high schools cite student discipline as their chief admissions criterion, and 80% require that entering students have successfully completed their previous year of school

(National Center for Education Statistics, 1987). In other words, these schools are not obliged to take all comers, as public schools must, and they are free to get rid of students who do not work out, who generally end up in the public schools.

So who are these students? They turn out to be children who should have given private schools an enormous edge over public schools in performance. In the sample of students tested by the NAEP (see Figure 7.1), about 50% more private school youngsters than public school youngsters have parents who were college graduates. For the nation as a whole, the difference between public and private school students in level of parent education is even more dramatic: 30% of parochial school kids' parents and 57% of the parents of kids in other private schools graduated from college, in comparison with 19% of public school students' parents.

If there is anything education research tells us, it is that higher education translates into higher incomes, and both are strongly associated with higher academic achievement (see Figure 7.2). Even on the basis of family income alone, private school students should have performed dramatically better. According to the latest national figures, about three times as many public school students as private and parochial school students had family incomes under $15,000, while twice as many parochial school students and more than three times as many other private school students had family incomes of $50,000 and more. Consider, too, that private schools in the NAEP sample and nationally are dramatically underrepresented in rural and disadvantaged communities, where the nation's poorest youngsters live, and that poverty is strongly associated with lower academic achievement.

Socioeconomic status makes a big difference in student achievement, but school counts too. And there are big differences in what public and private school students take in school. For example, 81% of the private school seniors and only 56% of the public school seniors in the NAEP sample were in an academic track. Taking more academic courses, like having better-educated and wealthier parents, is strongly associated with higher scores, so how come public and private schools had an identical record in the percentage of students they produced who were prepared to handle college-level math? And why were the average scores of private school seniors so close to those of public school seniors?

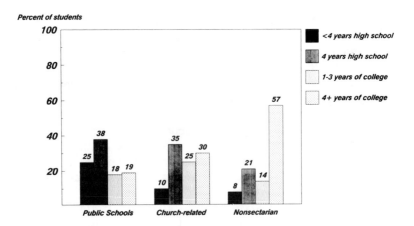

Figure 7.1. Parental Education Levels of Elementary and Secondary Students in Public, Parochial, and Other Private Schools
SOURCE: National Center for Education Statistics (1991, figure 3-6, p. 47).

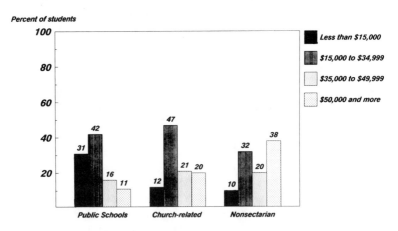

Figure 7.2. Family Income of Elementary and Secondary Students in Public, Parochial, and Other Private Schools
SOURCE: National Center for Education Statistics (1991, figure 3-5, p. 46).

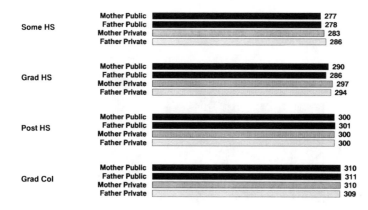

Figure 7.3. Mathematics Achievement at Grade 12 by Level of Parental Education, Public and Private Schools
SOURCE: National Assessment of Educational Progress (1991) and American Federation of Teachers.

In fact, these considerable differences between the family and academic backgrounds of public and private school youngsters explain why, when you look only at *average* scores, private school students do somewhat better—though well below what you would expect, given their advantages. But what happens when you compare the NAEP scores of public and private school students who have similar family backgrounds and who have taken similar courses—if you compare apples with apples? Their achievement is almost identical.

For example, when you compare the scores of public and private 12th graders whose parents have similar education levels, the sector differences become even narrower (see Figure 7.3). Or look at the results when eighth graders are matched according to the math courses they have taken: Public school students who have had pre-algebra score 274 and private school students score 273. The results are similar for eighth graders who have taken algebra, except that public school kids score four points better than kids from private schools: 298 as opposed to 294 (see Figure 7.4).

It's the same story when you compare the scores of public and private school seniors who have taken similar courses (see Figure 7.5). Among kids who have gotten only as far as Algebra I, private school students score slightly better; among kids who have taken

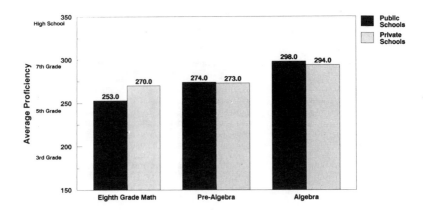

Figure 7.4. Average Overall Mathematics Proficiency by Students Taking Similar Courses: Grade 8
SOURCE: National Assessment of Educational Progress (1991) and American Federation of Teachers.

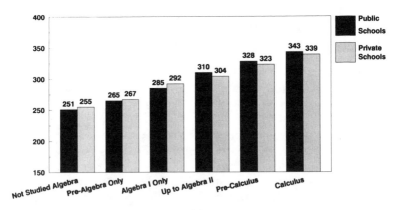

Figure 7.5. Average Overall Mathematics Proficiency by Students Taking Similar Courses: Grade 12
SOURCE: National Assessment of Educational Progress (1991) and American Federation of Teachers.

more advanced courses, public school students score slightly better. But the point is that, when you look at private and public school kids who have done the same course work, there are no big differences in their achievement; there is no "private school advantage." And when you consider that these comparisons by courses taken did not factor in the big differences in public and private school students' backgrounds, the proposition that public schools are adding more value to their students than are private schools becomes even stronger.

Are the 1990 national NAEP results in mathematics an anomaly?[1] Although this was the first time that the NAEP reported public-private school comparisons, it is not the first time that the NAEP collected private school data. In 1988, Chester E. Finn, Jr., now an adviser to Secretary of Education Lamar Alexander and then Assistant Secretary of Education, presented unpublished public-private school comparisons from the 1986 NAEP assessments of reading, history, and literature achievement to the annual meeting of the National Association of Independent Schools. According to Finn, private school students (including parochial school kids) scored, on average, only about four points higher than public school students on reading and six points higher on history and literature. He also said that the soon-to-be-released 1986 math exams would show similar results. "There's a differential," he said, according to *Education Week,* "but it's a very small differential, in an area where the public school performance is scandalously low" (Goldberg, 1988, p. 1).

Finn then pointed out that twice as many private school students as public school students taking the tests had parents who were college graduates, and that this probably explained the slightly higher average private school score: "With differences that large in parent education, it is conceivable that there's no school effect showing up here at all." His advice to the private school audience? "You need to improve faster than the public schools if you expect to continue to have people paying an average of $6,200 a year for day schools . . . in order to get a presumably better educational product."

Even James S. Coleman, whose 1981 analysis of public-private school performance is cited as the premier source of scientific evidence of private school superiority, warned that "one should not make a mistake: Our estimates for the size of the private-sector effects show them not to be large" (Coleman, 1981, p. 19). A small army of other researchers have shown that the small private school edge found by Coleman disappeared when differences in students' family background and course taking were examined.

That leaves John Chubb and Terry Moe, authors of *Politics, Markets, and America's Schools* (1990) and the present-day purveyors of "objective proof" of private school superiority. Lots of politicians and op-ed writers have repeated their findings as gospel, and many individuals have become converts to public aid for private education on their authority. But, as their peer reviewers and even a few statistics-savvy journalists have pointed out, Chubb and Moe's study of public and private high schools also did not find a private school advantage once students' background characteristics and academic courses were taken into account; their "choice" recommendations were not supported by the results of their analysis.

The failure of Chubb and Moe's analysis to yield them support for their conclusions is not particularly surprising. The evidence they use comes exclusively from the High School and Beyond Study, the same data that failed to yield Coleman sizable private sector effects. Moreover, despite the considerable print they expend on discussing why their handling of this data is an advance over other researchers' methods, Chubb and Moe virtually ignore all that has been learned about how to work responsibly with what is now acknowledged to be this deeply flawed, if not worthless, data set. What they do instead is highly unorthodox. A short list includes throwing in elite private and other private schools along with Catholic schools in a way that automatically conferred a private school advantage in their public-private analysis; constructing a school organization measure comprising 50 variables, making it almost impossible to single out the effects of any one variable; pioneering the use of a dependent variable that measures achievement change in a way that exaggerates high and low performance differences, and then conceding, in a footnote in the back of their book, that this has no substantive meaning; and reporting results in terms of average differences between schools in the highest quartile of performance (87.5th percentile) and the lowest quartile (12.5th percentile), which makes for very extreme comparisons. And, as John Witte (Chapter 6 in this volume) forcefully points out,

> They never directly test the differential effect of public and private schools on achievement. . . . [P]rior studies either ran separate regressions for public and private school students or analyzed all students together but included a variable indicating whether the student was in a public or private school. They did neither.

Methodological pyrotechnics notwithstanding, Chubb and Moe still fail to prove their hypothesis: All of their variables taken together explain only about 5% of the variation in achievement; and even when they ask what would happen if we moved students from a school in the lowest quartile of effective organization to the highest, the answer is that they would get less than 1 more answer correct on a 115-item test (Witte, 1991, p. 21; also Rosenberg, 1990-1991; Shanker & Rosenberg, 1991; Witte, 1990).

The latest pieces of evidence debunking the private school superiority myth both come from Milwaukee. The first concerns Catholic schools, and it is especially noteworthy because Catholic and other private schools are not required to report their students' test scores to the public. When Catholic schools do on occasion, it is always in terms of average scores aggregated at the district or national level. But the *Milwaukee Journal*'s religion reporter, Marie Rohde, persisted in asking the Milwaukee archdiocese to provide a finer breakdown, and her request was eventually granted. In a story that ran in the *Journal* on August 1, 1991, Rohde reported that, "Minority students enrolled in Milwaukee's Catholic elementary schools suffer the same lag in achievement test scores as their counterparts in the public schools, according to test results made public for the first time" (p.1). The test was the same one used by the Milwaukee public schools, the Iowa Test of Basic Skills. The scores, Rohde continued, "run counter to longstanding claims by most Catholic educators that they are doing a superior job of teaching disadvantaged children." In fact, while the scores of public school minority students have been stable, those of minority children in the Milwaukee Catholic schools have declined.

According to Rohde, John Norris, superintendent of the Catholic schools, blamed the gap on "socioeconomic factors" and said that test scores of Catholic and public schools "should not be directly compared." But two years earlier, when the archdiocese used a test different than the one in the public schools and reported the scores without breaking them down by race or individual school, it had no qualms about making such a comparison: "The bottom line is, in our system we perform better than the national average, and we are dealing with minority people in an inner city situation." The real bottom line is that averages can obscure as much as they illuminate, and in this case the higher scores of advantaged Catholic school students masked the poor achievement levels of minority Catholic school students, most of whom were concentrated in separate schools. The other piece of evidence from Milwaukee comes from its much vaunted, state-initiated voucher experiment. The product of a coalition between Polly Williams, a Democratic state legislator from Milwaukee and the former chair of Jesse Jackson's presidential campaign efforts in Wisconsin, and Governor Tommy Thompson, a conservative Republican, the Milwaukee voucher program began in September of 1990 and was open to a maximum of 1,000 low-income children in a district where about 60,000 children met the law's definition of poverty. Religious schools were excluded from the program, and only 7 of 21 eligible private schools volunteered to participate. The voucher was worth $2,500, paid out of the public schools' budget.

Estimates of how many families applied for the voucher vary from 600 to 750 families, but in the end 341 students were accepted by the seven private schools. By June, 249 students remained, in part because one school, which had been a religious school until shortly before the program began, went bankrupt and its 63 voucher students returned to the public schools; some voucher students were expelled, while others dropped out or moved. The following September, 86 of the remaining 249 voucher students did not return to their private schools.

According to the first-year evaluation of the program, while the parents of the participating students met the low-income criterion, they also tended to be more educated than either the Milwaukee public school parents on the whole or the low-income public school parents. Voucher parents had also been more active in the public schools and more dissatisfied with them than the average public school parent. Their involvement in the private schools was even higher than it had been when their children attended public schools, and their satisfaction levels were greater. Why so many of them did not return their children to the private schools begs further exploration.

What about the achievement of the voucher students, the prime justification for the experiment? One-year evaluation results do not make for conclusive evidence, but these certainly undermine the argument that private schools do a better job of educating low-income students than public schools. There were no dramatic gains in achievement among the voucher students, and their performance was about equal to that of the low-income students in the Milwaukee public schools (Witte, 1991).

Although all the talk about how private schools are doing a better job than public schools, especially with disadvantaged students, turns out to be just talk, that does not mean private schools have nothing to teach public schools. For instance, public schools could stop giving students a choice of curriculums—they choose easier ones—and insist that they take more academically challenging courses, the way they do in Catholic and other private schools. The public school system also could start heeding the message many parents, especially poor minority parents, have been trying to convey when they remove their children to Catholic and other private schools: Teachers can't teach and students can't learn when a handful of violent or disruptive kids are allowed to terrorize the school community. Something needs to be done for those kids, but right now the failure of many school boards to face up to the issue means that public school youngsters who want to achieve, and that's a majority, are being held hostage by a small minority of destructive kids. Private schools do not tolerate that, and neither should public schools.

Private schools also have a lesson to teach policymakers and the public, and the subject is children in poverty. As the NAEP results indicate, most of the advantage private schools have in average scores is due to their more advantaged student body. In fact, the results of the NAEP and other assessments demonstrate that childhood poverty is not only bad for America morally and socially but educationally, as well. Of course, many poor children do very well in school, and education continues to be a major route out of poverty. But it is also the case that poverty, especially when it is accompanied by family and community disintegration, is associated with lower academic achievement. Overcoming childhood poverty may not solve our crisis in education, but it would take us a good stretch down that road.

Would permitting public dollars to follow children to private and parochial schools turn our education system upside down? Would it destroy neighborhood schools and transform public education into a system for the have-nots? Would it violate the separation between church and state to the detriment of both? Could it lead to public money going to cult schools, radical schools (of the left and the right), and crassly commercial schools thrown together by people out for a quick buck? Would it mean less accountability in education because private and parochial schools, unlike public schools, are not required to publicly report their test results or their finances? Might it sanction a school system stratified by class, religion, ethnicity, and race and thereby undermine our pluralistic democracy?

The risks involved in public aid to private education are substantial, and they are not balanced by any evidence of educational benefit. In fact, the results of the NAEP and other national studies show that, if we want American children to meet world-class education standards—or even be able to do seventh-grade math by the time they leave high school—then spending tax dollars to send them to private and parochial schools is a bankrupt strategy.

The dismal performance of private schools also means that those who have charged that bureaucracy or teacher unions or desegregation orders or democratic control is chiefly responsible for our crisis in education had better look elsewhere because private schools are not constrained by any of these. On the other hand, it means that public schools cannot blame their dismal performance chiefly on the deterioration of families and communities. Even if we were to get the kinds of kids private schools have—handpicked and with parents who are relatively well educated and motivated to spend money on schooling—and even if we, like the private schools, were to have smaller class sizes or more flexibility in removing troublemakers, the evidence indicates that student achievement would still be at a level that is far below world standards.

That is shocking, but it should not cause us to despair. Rather, it underscores, and in the strongest possible way, the case for restructuring our schools, both public and private. The majority of our youngsters—and even the handpicked, more academically tracked students in private schools—are not achieving at the levels they and this nation need. As surprising, then, as the results of the public-private school comparisons may be, they are not really shocking: Public and private schools by and large have the same textbooks, the same curriculum, the same tracking methods, the same internal organizations—and the same indifferent standards. Exceptions exist in both sectors, which, of course, means they are not sectoral differences.

Public and private schools also have students who are subject to the same incentives for working hard in school—that is to say, very few such incentives. College-bound students in both public and private schools know they'll be able to find a college that will accept them, no matter how poor their grades are or how little they know, as long as they have a high school diploma and, usually, money— and in the latter case, the private school kids do have an advantage. The one exception is students, in either school sector, who hope to attend elite universities; they have to work very hard indeed.

As for going to work from high school, students in both public and private schools know that employers don't ask to see high school transcripts and don't even offer decent jobs to high school graduates until they are 24 or so, if then. So a student who has worked hard at rigorous courses will be competing for the same poor job at the same low pay as a student who has filled his schedule with soft courses that he barely passed. And these bad lessons are being learned by students in public and private schools alike.

What about parents? Why aren't they making sure youngsters apply themselves? That's easy. Whether kids are in public or private schools, most parents won't be successful at pressuring them to work harder when the kids can tell them, "I've already done what I need to do to get what I want."

As for teachers, they have a hard enough time, under the best of circumstances, persuading kids that history or physics or even regular attendance is "relevant" to their future lives. But, when the kids can say, "I don't need that to get into college or to get a job; it doesn't count" or "taking that course will pull my average down," the battle is lost before it starts.

One solution—though it's by no means the only one—is for American businesses to link getting jobs with high school achievement and for colleges to do the same thing in setting admission standards. Elementary and secondary schools would then have support for upholding standards. Parents and teachers would have support when they say, "Unless you turn off the television set and work harder, you're not going to make it." And our students would have evidence that working hard and learning something are essential to getting what they want. At the very least, they would see a reason to achieve and, because they're no less able than students in our competitor nations, they would.

The poor outcomes of both public and private education also indicate that there is not much to the argument that the competition school choice would produce would in turn serve as an excellent accountability system. As the argument goes, parents would make school decisions on the basis of educational excellence, so bad schools would go under and good schools would thrive and be replicated.

But there are parents who choose private schools and who keep their youngsters there despite, as the NAEP tells us, their mediocre performance, and this suggests that, if school choice produces accountability, it is not primarily or always on the basis of educational quality and outcomes. Certainly, parents in both public and private schools by and large do not seem to think their youngsters are not performing well enough.

Choice, then, may be an excellent incentive for schools to work hard to attract customers, but it is a dubious incentive for getting them to focus on improving student achievement. The only way to do that is to do so directly, that is, to design schoolwide incentives in which there are rewards for improving student achievement and consequences for failure.

The idea of an accountability system for schools that involves rewards and consequences is radical and very controversial, and it would need to be tested to see what works, when, and how. But the idea of an accountability system based on private school choice is also radical and very controversial, and the NAEP and other results tell us it would not work. This much is very clear: Even if the public rejects private school choice, it will not stand for the status quo in public education. Either there will be a new kind of accountability system in education that both the public and educators can believe in, or some crazy accountability scheme that would not be good for education will be imposed on us.

The private school choice packages that are being pushed across the nation will not help kids find out that they need to work in school to get what they want, just as they must on the athletic field and in the world of work. They will not stimulate schools to focus on improving student achievement and to experiment with new ways of doing so. They will not produce greater accountability in education, and they will no doubt yield less. They certainly will not eradicate the effects of childhood poverty. And they will not solve the crisis in education because that crisis afflicts public and private schools alike.

Note

1. The results of the 1990 NAEP science examination, which were released after this article was written, bear out the points we have made in connection with the NAEP math scores. If you look only at average

scores for 12th graders on the NAEP science examination, private school students do slightly better. But when you compare the achievement of public and private school students in grades 9-12 who have taken science cources, the difference in achievement disappears (NAEP, 1992, table 3.8).

References

Chubb, J. E., & Moe, T. M. (1990). *Politics, markets, and America's schools.* Washington, DC: Brookings Institution.

Coleman, J. S. (1981). Response to Page and Keith. *Educational Researcher, 10,* 18-20.

Goldberg, K. (1988, March 9). "Gravest threat" to private schools is better public ones, Finn warns. *Education Week,* p. 1.

National Assessment of Educational Progress. (1991, June). *The state of mathematics achievement: NAEP 1990 assessment of the nation and the trial assessment of the states.* Washington, DC: U.S. Department of Education, National Center for Education Statistics, Office of Educational Research and Improvement.

National Assessment of Educational Progress. (1992, March). *The 1990 science report card: NAEP's assessment of fourth, eighth, and twelfth graders.* Washington, DC: U.S. Department of Education, National Center for Education Statistics, Office of Educational Research and Improvement.

National Center for Education Statistics. (1987). *Private schools and private school teachers: Final report of the 1985-86 private school study.* Washington, DC: U.S. Department of Education.

National Center for Education Statistics. (1991). *Private schools in the United States: A statistical profile, with comparisons to public schools.* Washington, DC: U.S. Department of Education.

Rohde, M. (1991, August 1). Minority test scores at Catholic schools mirror lag in city. *Milwaukee Journal,* p. 1.

Rosenberg, B. (1990, December-1991, January). Not a case for market control. *Educational Leadership, 48*(4), 64-65.

Shanker, A., & Rosenberg, B. (1991). *Politics, markets and America's schools: The fallacies of private school choice.* Washington, DC: American Federation of Teachers.

Witte, J. F. (1990, August 30-September 3). *Understanding high school achievement: After a decade of research, do we have any confident policy recommendations?* Paper presented at the annual meeting of the American Political Science Association, San Francisco.

Witte, J. F. (1991, September). *Public subsidies for private schools.* Madison: University of Wisconsin.

8

Private Citizenship and School Choice

MICHAEL JOHANEK

Sometimes a public debate is actually about the matter discussed. But when ideological extremes meet on a new common proposal, when the issue clearly implies fundamental notions of governance, when the central terms mean considerably different things to different proponents, and when proponents share few reasons for their common stance, the debate may not actually concern the subject ostensibly at hand.

So it seems in the current debate over school choice plans. The terms of choice—including *controlled choice, limited choice,* and *public choice* —each indicate a variety of positions on such issues as inclusion of

AUTHOR'S NOTE: This chapter previously appeared in *Educational Policy* (in June 1992); copyright © 1992 by Corwin Press. Quotations from *The Wall Street Journal* are reprinted with permission, © 1991 Dow Jones & Company, Inc. All rights reserved. Quotes from *The New York Times,* copyright © 1991 by The New York Times Company, are reprinted by permission.

private schools, allowance for interdistrict choices, equalization of expenditure levels, formation of new schools, and the review or dissolution of undesired schools. Some proponents emphasize the power of parental choice as central, even as an end to be sought, while others support it simply as a present tactic protecting "alternative schools" against entrenched bureaucracy. Many have expressed support for choice explicitly as a means of scaring public educators into action on other reforms of more substantial curricular or structural nature. In spite of all of this, we continue to speak of "the" choice debate, a curious phenomenon to be explored here.

Choice proponents not only support widely ranging schema, but they do so with equally varied rationales. The current cast of supporters comes from various political persuasions. Radical conservatives such as Chester Finn claim the need for more "consumer-oriented" schools. Progressive reformers such as Joe Nathan recall the roots of controlled choice in the civil rights struggle and alternative schools movement. Former Governor Pete du Pont advocates choice claiming that "if anything, the 1980's showed that the marketplace works" (DeWitt, 1990). And East Harlem principal Deborah Meier (1991) urges liberal colleagues to avoid a knee-jerk reaction against choice and rather look to how regulated choice can empower the disadvantaged.[1] Add to all this a conservative Republican president taking the issue center stage with calls for "revolutionary" change: "We can encourage educational excellence by encouraging parental choice," declared the president in unveiling "America 2000." Vaguely reminiscent of recent sneaker ads, the slogan of school reformers today, says the president, is "Don't dither, just do it" (Bush, 1991). A fuzzy issue with odd alliances gained a new political currency.

The Issue

"These are difficult times because we are difficult people," according to Amy Gutmann (1990, p. 7). Americans want the education of their children "to maximize both their freedom and their civic virtue." We demand that school fulfill our personal goals as well as our social aims.

The nature of the relationship between a government and its people lies at the heart of the choice issue—the role of citizens in shaping the structures and functions of a central public institution. More specifically, it concerns *how* a government is to fulfill a generally accepted responsibility, for almost no one demands that government stop paying for compulsory education.[2] We accept the *public* responsibility of government and accept education as having *public* characteristics. Choice raises the question of whether or not we should use what has been labeled a *private* mechanism, namely, "the market," in the pursuit of this common *public* goal.[3]

The problem thus revolves principally around our understanding of the respective realms of "private" and "public." The understood boundaries between public and private certainly have varied over time, frequently blurring. This chapter suggests that public and private spheres have so intermingled during the post-World War II period that they have spawned a different mode of carrying out traditionally "public" functions. This is not to say that the private and public realms have been necessarily replaced by this realm. Apparently, there still exist institutions and practices we wish to designate as just private or public. But the interactions between private and public worlds have become so intense, so interpenetrating, that the borders have done more than blur. We have slowly developed a new manner or mode of carrying out public functions that can be called neither *public* nor *private*. It represents a different and hybrid realm. Significant social-geographic changes over the post-World War II period have changed the meanings of our terms *public* and *private*. For want of a better term, this new mode of carrying our certain social functions will be designated *private citizenship*.[4] The designation derives from the oxymoronic nature of the term *private citizen*, given the explicitly public nature of citizenship. That we have become accustomed to the use of *private citizen* in our discourse lends evidence to my thesis; it seems to make sense to us, though it cannot under past designations of public and private. Use of a term that is contradictory may not aid us in completely resolving this contradiction, but I am not convinced it is an unhealthy or avoidable tension for democratic society.

Given that the choice debate pivots around our understanding of public and private, this reformulation offers a means of clarifying the rhetoric of the controversy and of placing the debate within a wider social context. The choice debate, though, does have a history that may help us better frame the current polemics.

Historical Context

The odd set of bedfellows arguing for family choice in publicly supported schooling dates back at least two centuries. Often based on rather different foundations, calls for choice have come from various points on the political spectrum. In *The Rights of Man*, Thomas Paine advocated a voucher plan for the poor of 10 shillings a year for six years, which included "half a crown a year for paper and spelling books." "It is monarchical and aristocratical government only that requires ignorance for its support," declared Paine in 1791. He did note as well, though, the double function of the voucher system: "To [the children] it is education, to those who educate them it is a livelihood," and "there are often distressed clergymen's widows to whom such an income would be acceptable" (1791-1792/1984, p. 245; see also West, 1967). Adam Smith, while recognizing the great influence of Paine, fought what he labeled "Paine's yellow fever" of egalitarian "democratical" philosophy (see Foner, 1791-1792/1984). Smith, though, also supported a voucher-style family choice plan but emphasized it as an efficient way of letting the market's creative energy stimulate stuffy pedagogues. John Stuart Mill, in turn, later advocated a voucher program for those in need but stressed personal liberty in arguing against the state actually providing the education. "A general State education is a mere contrivance for molding people to be exactly like one another . . . [it] should only exist, if it exist at all, as one among many competing experiments." Current national test advocates appear rather limp-willed next to Mill. Compulsory education would be tested yearly, starting at an early age, and poor test scores might result in a fine to the family or suspension of free education! Mill, of course, wished to avoid state imposition of belief and thus insisted that tests be limited to "facts and positive science exclusively" (1947, pp. 107-110).

Since the Supreme Court's 1925 *Pierce* decision assured private schools' right to exist, the odd set of bedfellows voicing support for choice programs has only grown in range. Milton Friedman's treatment of vouchers in his classic *Capitalism and Freedom* added formal economic trappings to the debate. Public education funding "can be justified by the 'neighborhood effects' of schooling," though state operation of schools is an unwarranted "nationalization" of the "education industry" (Friedman, 1962, chap. 6). Southern segregationists' support for choice had other noneconomic "neighborhood effects" in mind. John Holt and other radicals saw choice as an escape from public school subjugation and a boon to the "free" school movement. The cacophony reached such a point by the early 1970s that Al Shanker, no novice to vociferous exchanges, reportedly complained that this motley "antischool coalition" included

> parochial school interests who see it as a source of money; political conservatives who feel nothing should be public if it can be private; Southern whites trying to weasel out of desegregation; black separatists; businessmen looking for a new market in education; middle-class parents who want a subsidy for their escape into private schools in suburbia; and "liberal new left anarchists." (cited in Coons & Sugarman, 1978, chap. 2, footnote 6)[5]

If we add the array of proposals calling themselves choice to the variety of arguments offered by its proponents, what are we to understand by "the choice debate"? While the curious alliances and eclectic mix of rationales are not new, they now address a dramatically reorganized world.

Recent Changes Contributing to the Development of Private Citizenship

> The confusion over public and private responsibilities lies at the heart of the ideological disarray and the feelings of breakdown in the contemporary political scene. What are the new rules of the game if there no longer are clear lines of demarcation between what is properly a public function and what is private? (Smith, 1983, p. 153)

Critical changes in the ways we organize our daily lives, particularly regarding the role of public and private forces, have occurred and/or accelerated since World War II.

Government has increased its role in the market and in "private" life. Government, in part as a result of Keynesian notions of "aggregate demand management" and increased public demand, participates in many areas formerly seen as sacredly private.[6] Government entered the domain of private housing, for example, spurring the market on through FHA-financed loans for "private" housing and "public" housing projects. Resultant neighborhoods reflected a new, more stringent economic and social segregation, with a homogenization of suburbs and a possible reduction in residential mobility (see Tobey, Wetherell, & Brigham, 1990). The relationship between a patient and doctor, long a private domain, saw new government involvement in Medicare and Medicaid. Care for our elderly became a conscious concern of the government through social security, in effect lifting the elderly out of their position of poverty within 20 years (see, e.g., Schwarz, 1988). The ivory towers could not escape, as private and parochial education accepted government funds and even rules from the GI Bill through to the Stafford loan program. Even for-profit schools received substantial sums in student aid (see, e.g., Palumbo, 1988; Wilms, 1983). The advent of sex education in public schools and, more recently, the controversy over public regulations regarding AIDS testing indicate the difficulty we have in drawing public-private lines. In many cases, the "public" sector has stepped actively into "private" shoes.

Individuals have lessened their involvement in "public" realms. Since the turn of the century, voter participation seems to have plummeted, as has participation in political parties.[7] Lack of voter participation in school board elections continues with dismal consistency. In schools, parental involvement in such groups as the PTA declined as more and more parents spent more time in a "private" sector, work (see, e.g., the 1990 PTA/Dodge National Parent Survey and others cited in *Newsweek*, Special Edition, Fall/Winter 1990).[8] Why U.S. citizens do not participate more in these activities remains unclear. The U.S. citizenry remains highly interested in politics, and it is quite optimistic politically when compared with other nations. Even those voters most distrustful of government vote almost as often as their more trusting peers (Uhlaner, 1991; Wolfinger, 1991).

Private life has been increasingly "marketized." Accelerated by communication innovations since World War II, the consumer market has saturated our personal lives. Our very sense of community has been

increasingly shaped by the goods we consume. "No American trans-
formation was more remarkable," claimed Daniel Boorstin nearly
20 years ago, "than these new American ways of changing things
from objects of possession and envy into vehicles of community. The
acts of acquiring and using had a new meaning" (1973, pp. 89-90).
The "consumption communities"—nonideological, democratic, public, vague, and malleable—meant people now "were affiliated less
by what they believed than by what they consumed." Even non-
consumption activities (e.g., jogging) have been segmented further
along the lines of the consumer goods chosen for the activity (Nike®'s
versus Woolworth® tennis shoes from the bin). The latest advertising slogans slip easily into and out of our vernacular.[9]

In terms of home life, a glance at the architecture and organization
of the house adds perhaps a more visible example of the increasingly
"marketized" private life, pulling individuals away from "public"
realms. Large front porches have slowly disappeared, first to back-
yard porches and sun rooms, then to electronically state-of-the-art
home entertainment centers in product-laden family rooms that
"Margaret Mead referred to . . . as giant playpens into which the
parents had crawled" (Jackson, 1985, p. 281). How to socialize from
within this audiovisual womb? Why not use the private phone, dial
"900," and purchase a social life via fiber optics and a credit card?
Or join fellow consumers on a home shopping network?

The market has also imposed itself more insistently on business,
forcing more responsive organizations and more flexible production. As one result, the borderline between production and consumer sectors blurred further. Corporations cut a swath through middle management and pushed greater authority to on-line workers
more sensitive to client concerns. Quality-obsessed managers link
design and production processes more intimately to consumers
through just-in-time and quality function deployment. Industries
continue deunionizing their work forces, exposing workers further
to the vagaries of a fluid market in search of "human capital." Even
within the nonprofit sector, many organizations have entered for-
profit markets, selling products and services to a paying market, a
"business-venturing trend" one observer terms the " 'profitization'
of the nonprofit sector" (Corman, 1987, p. 103; see, e.g., special 1991
bonus issue of *Business Week,* October 25, 1991).[10]

The private sector has been increasingly active in public realms. Not all post-World War II change has had the effect of private withdrawal into sophisticated consumption; if this were so, "private citizenship" would simply represent a change in degree, not of kind. Since at least the turn of the century, we have witnessed more "private" participation in certain "public" realms. Malls indicate a private market-based arrangement that fulfills many public social functions. Private businesses increasingly invest in markets and activities traditionally provided by governments. A rising number of cities, such as New York, Los Angeles, and Dallas, contract out to private firms such "public services" as street resurfacing, foster care, park maintenance, and delinquent-tax collection (Bartlett, 1991).

In education, public schooling depends on privately produced products and services, such as tests and textbooks. Media entrepreneur Chris Whittle plans to spend more than $60 million in researching a new model of schooling, with hopes of later investing $2.5-$3 billion in a chain of 200 private for-profit schools that would admit students in a random selection process (Walsh, 1991). Florida's Dade County school board has turned to a private for-profit firm, Education Alternatives, to design and start up its new South Pointe Elementary School (Bradley, 1990).

In politics, private polls regularly influence public policy. Private organizations such as the Educational Testing Service, the College Board, the Carnegie Foundation, the Heritage Foundation, the Brookings Institution, and even the New American Schools Corporation indicate the range of policymaking responsibilities handled by private enterprises working "in the public good" (see, e.g., Lagemann, 1989). Few dispute that private corporations should practice, or at least appear to practice, good citizenship and social responsibility. Most professions in "public service" accredit their membership privately. Desert Storm demonstrated again the private corporate role in the maintenance of public defense. Should any controversy arise over that role, count on the innumerable corporate and private PACs to enter the public fray. Should you personally wish to participate in such public issues, private media occasionally holds teleconference "town meetings" and open phone line talk shows.

The combined effect of so many shifts in how and where private and public sectors act cannot but have affected our understandings of what constitutes those sectors. From where else would we derive their meanings? In addition, the post-World War II period shaped a new public-private arrangement: The government provides the funding—in housing subsidies, student aid, military contracts, medical care—and the market distributes those funds. We have arrived at a means of merging a favored myth with stubborn reality. We have teamed up our fascination with the mythical market, which harkens us back to glory days of greater individual autonomy, with our realization of the gross inequities and segregation our oligopolistic reality produces.

What might this new public-private model "private citizenship" look like in more detail?

The New Character of Private Citizenship

> To identify democracy, as Bryce does, with "the rule of the whole people expressing their sovereign will by their votes," is to invite the danger of accepting the form for the substance. Forms are important only in so far as they become a means for cultivating a democratic attitude. (Bode, 1927, p. 13)

We are in the midst of redefining how we might cultivate our democratic attitude. For purely heuristic reasons, I offer the schematic shown in Table 8.1 as a means of identifying some key features of private citizenship. It suggests that a variety of societal functions have been handled in distinct manners in the public and private realms and that private citizenship entails new means of carrying out such functions.

Malls offer a paradigmatic example of private citizenship. Private institutions on private property existing primarily as centers for intensive shopping now serve many of the purposes of the old public town squares. Community organizations hold concerts, many young and old socialize, and next-door neighbors finally meet each other in the mall. Malls certainly do not reproduce town squares though; this "public" realm reflects the market-organized lives of private citizens. Political rights of free speech do not apply in the same way in malls, where private guards enforce the social order. Participation in mall life practically demands consumption, and the social consumer hierarchy shines through, if imperfectly, from the gilded windows of specialty boutiques to the bins of bargain base-

TABLE 8.1 Key Features of Private Citizenship

Social Function	Private Realm	Public Realm	Private Citizenship
Control/ setting limits	market (especially for excellence)	government (especially for equity)	market *as* democratic control
Asserting rights	consumer rights movement	civil rights movement	consumer rights *as* civil rights
Setting up organizational structures	as client oriented, flexible	as social needs oriented, bureaucratic	client oriented with government check
Designating role of economic activity	as productive	as expenditure, consumption	productive expenditure
Setting dominant values	via diverse interests	via common duties	duty to affirm diversity
Schooling citizens	as a right, a service, product	as an obligation, a relationship	a right to choose, but obligation to develop economically productive skills
Assessing education standards	in terms of clients aims/ desires	in terms of common citizenship requirements and role as economic agents in national economic competitiveness	minimum competency for economic competitiveness
Getting people to participate in realm	largely via consumption	largely via voting	by consuming responsibly

ments. Consumers scrutinize the buying habits of others, insist on equal treatment (especially in close-out sales!), and relish the endless variety of choices, bound to each other in perpetual consumption. The mall may share functions of the old town square, but private citizenship has distinctively reshaped its popular character.

The consumer's market seems to have in fact become perceived as a primary means of democratic participation or popular control. The contradistinction between democratic mechanisms and market mechanisms appears to be giving way to a view of the market as the means by which individuals can make their voices heard. My vote may not count (all the politicians are the same anyway!) but, when I ask the store owner for a certain brand name, she either provides it or I go elsewhere where someone will. In addition, politicians up to the president alter their behavior and even their views based on privately conducted polls, little more than consumer market research applied to democracy. Low voter turnout may be, in part at least, acquiescence to the more efficient means of voicing public opinion via polls (Ginsberg & Shefter, 1990). Recall President Johnson's suggestion of extending congressional terms from two to four years because the accuracy of public opinion polls kept politicians so well informed of constituent wishes (cited in Boorstin, 1973, p. 156). Private citizenship may be a way of understanding what Irving Horowitz calls the "special character of a democratic dialectic" located "in the very disparity between systemic legitimacy and active participation" in the United States (Horowitz, 1991).

As consumers, we have found ways of protecting our interests. The consumer rights movement has become the way private citizens use public means (government regulation) to protect personal interests (health, safety, environment, and so on). More and more, consumer rights represent civil rights, given the market as an increasingly "public" sphere. Where in the past we might have seen voting as the key means of affecting policy, we see a more genuine and sustainable public participation through the many private acts of consumption. Whereas few citizens lobby their members of Congress actively on environmental issues, for example, they much more often will alter buying habits toward recycled paper products or non-animal-tested cosmetics. We need only look at our advice to developing nations throwing off the shackles of communist rule: Yes, work for democratic reform, but first bring in the free market!

Viewing the market as a democratic mechanism underlies private citizenship; my consumer rights, primarily of product choice and quality, then form a key component of my civil rights. My liberty demands the freedom to choose products and services, to not suffer imposition by some unresponsible monopoly, a dictator of the market. Witness the countless stories on Eastern Europe featuring the hapless Trabants on trash heaps. These rights of course imply responsibilities as well. Not only must my right to consume be protected via truth in advertising and product liability laws; I as consumer must also recognize that my "private" acts of consumption have "public" consequences. Seen optimistically, this represents a heightened awareness of the wider impact of our individual lives.

Does buying styrofoam cups doom my children to live among waste dumps? If I "buy American," will I help the economy? Will my use of certain propellants drive a further wedge in the ozone? We may exaggerate cause and effect ties, but we have learned to link local fast-food burgers to Amazon rain forests, or certain chocolate bars to aggressive Third World marketing practices. Consuming well has become a cultivated craft, an active pursuit with ample media time devoted to its development. Increasingly, consuming well means consuming responsibly. This is hardly then a retreat into materialistic solipsism; we recognize more and more the social effects of our consumption, whether or not we fully act on that recognition. We strive to be educated consumers as the best defense of our individual rights and as one means of promoting our collective rights. Civil rights often appear too fuzzy and awkward, forcing historical analysis as well as long-winded politicking. Consumer rights appeal to our notions of fair play, are tangible and visible, and reflect the world's interconnectedness that we see nightly on CNN.

An ironic effect of private citizenship on education can be seen in the current debates on choice and multiculturalism. Accepting our responsibilities, we recognize the social effects of our education consumption, an internationally competitive domestic economy. Bad consumers threaten all of us, polluting our human capital supply. But, as responsible consumers, how can we be forced to shop for our education in one store? Also as responsible consumers, how can we be forced to consume one history that might not reflect the varied market to which it is directed? The irony of the current debate is that many arguing for "choice" argue most ardently against "multiculturalism," and yet each share roots in private citizenship. *Both spring from responsible consumption and seek to satisfy the demands of market diversity!* One targets the market for schools; the other, the market for curriculum.

The post-World War II period has increased our tendency to see the market as a public means of expressing and protecting individual (read: consumer) sovereignty.[11] We increasingly view government and bureaucracy in one corner and democracy and the market in the other. School choice does fit within such an outline of private citizenship, and our reaction to choice plans should recognize this broader context.

Education Within Private Citizenship

Private citizenship applied to schooling offers a way to address the tensions between the traditional public and private sectors.[12] If one is operating within private citizenship, how will the current education debate be understood? Specifically, how does this model relate to the themes of diversity versus unity and school accountability?

Diversity Versus Unity

Demographic reports and daily experience constantly remind us that the United States is experiencing a significant shift in ethnic composition. On the one hand, the diversity offers great benefits, a richness all can enjoy. On the other hand, news of civil war in Yugoslavia and street battles in New York City remind us of the demand for unifying forces, common beliefs. This presents an uncomfortable tension, as evident in recent discussions of multiculturalism and political correctness. What beliefs do we truly hold in common? How do we maintain unity while affirming diversity?

Common agreement does seem to exist at one level for education. As Coons and Sugarman suggest:

> If there ever was a national understanding about adult society's responsibility for the young, there is no longer. There remains, nevertheless, a general conviction that a just society makes ample provision for the formal portion of children's education and assures a measure of fairness and rationality in its distribution. (1978, pp. 1-2)

Further, widespread acceptance apparently exists for certain principles of the "market," perhaps what Thurow (1983) has referred to as a fundamentalized "theology," and this combines with government support for an appealing alternative: school choice. When everyone wants cars and yet each wants a different type, the market will diversify at least to some extent to meet the demand for variety. Government provision of funds for schooling should then allow everyone to enter the education market, in itself a recognition that markets fail to provide the means of entry for participants. Those dissatisfied with the results cannot allege injustice, as no one person or group of persons designed the outcome, though they certainly shaped the market rules. As a result, no one can be directly blamed, a great appeal to a society that enjoys the "no-fault" approach in other areas.

Choice appears to offer a chance to bring the structure of schooling more into line with private citizenship. While some extremists may wax romantic about the marvels of the market, most will favor choice while still recognizing market failures. Educated consumers know to keep their guard up against business; they also recognize that only a few drive BMWs. Market-oriented solutions appeal to many not because they represent an ideal arrangement; they appeal because they offer a better-than-the-current arrangement, one in which income plays a large role in determining educational opportunity and the ability to move to the suburbs allows de facto choice.

Private citizenship suggests that a publicly funded market-oriented solution like choice may create more ethnic diversity within schools. Legitimate concerns do exist, though, as to an unregulated choice system's ability to promote ethnic diversity within schools, and advocates of controlled choice rightly include integration, guidelines among their proposed regulations of choice (see, e.g., Alves & Willie, 1987; Henig, 1990; Kirby & Darling-Hammond, 1988; Rossell & Glenn, 1988; Sandler & Kapel, 1988). Citizens should fear further separation by income and race in the United States. The question for most, however, is not whether integration will result but whether less economic and racial segregation will be stimulated. Commonly held educational faiths may integrate schools more effectively than a perhaps less commonly held faith in integration per se. But the private citizen may look down the street for the answer: While policymakers discuss multiculturalism in schools, McDonalds has been selling Breakfast Burritos® nationally for months! This may be a small accommodation to changing clients, but private citizens may see in it the market's capacity to incorporate diversity and thus increase school choice's appeal on exactly the grounds for which critics often feel strongest.[13]

Accountability

Accountability is rooted in the idea of measurements. Business employees are constantly measured, trained and retrained, and it makes no sense to exempt education from this worthy principle. (John F. Akers, Chairman of IBM Corporation and the Business Roundtable Education Task Force, 1991, p. A22)

Advocates for choice insist that competition will make schools more accountable to both parents and students. Schools will be forced to reorganize to deliver services more efficiently and more effectively. If not, they will go the way of Edsels. Yes, citizens can vote for public school board members, but private citizens prefer the immediacy of taking their business elsewhere. Few who have experienced the exasperating bureaucracy of many public schools will fail to cheer such an argument.

It is exactly on this point of accountability that private citizenship may be most illustrative. Critics of choice bemoan the business rhetoric as cheapening the lofty goals of democratic education, converting education into just another product, and warn of public schools falling prey to shoe salesmen-turned-educators. Invocation of the "invisible hand" by economists and executives leads critics to charge the deification of a human-regulated mechanism. Most others listen unmoved but with the lingering suspicion that dramatic change is needed. The bold language of choice in a bland political atmosphere makes the debate appear a sideshow of quibbling.

Opponents of choice miss the opportunity private citizenship offers to insist on true accountability. The vast majority support public funding for basic education because they recognize that education has some public characteristics. Responsible consumption then demands an accountability for education's public as well as private ends. Otherwise, we face a profound "accountability gap."

Many choice advocates stress assessment and accountability as twin pillars of reform; America 2000 teams up tests, innovation, and choice. To private citizens, national student tests appear quite reasonable, little more than consumer safety legislation. Some districts have already made the logical extension to what are essentially refund policies by promising to retrain poorly skilled graduates; others will guarantee job training placement or a seat in college with a certain grade average (e.g., the Milwaukee Guarantee; see Johnson, 1990). But national exams are to measure student achievements and will largely test their mastery of five core subjects. Certainly some of these mastered skills have benefits for the rest of us, but how will we assess whether or not the schools fulfill explicitly public aims?

TABLE 8.2 The "Accountability Gap"

	Goals/Aims	*Assessment*
Personal[a]	Subject matter mastery, cognitive skills, and so on	Achievement tests
Common	Citizenship, economic productivity, and ?	??????

a. Certainly I am not suggesting that a clean distinction can be made between personal and common goals in education. It is only necessary to my argument that some common, "public" goals be recognized.

To assess public aims, of course, they must first be known in greater detail than the current debate allows. Table 8.2 illustrates this "accountability gap."

The gap involves no means of assessing our public or common aims for schooling. If citizenship is one of our stated goals, how will we hold schools accountable for its achievement?[14] If we aim to "ensure that every American adult . . . has the skills necessary to compete in a global economy," how will we measure their ability to compete? Adult Americans earning less than the poverty level "compete" in a global economy, but surely our collective aim is to move more Americans into higher-skills, higher-pay professions. How will we assess our progress in the year 2000? Do we wish to set income distribution goals or wage differential standards reflective of an increased collective "ability to compete in a global economy" (U.S. Department of Education, 1991)? From the perspective of private citizenship, if citizens pay for this education product offering such public benefits as ensuring the ability to "exercise the rights and responsibility of citizenship," how will they know if they are getting what they bought? Might a private citizen sue publicly funded schools for "truth in advertising" if responsible citizenship declines by the year 2000?[15]

If the choice debate fails to address accountability for public goals of education, beyond the benefits to individual students, it will attempt to avoid the unavoidable—the definition of public purposes for democratic education. To the degree that the social reproduction of democracy remains a goal of schooling our youth, practicality demands a means of gauging our progress on what cannot pretend to be an "externality" to the education market. It is the least private citizens should demand as educational consumers.

Some Conclusions

Jennings Wagoner, Jr., declares that the choice debate reflects a "crisis of faith" in the "unofficially established national church"—the public school. Though choice seems the "issue of the moment," it

> may be that we are caught in the throes of a continuing and fundamental challenge to (if not reordering of) the faith, form and functions of the public school as our national church and are witnessing the emergence or reemergence of dissenting sects engaged in a deep struggle with the established order. (Wagoner, 1986)

If this faith lies in a form, in the current assigned comprehensive public school, then yes, such a struggle exists and has existed for some years. The faith in publicly supported education shows no such crisis though; if at all, the stress on technological change combined with tighter family incomes promises greater support for public funding. Educators must not let the fact that the *means* of public education may change force a concession on the *ends* of public education. We must insist on full accountability for public schooling, and that includes the public goals we set for it. The struggle reflects the dramatically changed public-private arrangements affecting all "public" institutions. The way public educators react will determine whether schism or reinvigoration will result. How might the context of private citizenship inform a richer exchange in the current choice debate?

First, we can recognize the limited utility of Chubb and Moe's opposition of "democratic control" to "market control." Market control is now seen as a means of democratic control. Their argument's appeal has rested more on the antibureaucracy sentiments of many beleaguered taxpayers than on a genuine desire to remove schools from "democratic control." Under private citizenship, people still demand government services, though they may insist on different ways of using them.

Second, educators should not fight the rhetoric of choice; rather, they should exploit it. The language of choice has wide appeal, and direct opposition by educators will not be understood by the public.[16] The appeal reflects, if it may be said, a "trickle down" of the concept from the many other areas of our lives, such as housing, Medicare, and student aid.[17] President Bush calls for "responsive schools, customer-driven schools," setting up the familiar relationship between customer and product (see Pitsch, 1991). Regardless of the validity of arguments against the legitimacy of total parental control of democratic schooling (Gutmann, 1987), few blinked twice when the president declared that "the concept of choice draws its fundamental strength from the principle at the very heart of the democratic idea" (Bush, 1991). Further, for those suffering from discrimination, consumer rights protection may sound like a far more practical, tangible, and enforceable base than civil rights laws, especially in the current political climate. By focusing on the assessment of common goals, the limits of the economics-inspired discourse can be stretched to a discussion of schooling's political ends. Instead of fighting the rhetoric of choice, why not propose truth-in-labeling laws for all schools?

Third, public support of education must not be equated with public provision of education. Some critics of current reforms warn that public education may be so undermined—either by the success or by the failure of current efforts—as to place its very existence in jeopardy (see, e.g., Boyd, 1991). Few cite any historical evidence of a decline in popular support for government funding of education, though many fear an aging population's loss of interest. By insisting on filling the "accountability gap," educators can redirect the discussion toward commonly shared goals for schooling, including providing the economic base with which to support the elderly. While private citizenship may undervalue that public spending that enhances economic productivity, choice systems may connect tax expenditures more clearly to their benefits, and thus may even lead to greater support for public spending. For, while choice pronouncements may be faulted for "historically selective attention" to the record of market use in the provision of public service, most private citizens are not as enamored of the market as are the Chicago economists (Starr, 1987). Private citizens have also been pushed to the market by a growing cynicism with politics. In this light, public support of public education does not equal public support of government-run schools. The resulting "private" schools reflect no more loss of support for a "public" good than the "private" provision of "public" defense goods.

Finally, private citizenship may offer a means of moving beyond the "phony polarization" E. J. Dionne (1991) laments in his recent work: "What is required to end America's hatred of politics is an organizing idea that simultaneously accepts the efficiencies of markets and the importance of a vigorous public life" (p. 354). By dissolving the boundaries between public and private, private citizenship may allow us to focus more systematically on the purposes, not the means, of the common life we wish to construct in our democracy. Instead of focusing on choice's excessive consumerism, why not tap private citizenship's possibility for merging liberalism and populism, the "democratic engagement" Harry C. Boyte (1991, p. 63) calls "essential for . . . a revival of a public world in which citizens once again become subjects and creators of history." Recent convergence of conservative and liberal views on such areas as welfare reform and health policy may augur well for such a synthesis.

Recent events dramatically challenge the roots of much of the political ideology with which we have understood our world. State Department analyst Francis Fukuyama (1989) called it the "end of history," a movement beyond dichotomies to technical solutions. Democratic party hopeful Governor Bill Clinton has spoken of the need for a "new choice" in U.S. politics; "traditional answers on the right and left do not work anymore" (quoted in Toner, 1991, p. A18). Choice, speaking directly to our reformulated notion of private citizenship, offers an ideological exit from both the social engineering of the 1960s and the libertarian hangover from the 1980s. Consonant with the new arrangements of our daily lives, the public will fail to understand opposition to its principles.

Often we seek to clarify new ideological boundaries by tapping reassuring myths (like the market), holding them up to the world, and choosing either to escape into the myths or to reconcile them to actualities. Choice offers this opportunity of reconciliation, to understand the limited options we have, to make an effort to expand the realms in which we do choose beyond those of consumption, and to move past market mythology to one based on a realization of the limited benefits guided market forces may have.[18]

Notes

1. Ms. Meier (1991, p. 268) recognizes that "in the political climate of the 1990's choice runs the risk of leading to privatization." The question for Meier becomes: How we can use choice to stimulate good public education?

2. Even Milton Friedman in his classic *Capitalism and Freedom* recognized the need for government to subsidize required education and the need to impart a common tradition of some sort. He recognized further that schooling was a public as well as private good: "A stable and democratic society is impossible without a minimum degree of literacy and knowledge on the part of most citizens and without widespread acceptance of some common set of values. Education can contribute to both. In consequence, the gain from the education of a child accrues not only to the child or to his parents but also to other members of the society. The education of my child contributes to your welfare by promoting a stable and democratic society. . . . both the imposition of a minimum required level of schooling and the financing of this schooling by the state can be justified by the 'neighborhood effects' of schooling" (1962, pp. 87-89).

3. The fact that many conservative advocates of choice acknowledge the need for some regulation of voucher systems—in fact, the very need for vouchers—indicates their acceptance of at least minimal public goals in schooling.

4. Whether this recently reshaped formulation represents a shift to a substantially new understanding, a return to an earlier understanding, or a mixture of both will not be a focus of this chapter. It seems that the mix of designations, that is, the realms and definitions accepted as public and private, corresponds to the distinct configuration of political organizations, housing arrangements, work patterns, educational systems (formal and informal), economic structures, church-state relations, family patterns, and so on during any given historical period at least in terms of the sociohistorical factors that may contribute to such understandings. Given the dramatic changes in these factors since World War II, it seems untenable that our public/private designations would not be affected. Perhaps simply having less government in the earlier periods had an effect on the designation of public-private domains; also, other now "private" institutions had a more "public" domain role (e.g., churches). Regional and subcultural variations would certainly need to be accounted for as well. I am cautioned in all this by such works as Michael Katz's social history of welfare, with his claim that public assistance has always been greater than private. See also Carl Kaestle (1983) concerning the different meanings given to *private/public* in education. For a provocative treatment of market tensions in schooling, see David Labaree (1988). Currently, I am not prepared to develop the broader historical pattern of private/public realms.

5. For brief historical accounts, see Coons and Sugarman (1978, chap. 2), Maddaus (1990), and Wise and Darling-Hammond (1984).

6. Recall, for instance, the reasons used in opposition to FDR's programs in his later terms.

7. For example, national election turnouts have dropped 25 percentage points this century; midterm congressional elections dropped to a 35% turnout in 1988 (see Ginsberg & Shefter, 1990).

8. Just over a third of eighth-grade parents self-reported attending a parent-teacher organization meeting in 1988 (National Center for Education Statistics, 1991; a still relevant article is Burges, 1977).

9. For a development of a similar line of thought, see the early chapters in Flacks (1988).

10. Perhaps too little has been said relating current reform proposals to wider deunionization trends; teaching stands out as one of the most unionized sectors of our economy.

11. By emphasizing consumer rights, competition appears here akin to *doux commerce;* ironically, it seems that the early appeal of (market) economic "interests" was in its calming, rationalizing effects on the "passions" more than in its innovative or energetic drives. See a discussion of its roots in Hirschman (1977). For a related investigation of the phenomenology of public-private involvements, see Hirschman (1982). As Denis Doyle put it: "There is in the popular mind a vision of cutthroat competition, of profit-taking buccaneers swashbuckling across the State, people who are . . . merciless, kind of Atlas Shrugged/Ayn Rand types. Well, there certainly is that type of competition, but there is competition which is closer to home . . . and that is the competition which emphasized the supremacy of the consumer, consumer sovereignty, and that, in fact, is what competition is all about" (cited in Paulu, 1989, p. 31).

12. As David Labaree (1988, p. 1) suggests, "The American public high school is the product of a continuing struggle between politics and markets. From its founding to the present day, it has embodied interests that are both public and private." Thus the school choice debate provides an opportune means of sounding out the evolving relationship of public and private spheres.

13. Perhaps, depending on the measure used, public schools are our most integrated institutions, and that may be due to involuntary measures (see, e.g., Hochschild, 1984). An interesting study to investigate private citizenship's potential for ethnic and racial integration might be to evaluate which of the two institutions receives a relatively more integrated population—local shopping malls or local public schools.

14. The brief mention of citizenship in the goals of the president and governors may not indicate much clarity or priority for a traditional public purpose of education. There is a near-total absence of discussion

in the work to date of the National Council of Education Standards and Testing on how achievement of citizenship goals might be assessed; voter registration percentages hardly seem an "authentic" evaluation.

15. There may be analogous ways in which private citizenship can demand accountability in other realms, such as health care and housing. Defense goods, in which actual "consumption" is more indirect (to say the least), may not submit so readily to such a model. In general, though, demanding such accountability may offer a way of strengthening what Boorstin calls the "more attenuated lives" we live "as members of more casual communities" than earlier citizens experienced. By focusing on assessing the achievement of public goals, U.S. citizens might reinforce the "countless gossamer webs knitting together the trivia of their lives" (Boorstin, 1973, p. 148).

16. The gap between the public and educators regarding approval ratings for choice is considerable, between 40-65 percentage points. See Lou Harris & Associates poll in *Agenda* (Fall, 1991, p. 11).

17. Earlier congressional health care debates seem to be affecting current school choice discussions (see Miller, 1991).

18. There may be an odd historical irony here. While the West celebrates ideological victory over communism, we extend the application of free market economic models into our most public concerns, perhaps coming closer to fulfilling Marxist prophesies of economic determinism than we ever did during Marxism's heyday. But *that* is another essay.

References

Akers, J. F. (1991, March 20). Let's get to work on education [Editorial]. *The Wall Street Journal*, p. A22.

Alves, M. J., & Willie, C. Y. (1987). Controlled choice assignments: A new and more effective approach to school desegregation. *The Urban Review, 19*, 67-88.

Bartlett, S. (1991, July 7). New York cost-cutting idea: City jobs, outside workers. *The New York Times*, pp. A1, A16.

Bode, B. H. (1927). *Modern educational theories.* New York: Macmillan.

Boorstin, D. (1973). *The Americans: The democratic experience.* New York: Random House.

Boyd, W. L. (1991). Public education's last hurrah? Schizophrenia, amnesia, and ignorance in school politics. In D. J. Vold & J. L. DeVitis (Eds.), *School reform in the deep South: A critical appraisal* (pp. 19-36). Tuscaloosa: University of Alabama Press.

Boyte, H. C. (1991). Democratic engagement: Bringing populism and liberalism together. *The American Prospect, 6,* 55-63.

Bradley, A. (1990, June 6). In Dade County, company gears up to help district run a public school. *Education Week, 9*(37), 1, 16-17.

Burges, B. (1977). Rx for school governance. *Journal of Education, 159*(1), 43-67.

Bush, G. (1991, April 18). [Remarks by the president at the presentation of the National Education Strategy, the White House; press release from the Department of Education, downloaded through OERI Bulletin Board].

Coons, J. E., & Sugarman, S. D. (1978). *Education by choice: The case for family control.* Berkeley: University of California Press.

Corman, R. P. (1987). The realities of "profitization" and privatization in the nonprofit sector. In B. J. Carroll, R. W. Conant, & T. A. Easton (Eds.), *Private means, public ends: Private business in social service delivery* (pp. 98-118). New York: Praeger.

DeWitt, K. (1990, November 14). Debate on choice continues. *The New York Times,* p. B8.

Dionne, E. J., Jr. (1991). *Why Americans hate politics.* New York: Simon & Schuster.

Flacks, R. (1988). *Making history: The radical tradition in American life.* New York: Columbia University Press.

Foner, E. (1984). Introduction. In T. Paine, *The rights of man.* New York: Penguin. (Original work published 1791-1792)

Friedman, M. (1962). *Capitalism and freedom.* Chicago: University of Chicago Press.

Fukuyama, F. (1989, Summer). The end of history? *The National Interest.* (Reprinted with commentary in K. M. Jensen, Ed., 1990, *A look at "The end of history?"* Washington, DC: U.S. Institute of Peace)

Ginsberg, B., & Shefter, M. (1990). *Politics by other means: The declining importance of elections in America.* New York: Basic Books.

Gutmann, A. (1987). *Democratic education.* Princeton, NJ: Princeton University Press.

Gutmann, A. (1990). Democratic education in difficult times. *TC Record, 92*(1), 7.

Henig, J. R. (1990). Choice in public schools: An analysis of transfer requests among magnet schools. *Social Science Quarterly, 71*(1), 69-82.

Hirschman, A. O. (1977). *The passions and the interests: Political arguments for capitalism before its triumph.* Princeton, NJ: Princeton University Press.

Hirschman, A. O. (1982). *Shifting involvements: Private interest and public action*. Princeton, NJ: Princeton University Press.

Hochschild, J. L. (1984). *The new American dilemma: Liberal democracy and school desegregation*. New Haven, CT: Yale University Press.

Horowitz, I. L. (1991). The glass *is* half full and half empty: Religious conviction and political participation. *Society, 28*(5), 17-22.

Jackson, K. T. (1985). *Crabgrass frontier: The suburbanization of the United States*. New York: Oxford University Press.

Johnson, D. (1990, February 7). Milwaukee plans a college guarantee. *The New York Times*, p. B6.

Kaestle, C. (1983). *Pillars of the republic*. New York: Hill & Wang.

Kirby, S. N., & Darling-Hammond, L. (1988). Parental schooling choice: A case study of Minnesota. *Journal of Policy Analysis and Management, 7*(3), 506-512.

Labaree, D. (1988). *The making of an American high school: The credentials market and the central high school of Philadelphia, 1838-1939*. New Haven, CT: Yale University Press.

Lagemann, E. C. (1989). *The politics of knowledge: The Carnegie Corporation, philanthropy, and public policy*. Middletown, CT: Wesleyan University Press.

Maddaus, J. (1990). Parental choice of school: What parents think and do. In C. B. Cazden (Ed.), *Review of research in education* (pp. 267-295). Washington, DC: AERA.

Meier, D. W. (1991, March 4). Choice can save public education. *The Nation*, p. 253, 266-271.

Mill, J. S. (1947/1859). *On liberty*. New York: Appleton Century Crofts.

Miller, J. A. (1991). House panel's vote marks a sea change on the choice issue. *Education Week, 9*(10), 1, 26.

National Center for Education Statistics. (1991). *Digest of education statistics, 1990* (OERI-NCES 91-660). Washington, DC: U.S. Department of Education.

Paine, T. (1984). *The rights of man*. New York: Penguin. (Original work published 1791-1792)

Palumbo, G. E. (1988). *Proprietary school interests and influence on the 1985-1986 reauthorization proceedings on Title IV of the Higher Education Act of 1965*. Unpublished Ed.D. thesis, Teachers College, Columbia University.

Paulu, N. (1989). *Improving schools and empowering parents: Choice in American education*. Unpublished report based on the White House Workshop on Choice in Education.

Pierce v. Society of Sisters of the Holy Names of Jesus and Mary, 268 U.S. 510, 45 S.Ct. 571 (1925).

Pitsch, M. (1991, March 6). Bush unveils "opportunity package" of domestic initiatives. *Education Week*, 24.

Rossell, C. H., & Glenn, C. L. (1988). The Cambridge Controlled Choice Plan. *The Urban Review, 20*(2), 75-94.

Sandler, A. B., & Kapel, D. E. (1988). Educational vouchers: A viable option for urban settings? *The Urban Review, 20*(4), 267-282.

Schwarz, J. E. (1988). *America's hidden success.* New York: Norton.

Smith, B. L. R. (1983). Changing public-private sector relations: A look at the United States. *The Annals of the American Academy of Political and Social Science, 466*, 149-164.

Starr, P. (1987). The limits of privatization. *Prospects for Privatization: Proceedings of the Academy of Political Science, 36*, 3.

Thurow, L. C. (1983). *Dangerous currents: The state of economics.* New York: Random House.

Tobey, R., Wetherell, C., & Brigham, J. (1990). Moving out and settling in: Residential mobility, home owning, and the public enframing of citizenship, 1921-1950. *The American Historical Review, 95*(5), 1395-1422.

Toner, R. (1991, May 8). Democrat session previews '92 race. *The New York Times*, p. A18.

Uhlaner, C. J. (1991). Electoral participation: Summing up a decade. *Society, 28*(5), 35-40.

U. S. Department of Education. (1991). *America 2000: An educational strategy.* Washington, DC: Author.

Wagoner, J. L., Jr. (1986, April 29). *Choice: The historical perspective.* Paper presented at the Conference on Choice in Education, Charlottesville, VA.

Walsh, M. (1991, May 22). Entrepreneur Whittle unveils plans to create chain of for-profit schools. *Education Week, 10*(35), 1, 14.

West, E. G. (1967). Tom Paine's voucher scheme for public education. *Southern Economic Journal, 33*, 378-382.

Wilms, W. W. (1983). Proprietary schools and student financial aid. *The Journal of Student Financial Aid, 13*(2), 7-17.

Wise, A. E., & Darling-Hammond, L. (1984). Education by voucher: Private choice and the public interest. *Educational Theory, 34*(1), 29-53.

Wolfinger, R. E. (1991). Voter turnout. *Society, 28*(5), 23-26.

9

The Dutch Experience With School Choice: Implications for American Education

FRANK BROWN

This chapter discusses a specific school reform, parental choice, which is currently being promoted in America by ideological political conservatives, and it reviews the experience with parental choice in the Netherlands (also known as Holland) for possible lessons to be learned by Americans. Parental choice in education is defined here as the right of parents to select from available public and private schools a school or schools for their child or children. Parental choice (hereafter referred to as *choice*) has always existed for Americans with economic means. Parents with financial means may move to the neighborhood they choose and enroll their children in the neighborhood school, enroll their children in a private school within reasonable commuting distance, or enroll their children in a private boarding school. I am aware of the argument by many educators and policymakers that parental choice options should be limited to selections among public schools, but, to explore the Dutch experience with school choice and to discover what Americans may learn from their experience, this discussion considers both public and private options. Before comparisons are made between the Dutch experience and the options for Americans, however, an examination will be made of the cultural, social, and political contexts in which choice exists. For example, what cultural, educational, social, and political problems might be caused by this reform effort?

This reform movement is a drastic departure from anything we have previously witnessed to improve elementary and secondary education in America, and the proposed reform could not be carried out without changes in our cultural, social, and political ideologies (Iannaccone, 1988). Iannaccone (1988, p. 52) places major shifts in our political ideology approximately 36 years apart beginning with the 1860 presidential election of Abraham Lincoln. Other major shifts took place in 1896, 1932, 1954, and 1968. The election of President Jimmy Cater is seen as an aberration in this trend caused by the Watergate scandal and Carter's perceived southern conservative thinking (Iannaccone, 1988, p. 52). In the 1970s, the rhetoric of equality was viewed by most white Americans as moving toward quotas in fighting racial, ethnic, and gender discrimination. This educational policy shift from equity to excellence is a component of a larger shift in political ideology in which the larger society is willing to tolerate some inequality (Iannaccone, 1988, pp. 60, 63). Other authors have drawn similar conclusions.

Boyd and Kerchner (1988, p. 1) saw the 1980 election of President Ronald Reagan as the turning point that produced a major shift in our political ideology, which redefined our national education policy, resulting in less support for education. President Reagan shifted the federal emphasis from equity and social justice to excellence in education, which he promised would increase industrial productivity and the country's competitive edge in world markets. Clark and Astuto (1990, p. 11), who follow federal educational policies, see President George Bush continuing the Reagan policy; and, despite Bush's claim to become the education president, they predicted "low priority, few initiatives, and declining fiscal support" for excellence in education as the dominant philosophy, which correlates with higher academic standards and testing, deregulation, and increased privatization of education. They also argue that President Bush is "ideologically comfortable" with this policy. Kirp (1982), in his research on equity and integration in five San Francisco area school districts, noted a nationwide decline in support among white Americans for increased equity and integration of public schools. Lewis (1978), in his study of educational equity and integration in a midwestern city, concluded that such a "pervasive system of inequality would not exist in America without the tact approval of the majority." The language of this debate about school reform is both symbolic and ideological in nature (Brown, 1990). Vergon (1990), Iannaccone (1988), and Clark and Astuto (1990), however, argue that this educational ideology is now accepted by most Americans and will be with us for a long time. Using Iannaccone's (1988) time table for major ideological shifts, the trend that began in 1968 will be with us until the year 2004.

This shift in the country's ideology away from equity and social justice parallels a similar shift that occurred at the end of the First Reconstruction era, when liberal legislation on equity issues was enacted by the Reconstruction Congress, 1865-1890, but was replaced by a conservative Congress and Supreme Court. By 1896, in *Plessy v. Ferguson*, the Court held that states were no longer obligated to support integrated public functions, and this rule remained in force until the Court's ruling in 1954 with *Brown v. Board of Education*. Since *Brown*, in the Second Reconstruction era, we are currently witnessing another shift in ideology similar to what took place at the end of the First Reconstruction period. This new ideology is being debated across the country and in Congress. For example, U. S. Secretary of Education Lamar Alexander, in a 1991 appearance before a congressional committee, sparked a debate on this conservative ideology among members of congress (DeWitt, 1991, p. A10). Liberal members of the committee asked Secretary Alexander why the Department of Education had deferred authorization of the Middle States Association of Colleges and Universities accreditation agency for using cultural diversity as one standard for accrediting colleges. But conservative members of the committee and Secretary Alexander saw diversity standards as promoting "hiring quotas." A brief review of this political ideology and changes promoted by this ideology should help us to understanding these educational reforms.

Education Problems

The major education problem (Boyd & Kerchner, 1988; Brown, 1990; Brown & Contreras, 1991; Carter & Sandler, 1991; Clark &

Astuto, 1990; Coons & Sugarman, 1979; Lewis, 1978; "What of the Children," 1991) in America has and continues to be how best to improve the literary skills of children from racial, ethnic, and language minority groups. Most of these minority children are located in urban centers along with many poor white children. Regardless of the political ideology, and the symbolic representation of that ideology, the issue is still one of equity and economics (Brown, 1990). Briefly, during periods of economic decline, equity measures that require a sharing of resources are not acceptable by the ruling majority. Equity measures are suppressed by a political ideology that does not promote a sharing of resources with disadvantaged members of society. Some policy issues supported by this new antiequity ideology are excellence in education with national testing standards, no new taxes for social programs, no increase in school desegregation, and no further sharing of resources with children of the disadvantaged. Also, the argument is made that improved equity standards will produce "quotas." Thus choice, as political symbolism, means minimum government efforts will be used to further integrate public schools; affirmative action programs will be opposed; and the well-to-do will not be asked to share additional resources to support the education of children from poor and minority groups.

Astin (1991), an internationally respected educational policy analyst, believes that, because there is no research evidence to support elementary and secondary education school choice plans, any decision to promote choice must be considered purely political. Astin, however, is applying rationality to a purely cultural phenomenon. On the other hand, Coons and Sugarman (1979, pp. 27, 40, 43), who are strong supporters of school choice, take a programmatic position by accepting this ideology; they argue that it "does not appear likely that affirmative integration will soon become either a constitutional norm or a social habit." They also agree with Lewis (1978) that school personnel, who are generally middle class and white, will continue to use the "hidden curriculum" to the disadvantage of minority students. Further, implicit racism is widespread in America and will also exist in schools of choice with legal safeguards, public or private, integrated or segregated (Coons & Sugarman, 1979, pp. 27, 110, 120). Coons and Sugarman (1979, p. 27) feel that, given the cultural, social, and political realities in America, society's perception of the poor is related to their "academic performance" and the best last chance for the poor is the opportunity to select or operate their own schools through a system of school choice. Recently, Coons and Sugarman (1990-1991) have argued that minority group children should be granted a percentage of private school enrollment of choice to protect them from discrimination. They may be correct in their appraisal of opportunities for the poor in America.

African Americans have reacted to this new conservative political ideology, which began after two decades of steady progress in race relations, by perceiving the current anti-affirmative action atmosphere as a conspiracy by whites to reduce opportunities for minority groups (DeParkle, 1990), a conspiracy that is generally referred to as "the plan." Many whites, however, are opposed to this conservative idealogy and school choice (Brown & Contreras, 1991; Davies, 1991; Levin, 1977; Martin, 1991; Timar, 1990), but there are many supporters (Chubb & Moe, 1990; Coons & Sugarman, 1979).

School Choice

Choice in education is supposed to improve education by injecting market incentives among schools, which would improve schools without significant additional costs by promoting innovations through the restructuring of schools and by increasing parental participation in the schooling process (Paulu, 1989). The symbolism used to promote choice is "market incentives." Most observers of choice in the social services, however, reject the notion of the classic market theory (Brown & Contreras, 1991; Coons & Sugarman, 1979; Drucker, 1985). There is evidence that competition among municipalities for residents, competition between public and private hospitals, and competition between public and private schools does not improve output (Arrow, 1951; Brown & Contreras, 1991; Coons & Sugarman, 1979; Drucker, 1985; Hirschmann, 1970; Liebermann, 1989). In education, a 50% reduction in the number of Catholic schools over the past two decades is strong evidence of a lack of market incentives in education (Brown & Contreras, 1991; Erickson, 1986). There are parents seeking choice options—the demand side—but we are unlikely to find available schools—the supply side (Brown & Contreras, 1991; Elmore, 1990; Levin, 1977; Liebermann, 1989). Although new fundamental Christian schools have been established in the past three decades, most were established by white parents to evade racially integrated schools.

In the United States, there is only one education program in which parents may enroll their children in private schools and attendance is supported with public funds. In 1990, Minnesota state law allowed a maximum of 1,000 students from low-income families to enroll in private schools in the Milwaukee area with tuition to be paid by the state. Of the 20 private schools in the area, 7 participated in the program. Of the 341 students who took advantage of the opportunity by enrolling in the private schools, 63 students returned to the public schools before the end of the school year (Chira, 1991b). But there are choice options within several large urban public school districts. Most public school choice plans involve the establishment of special-focus schools called "magnet" schools designed to promote racial integration without involuntarily busing of students and to improve students' academic performance.

There is no empirical evidence to support the success of choice programs (Astin, 1991; Brown & Contreras, 1991; Chira, 1991a; Hermann, 1991; Timar, 1990). Some researchers (Furhrman, 1989; Metz, 1990) have observed that educational innovations are often rejected because "innovative" schools are not perceived as "real schools." The rituals and symbols in traditional schools are important to the elites who were successful in "real schools" (Metz, 1990). Few parents change their children's schools because of innovative programs but they will change schools to be in a better neighborhood, close to child care facilities, or close to a job (Erickson, 1986; Hermann, 1991). Also, many choice programs are stressful for teachers and students (Hermann, 1991). People of influence attended "real," and not innovative, schools and they expect others to attend "real" schools. Parents continue to use the social class and race of peers in selecting schools for their children and in judging a school's quality. In addition, pressures to reform tend to strengthen the grip of "real" schools opposed to innovative ones (Metz, 1990, pp. 85-87; Timar, 1990).

Timar's (1990) research on restructured (innovative) schools showed the image of the "real schools" to be powerful and to cause resistance to any departure from this image. Opposition to change comes from parents, teachers, students, and administrators, who attempt to protect the image of "real schools." Real schools are usually those attended by children of well-to-do parents, public or private.

Despite resistance from school people, parents, and school board members, the dominant political ideology demands that choice be used to counter forces pushing for improved equity and social justice.

Thus it is important that we draw upon experiences with school choice in other countries. The Netherlands is the only country with a nationwide school choice program involving public and private schools supported with public funds. I will also briefly review choice programs in Canada and Australia.

School Choice in Other Countries

The Netherlands

The Netherlands is located in the low country of Europe. It is a compact country slightly larger than the state of Maryland and, with 14 million inhabitants, is the most densely populated country in the world. Holland is unique in that education and most other social services are financed by the government but are generally operated by private nonprofit organizations, often religious in nature. A small fraction of social services are delivered by the government (James, 1986; Louis & Van Veizen, 1990-1991). This delivery system is derived from a special feature of the Dutch society, "pillarization," which is the tendency for Catholics, Protestants, and other groups to exist separately in every aspect of Dutch life, including residence, jobs, friends, and politics (James, 1986; Louis & Van Veizen, 1990-1991).

In 1917, a coalition between Catholics and Protestants (mainly Calvinists) produced a national constitution that provided public support for religious schools. In 1920, a national education law was enacted to implement this education policy. In the Netherlands today, there are 4,000 independent governing school boards for 8,050 elementary schools and 2,000 secondary schools. Approximately 69% of all elementary pupils attend privately operated, publicly funded schools and 31% attend public schools. At the secondary level, 72% attend privately operated schools and 28% attend public schools. The average enrollment for an elementary school is 175 and is 545 for a secondary school. Most, 95%, of the privately operated schools are church related. Choice has existed in Holland for 85 years but has not been replicated in any other European country.

To establish a private school in Holland with public funding, a group of parents, 50 to 125, depending upon the size of the municipality, and usually with the assistance of their church, petition the government for a school. If the request is granted, the central government pays all costs on a per pupil basis for current expenses, and the municipality provides a building for the school. There is parity in funding between public and private schools, and teacher salaries may not be a supplemented by schools. Private schools, however, may charge a small fee for nonpersonnel expenses. Teacher salaries, which constitute 80% to 90% of school budgets, are paid directly by the national government. Public schools are initiated by municipalities. All schools are funded using a standard teacher-to-student ratio of 31 to 1.

What can we learn from school choice in the Netherlands? Parents may choose any school for their child but private schools may select from among applicants. There is less social conflict over education, and experimentation is possible but is rarely found in Dutch schools. Curriculum, pedagogy, and school organization are generally uniform throughout the country. The Dutch schools conform to the desire for pillarization in Dutch society. Religious affiliation and residence are the strongest factors influencing school choice. Less popular schools do not disappear, as market incentives would dictate. Pedagogy is in the hands of professional educators, with almost no parent participation. Parents determine a school's quality more on the visible social-economic mixture of students and less on a school's academic performance. All schools, public and private, must follow rigid central government regulations on the curriculum but pedagogy is left to teachers. All students must take a national exam at the end of elementary school and at the end of high school. Teacher salaries, teacher credentials, and working conditions are regulated by the central government.

One must remember that a Catholic school is generally located in a Catholic neighborhood; teachers are affiliated with the Catholic church and have been trained in privately operated Catholic teacher education colleges. Students may engage in religiously related curricula activities. The same is true for the Calvinist and other religiously oriented schools.

What are some of the negatives? Private schools may select from among student and teacher applicants. With choice, schools with high immigrant enrollments are experiencing "white flight" (Louis & Van Veizen, 1990-1991, p. 69). One public elementary school reached almost 100% non-Dutch enrollment soon after the non-Dutch enrollment had reached 50%. Dutch parents are using choice to desert "black schools" (Louis & Van Veizen, 1990-1991, p. 69). In recent years, there has been a tendency for Muslim residents to establish their own schools and, in the past three years, more than 10 Muslim elementary schools have been established (Louis & Van Veizen, 1990-1991, p. 70). The children of most "guest workers" are enrolled in public schools. "Creaming" or "tracking" takes place at age 12 via a required national examination, which results in academic sorting by social class for subsequent schooling (James, 1986).

Canada and Australia

In addition to school choice in Holland, we may draw upon the experiences of choice programs in Canada and Australia. Erickson (1986), a specialist on private education in Canada, found in his research that religious schools in operation at the founding of the Canadian Federation in 1867 are protected and continue to operate with public funding. Newly established private schools are privately funded, and privately operated public schools are de facto "public schools." Canadians do not increase innovation or diversity in the student population by extending public funds to private schools.

In British Columbia, there is government support for "unprotected" private schools. In 1978, British Columbia enacted a law to provide partial public funding for nonconstitutionally protected private schools. British Colombia offered 39% public financial support to private schools (which are mainly Catholic schools). With partial state funding, the schools increased teacher salaries and consolidated some schools to save money, saw increased state regulations, and found increased client dissatisfaction with the schools as religious institutions. The schools found themselves "hooked" on public funding and could not reverse their course. Dissatisfaction resulted from the hiring of more teachers with little interest in the religious doctrine once salaries were raised with the help of state funds. And a state-required curriculum left little time for religious activities (Erickson, 1986).

Erickson (1986, p. 104) found that client dissatisfaction with publicly funded private education in British Columbia compares with negative feelings by former Dutch citizens living in Canada toward Dutch publicly funded Calvinist schools. These ex-Dutch citizens felt that the schools were private in name only and were public schools in reality. They expressed a strong desire for private schools without public support. One must also remember that, in Holland and in Canada, there is not a constitutional separation of church and state. Therefore one would expect public schools also to engage in religious activities. With a uniform state-mandated curriculum, the distinction between public and private schools may be minor. Unlike those in the Netherlands, however, Canadian private schools may not use religious affiliation as a criterion for accepting students or for hiring teachers.

Erickson (1986) also found that the most active choosers of private education in Canada were the better educated and wealthier parents; this was also true for parents who selected public schools. He also found that protected private schools with full state funding were significantly "deprivatized" and de facto public schools. In my experience in visiting private schools in Ontario, I found that the terms *Catholic* or *private* are rarely used in referring to Catholic schools. These schools are in every way public schools. Residents in Toronto refer to their schools in terms of the public school district and the "separate" school district (Catholic). Constitutionally protected private schools and public schools in Canada receive equal public funding.

The Australians have also experimented with school choice (Birch & Smart, 1990; Boyd, 1987). Beginning in 1973, the national government initiated the funding of private elementary and secondary schools on a need basis. Today in Australia, 30% of all students attend private schools, of which 75% are Catholic schools, and 70% attend public schools. The schools are funded on a need basis with the poorest private schools receiving approximately $3,200 per pupil from the national and state government and the wealthiest schools receiving approximately $1,000 per pupil (Birch & Smart, 1990, p. 49). This support accounts for about 75% of the operating expenses for the poorest private schools, which are mainly Catholic schools. Boyd and Stuart (1987, p. 3) sum up the impact of choice on education in Australia:

> What is critical is who goes to private schools. In Australia, three-quarters of the students still go to government schools. But the prestige and career advantages of attending the elite private schools (which charge substantial fees despite receiving state aid) foster a creaming-off process that drains government high schools of most

of their upper-middle class students. This creaming off process reduces the reputation of state schools and sets in motion a dual school system by race and class.

Political Climate in the United States

U.S. supporters of parental choice in schooling usually fail to take advantage of lessons learned from choice plans in other countries. Nor do school choice advocates view educational reform as part of a larger political movement but, instead, view it solely as an isolated educational reform movement. A review of the literature on this subject leaves only one conclusion: The current educational reform movement in the United States is a component of a larger political movement. Researchers on this topic are in agreement that a radical shift in ideology has occurred in America over the past several decades regarding the allocation of opportunity for the poor, racial, ethnic, and language minority groups (Astin, 1991; Birch & Smart, 1990; Boyd & Kerchner, 1988; Brown, 1990; Clark & Astuto, 1990; Davies, 1991; DeWitt, 1991; Iannaccone, 1988; Mazzoni, 1988; "What of the Children," 1991). Education plays a major role in the politics of opportunity allocation in America. The conservative ideological consensus in operation today is similar in character to the dominant ideology of the 1890s. Presidents Reagan and Bush were the first U.S. presidents to veto civil rights legislation since President Andrew Johnson, who succeeded Lincoln in office. With strong support for this ideology by President Bush and the current U.S. Supreme Court, it will be difficult for a less conservative Congress to protect and improve educational opportunities for racial, ethnic, and language minorities who reside in our urban centers.

With the country's economic problems (Brown, 1990), I find it difficult to envision a significant positive change in the educational opportunity allocation process in America for at least a decade or more. The cause of the new ideology is based mostly on economics mixed with racism. Capital markets wishing to maximize profit are seeking cheaper labor markets, mainly outside of the country. To counter this economic trend, domestic workers must settle for lower wages, which results in less taxes to support social services such as education. A less credentialed domestic work force is produced, which must accept lower wages. Therefore the poor will get "symbolic" equity through choice.

Lessons From Other Countries

What can we learn from the Dutch, Canadian, and Australian experiences with choice in education? First, we must remember that these countries wanted to legalize the delivery of public-supported social services by religious groups. The U.S. Constitution calls for the opposite approach, the separation of church and state. The U.S. Supreme Court, however, has interpreted this constitutional provision on public funds for use by private religious organizations as being "legal" as long as their activities are not used to indoctrinate participants. For example, it is constitutionally permissible for religiously affiliated colleges and universities to receive public funds, although elementary and secondary religious schools may not. It is conceivable, however, that the current U.S. Supreme Court might extend this interpretation to K-12 schools. The Court could interpret a state-mandated curriculum for both public and private schools as meeting the constitutional requirement for the separation of church and state.

Second, two of these comparison countries also require fiscal parity between all schools, public and private. In Holland, fiscal parity exists between all schools in the country. In Canada, fiscal party exist between public and private schools within each province. In Australia, a need-based funding formula is in use and fiscal parity is not required.

Third, schools in these countries were established for racially homogeneous populations, while in the United States most schools were legally racially segregated until the 1960s. America was the last industrialized country to eliminate de jure racially segregated schools.

Fourth, neighborhoods in Holland are generally segregated by religious affiliation and social class; and it is to be expected that neighborhood parents, with local church assistance, organize schools for *their* neighborhood and largely restrict admission to children from that neighborhood and those affiliated with their religion. In Canada, there are administratively private school districts rather than individual schools as in Holland, and neighborhoods in Canada are generally religiously integrated. In practice, cities in Canada have two publicly funded school systems within their borders, one public and one private. The Australian communities are also generally religiously integrated.

In the Dutch experience, we found that (a) most schools are affiliated with a religious group; (b) private schools are funded on a per pupil basis, the same as public schools; (c) private schools have selective admissions while the public schools must accept all applicants; (d) "white flight" has left some public schools racially and ethically segregated; (e) private schools may select their teachers based upon religious affiliation; (f) because of the small average size of schools in Holland, education is very expensive; (g) there is a uniform curriculum in all schools, public and private, and an almost total absence of innovation; (h) there is little parental involvement with schools, public or private; (i) professional educators have almost complete control over the schools; (j) private and public schools must follow state regulations; and (k) parental choice is influenced more by religious affiliation and visible assessment of the social class mix of the student body and the school's neighborhood, and not the academic record of the school. Also, because teacher salaries are paid by the natural government, teachers through their professional organizations hold the most political influence over education. Finally, private schools in Holland are de facto public schools.

In Canada's publicly funded, privately operated schools, (a) the constitutionally protected religious school districts ("separate" schools) are de facto public schools; (b) there is fiscal equity between private and public schools; (c) private schools in Canada do not restrict student admission or teacher hiring based on religious affiliation; (d) the schools are integrated by race and social class; (e) except for experiments in British Columbia with the funding of non-constitutionally protected schools, private school enrollment in Canada has reminded fairly steady; (f) the private schools are not innovative; (g) private schools must follow state-mandated regulations; and (h) parents select schools based upon neighborhood and the social class mix of the student body.

British Columbia's experiment with partial public funding (30%) of previously unprotected schools showed that (a) state regulations followed public support; (b) the schools lost their religious character, and parent satisfaction decreased; (c) innovation did not occur; (d) state support gave rise to better teacher salaries, and more lay teachers sought employment in the private schools; and (e) despite client dissatisfaction, the schools are hooked on state funds and are likely to end up as de facto public schools like state-funded "separate" schools.

In the Australian experience with public and private school choice, (a) unequal public support among private schools resulted in a dual educational system, one for the poor and one for the rich; (b) most children from wealthy families attend elite private schools; (c) private schools do not receive equal public support but are funded based upon 12 categories of need; (d) innovations are missing from private and public schools; and (e) all private schools that accept state funds must follow state-mandated regulations.

School choice in Holland, Canada, and Australia that allows the use of public funds to support privately operated schools is derived from each country's dominant political ideology. The current ideology in the United States, however, is aimed at protecting advantages enjoyed by the dominant social classes, and efforts to reform education through choice are symbolic politics at its best. Review of the experience with school choice in the three countries discussed strongly supports the following conclusions: Choice will not result in market incentives to improve education. Choice will not improve educational opportunities for the poor. Choice will promote traditional schools, not innovative ones. Choice will not alter the influence of professional educators or increase the influence of parents in the schooling process. Private choice schools will become de facto public schools. Parents, students, and teachers still prefer "real" schools whether they are public or private, not radically innovative schools. Fiscal parity between schools is more likely to improve education than any other known reform. Parents will continue to use a school's social class mix of students and the neighborhood where the school is located to select a school for their children, and not the school's academic performance.

School choice may be a good political mechanism for reducing social conflict over education but it is a poor instrument for improving education for children from disadvantaged populations. With the first revolutionary, racially conservative, political-ideological shift since the 1890s firmly entrenched, I do not expect that an educational reform plan designed to improve schools for our urban poor will be acceptable to a majority of the Americans who support this ideology. If a choice plan is adopted, it will probably resemble the

Australian plan, which produced a dual school system, one for the rich and one for the poor. A publicly funded school is a public school, whether it is publicly or privately administered. We should expect public officials to demand accountability in the expenditure of public funds, a process that will turn any privately operated, publicly funded school into a "real" school and a public one.

If choice is a symbol used by politicians to send a signal that they intend to protect the educational, social, and economic advantages enjoyed by upper-class households, can we still learn from experiences with choice in other countries? Yes. We have learned that fiscal parity between schools is important; neighborhood control of schools helps resolve social conflict over education; and all people desire "real schools." Choice policies, however, may not reduce racial and social class discrimination, between schools and within schools (Coons & Sugarman, 1979; Oakes, 1985; Ogbu, 1978), or improve urban schools for racial, ethnic, and language minority group children. Coons and Sugarman (1979) saw neighborhood control of schools through choice as the only avenue left to improve urban schools, private or public, segregated or integrated, given discriminatory practices against minority students so common in our schools. We have learned, however, that privately funded schools become de facto public schools, and we need to go beyond the "public-private" model to significantly improve urban education. We need a model that includes fiscal parity with additional compensatory funding for the disadvantaged, more minority teachers, and a multicultural curriculum to reduce the impact of the "hidden curriculum" (downward academic tracking and culturally biased pedagogy).

In a recent debate on choice and school restructuring between Michael Kirst, a professor of education from Stanford University, and Chester Finn, a former U.S. Department of Education official with the Reagan administration (Kirst & Finn, 1991), Kirst argued that the conclusion drawn by Chubb and Moe (1990)—that schools need major restructuring to become effective—is contrary to public opinion. Except for big city schools, people are generally satisfied with their schools and, under these conditions, major changes are not likely to occur. Finn, on the other hand, argued that, while Kirst is correct about public opinion, the public's satisfaction is not based upon rational decision making, due to a lack of good information for parents. This debate seems to characterize feelings on the issue of choice by proponents and opponents.

But most professional educational groups have already expressed opposition to choice involving private schools. Some supporters of choice are beginning to call for a go-slow approach by conducting experiments with choice before full implementation. For example, Owen B. Butler (1991), chair of the Committee for Economic Development and former chair of Proctor and Gamble Corporation, feels there are too many questions to be answered before we implement choice programs. Butler adds that, under a voucher plan, all students in private schools will qualify for public support for their schooling, and publicly funded private schools will have to meet the same accountability standards in the use of public funds as public schools. Who will pay for the added cost of educating all students currently enrolled in private schools? Will private school clients continue to support these new "private" schools?

If choice schools are desired only in a theoretical sense, but not in "my" neighborhood, and if few expect choice schools with a private option to become a reality, then why is this such a hot topic? School choice may be seen as symbolic of a general conservative political philosophy that endorses prayer in public schools, supports public funding of private education, and supports reductions in affirmative action. Political symbolism is not new in America. Edelman (1977) discusses the extensive use of political symbols in his book *The Symbolic Uses of Politics.* I prefer to call the use of choice as a political symbol the "economics of politics" in which the haves are informed that they will no longer be called upon to increase support for the have-nots and "choice" is the political signal.

I also believe that the current conservative U.S. Supreme Court is likely to approve direct funding to private schools that are willing to implement a state-mandated curriculum, making the concept of vouchers obsolete. Private schools will become de facto "public" schools as evidenced in the experience with similar practices in Holland, Canada, and Australia. Under this scenario, big city schools will remain disadvantaged. Translated: Choice as a political philosophy means that current social inequalities are acceptable, at least for the duration of what is perceived to be a long period of general economic decline for America.

References

Arrow, K. (1951). *Social choice and individual values.* New York: John Wiley.

Astin, A. W. (1991, May 14). The education president stumbles. *Los Angeles Times,* p. B11.

Birch, I., & Smart, D. (1990). Economic rationalism and the politics of education in Australia. In D. E. Mitchell & M. E. Goertz (Eds.), *Education politics for the new century* (pp. 137-151). New York: Falmer.

Boyd, W. L. (1987). Balancing public and private schools: The Australian experience and American implications. *Educational Evaluation and Policy Analysis, 9*(1), 183-193.

Boyd, W. L., & Kerchner, C. T. (Eds.). (1988). *The politics of excellence and choice in education.* New York: Falmer.

Boyd, W. L., & Stuart, D. (1987). *Educational policy in Australia and America: Comparative perspectives.* London: Falmer.

Brown, F. (1990). The language politics education, and the disadvantaged. In S. L. Jacobson & J. A. Conway (Eds.), *Educational leadership in an age of reform* (pp. 83-100). New York: Longman.

Brown v. Board of Education of Topeka, 347 U.S. 483 (1954).

Brown, F., & Contreras, A. R. (1991). Deregulation and privatization of education: A flawed concept. *Education and Urban Society, 23*(2), 144-158.

Butler, O. B. (1991, July 5). Some doubts on school vouchers. *The New York Times,* p. A11.

Carter, D. G., & Sandler, J. P. (1991). Access, choice, quality and integration. *Education and Urban Society, 23*(2), 175-184.

Chira, S. (1991a, April 10). Rochester: An uneasy symbol of school reform. *The New York Times,* p. B8.

Chira, S. (1991b, June 12). The rules of the market place are applied to the classroom. *The New York Times,* pp. 1, B9.

Chubb, J. E., & Moe, T. M. (1990). *Politics, markets, and America's schools.* Washington, DC: Brookings Institution.

Clark, D. L., & Astuto, T. A. (1990). The disjunction of federal educational policy and national education needs in the 1990s. In D. E. Mitchell & M. E. Goertz (Eds.), *Education politics for the new century* (pp. 11-25). New York: Falmer.

Coons, J. E., & Sugarman, S. D. (1979). *Education by choice: The case for family control.* Berkeley: University of California Press.

Coons, J. E., & Sugarman, S. D. (1990-1991). The private school option in systems of educational choice. *Educational Leadership, 48*(4), 54-56.

Davies, G. K. (1991, May 15). The president's bold educational reform is a sham. *The Chronicle of Higher Education*, p. A44.

DeParkle, J. (1990, October 29). Talk of government being out to get blacks falls on more attentive ears. *The New York Times*, p. A12.

DeWitt, K. (1991, June 27). Democrats challenge new education policy. *The New York Times*, p. A10.

Drucker, P. F. (1985). *Innovation and entrepreneurship*. New York: Harper & Row.

Edelman, M. (1977). *The symbolic uses of politics*. Urbana: University of Illinois Press.

Elmore, R. F. (1990). Options for choice. In W. L. Boyd & J. J. Walberg (Eds.), *Public education in choice in education* (pp. 21-42). Berkeley, CA: McCutchan.

Erickson, D. A. (1986). Choice and private schools: Dynamics of supply and demand. In D. C. Levy (Ed.), *Private education: Studies in choice and public policy* (pp. 82-109). New York: Oxford University Press.

Furhrman, S. H. (1989). State politics and education reform. In J. Jannaway & R. Crowson (Eds.), *The politics of reforming school administration* (pp. 61-75). New York: Falmer.

Hermann, M. (1991, May 17). Blackboard jungle: The rise and fall of the Richmond (CA) Unified School District. *Express: The East Bay's Free Weekly, 13*(32), 1, 17-19, 25-29.

Hirchmann, A. O. (1970). *Exit, voice, and loyalty*. Cambridge, MA: Harvard University Press.

Iannaccone, L. (1988). From equity to excellence: Political context and dynamics. In W. L. Boyd & C. Kerchner (Eds.), *The politics of excellence and choice in education* (pp. 49-65). New York: Falmer.

James, E. (1986). Public subsidies for private and public education: The Dutch case. In D. C. Levy (Ed.), *Private education: Studies in choice and public policy* (pp. 113-137). New York: Oxford University Press.

Kirp, D. L. (1982). *Just schools: The idea of racial equality in American education*. Berkeley: University of California Press.

Kirst, M., & Finn, C. E. (1991). Have the politics become too political? *Politics of Education Bulletin, 17*(3), 4, 5, 8-10.

Levin, H. M. (1977). Educational vouchers and educational equity. In M. Carnoy & H. M. Levin, *Schooling in a corporate society* (2nd ed., pp. 293-309). New York: David McKay.

Lewis, M. (1978). *The culture of inequality*. New York: Meridian.

Liebermann, M. (1989). *Privatization and educational choice*. New York: St. Martin's Press.

Louis, K. S., & Van Veizen, B. A. M. (1990-1991). A look at choice in the Netherlands. *Educational Leadership, 48*(4), 66-72.

Martin, M. (1991). Trading the known for the unknown: Warning signs in the debate over schools of choice. *Education and Urban Society, 23*(2), 119-143.

Mazzoni, T. L. (1988). The politics of educational choice in Minnesota. In W. L. Boyd & C. T. Kerchner (Eds.), *The politics of excellence and choice in education* (pp. 217-230). New York: Falmer.

Metz, M. H. (1990). Real school: A universal drama amid disparate experience. In D. E. Mitchell & M. E. Goertz (Eds.), *Education politics for the new century* (pp. 75-91). New York: Falmer.

Oakes, J. (1985). *Keeping track: How schools structure inequality.* New Haven, CT: Yale University Press.

Ogbu, J. V. (1978). *Minority education and caste.* New York: Academic Press.

Paulu, M. (1989). *Improving schools and empowering parents: Choice in American education.* Washington, DC: U.S. Department of Education.

Plessy v. Ferguson, 163 U.S. 537 (1896).

Timar, T. B. (1990). The politics of school restructuring. In D. E. Mitchell & M. E. Goertz (Eds.), *Education politics for the new century* (pp. 55-74). New York: Falmer.

Vergon, C. B. (1990). School desegregation: Lessons from three decades of experience. *Education and Urban Society, 23*(1), 22-49.

What of the children left behind [Editorial]. (1991, June 17). *The New York Times,* p. A12.

10

Issues of Choice:
Canadian and American Perspectives

STEPHEN B. LAWTON

The key difference between the Canadian and American approaches to choice in education is found in the emphasis on collective rights in Canada and individual rights in the United States.[1] The remainder of this chapter is concerned with explaining this distinction and illustrating its implications for the organization and operation of educational systems. The Canadian situation receives the greatest emphasis in that the U.S. situation is the focus of the volume's other chapters.

Origins of Educational Rights

It is difficult, if not impossible, actually to speak about "Canadian" education because there is tremendous variability from province to

AUTHOR'S NOTE: This chapter was originally prepared for the conference, "Schools of Choice: Canadian and American Perspectives Colloquium," State University of New York at Buffalo, April 20, 1991 (revised August 2, 1991).

province. Under the Canadian Constitution (originally the British North America Act, 1867, and now the Constitution Acts, 1867 and 1982), responsibility for education was delegated to provincial governments, albeit with several restrictions. The restrictions varied from province to province (depending on their arrangements for education in 1867 or at the time that a province entered Confederation) but dealt primarily with the question of the federal protection of religious schools. The Charter of Rights and Freedoms, adopted with the 1982 patriation of the Constitution, came into effect in 1985 and extended federal protection to linguistic (French or English) minorities. The charter, however, did not deal with absolute rights, in that a province can opt out of specific provisions of the charter by passing legislation applicable for five years at a time.

In Ontario's case, the 1867 Constitution provided for the continuation (and federal protection) of what are termed "separate school boards." These boards are formed when a religious minority (Roman Catholic or Protestant) in a community chooses to separate from the public school system because of religious differences. The "public" or "common" school was the first school board formed in a community; if the majority of residents were, say, Roman Catholic, they would hire a Roman Catholic teacher (often a member of their religious order) to operate the school. If local Protestants so chose, they could then organize their own "separate" school, withdrawing their children from the local Roman Catholic "public" school and directing their property taxes to their Protestant separate school board (Lawton, 1987).

Most often this system worked in the opposite manner, with Roman Catholics withdrawing their children from the Protestant-dominated public system, but the legislation of the day pertained to both. Today, there remains one Protestant separate school board in Ontario. It operates a single elementary school in Penetanguishene, near Georgian Bay, north of Toronto. There are no "public" Roman Catholic school boards in Ontario, although two remain in Alberta, where the public-separate distinction also applies. For the most part, when people refer to "separate school boards" in Ontario, they mean Roman Catholic school boards.

What is notable about the arrangement for public and separate schools, as they operate in Ontario, Alberta, Saskatchewan, and Quebec, is that the right to schooling of a particular type is granted to groups rather than individuals; that is, it is a collective right granted to the minority religious group, Protestant or Catholic, in a given community.

This collective right did not come about because of the magnanimity of the dominant English Protestants in Ontario. In fact, it was part of a political deal at the time of Confederation that also protected the English Protestant minority's right to its own system of education in Quebec. It was a quid pro quo, if you like. Canada would not have been possible as a nation without this de jure guarantee for the protection of religious rights in education and de facto guarantee for the protection of language rights.

This history sets the stage for Canadian thinking about "choice" in education. Five parameters define the operation of choice in Canada. First, as noted at the beginning, choice is thought of as protecting group or collective rights: rights of subgroups in society with some identifiable trait. Second, the key traits of social salience have been religion and language (as opposed, say, to race, caste, gender, or disability—other traits that have been proposed as entitling one to collective consideration). Third, while these rights operated at the provincial level, it was the federal government's responsibility to protect these rights. Fourth, the right to a particular type of education is what Gairdner (1990) refers to as a "positive right"—the right to receive some service from government. And, fifth, the educational rights were obtained primarily on the basis of political power and pragmatism rather than commitment to some sort of transcendent ideal.

In Ontario, at least, there was a residual concern about individual rights as far as education was concerned. The individual Roman Catholic (or Protestant) retained the right to attend the public school even if other members of his or her minority had decided to create a separate school in the community. To do so, however, the child's family had to direct their property taxes to the public system and all children had to attend the public system, unless parents were willing to pay the cost of tuition at the separate school. Taxes could not be split and, in the case of mixed (Catholic/Protestant) marriages, one system or the other had to be supported.

Separate and public school systems differ slightly in each of the provinces where they exist. In some cases (e.g., Alberta and Saskatchewan), they approach the character of denominational systems, such as exist in Newfoundland, where there are four denominational systems: Protestant Integrated, Roman Catholic, Pentecostal, and Seventh Day Adventist. Children of members of each religious group in Newfoundland are required to attend the system that reflects their families' religion. There is no choice without religious conversion. In Alberta and Saskatchewan, Roman Catholics must support the Catholic system, if it exists, and they do not have the right, as Roman Catholics do in Ontario, to support the public system. Also, children of mixed Catholic-Protestant marriages have a choice of school systems and their taxes are split between the two. Those individuals who are neither Catholic nor Protestant have a choice of school systems and where to direct their taxes in Alberta, Ontario, and Newfoundland, but, in Saskatchewan they must, by law, be supporters of the public system (Lawton, 1987).

Public and separate systems have evolved over the years. Public systems (except in Quebec) are essentially nondenominational or secular systems much like public schools in the United States. They have lost their Protestant character, for the most part, although a lack of separation of church and state in Canada means that religion is not forbidden in the schools. Courts have ruled, however, that no particular religion may be favored in public schools.

Extension of Rights in the 1980s

The five operating principles affecting choice in education in Canada came into play during major changes to the educational system in Ontario during the 1980s. Two key events occurred: Roman Catholic separate schools were allowed to extend their range from elementary grades only (effectively grades 1 to 10) to offer a complete secondary system, and French-language school systems began to be formed. The first change was initiated as a political act of the provincial legislature (which followed more than a century of lobbying and court cases), and the second was initiated to comply with the new Charter of Rights and Freedoms guarantees for minority language rights. In both cases, the courts played a major role; in the first, the Supreme Court of Canada upheld the legislation that extended the Catholic system without granting parallel rights to other religious groups; in the second, the Appeal Court of Ontario effectively told the Ontario legislature the type of legislation that was necessary to implement the charter (Lawton, 1989, in press).

In both cases, collective rights were at issue: the rights of Roman Catholics and the rights of individuals who speak French or English as their first language. More specifically, the language rights were guaranteed for the children of francophones or anglophones who were educated in these languages in Canada; the rights do not apply to immigrants. Second, language and religion continued to be the defining traits. Third, action was taken at a provincial level, with the federal courts acting as the arbiter when disputes arose. Fourth, the rights were again positive rights, granting new claims upon government's resources. And, fifth, no new groups were able to win similar rights, even though the charter guarantees "equal benefits" for all and holds that it is to be interpreted "in a manner consistent with the multicultural heritage of Canadians."

Some concern about *individual rights* was recognized in the extension of the Roman Catholic system. First, secondary schools (covering grades 9 to 13 at that time, and now grades 9 to 12/OAC—or Ontario Academic Credits, which are fixed syllabus university preparation courses) are open to all regardless of religion. Second, for a 10-year period, teachers displaced from the public system due to enrollment shifts to the Catholic system are required to be offered places in the latter system. The former requirement has given way to large numbers of "open access" students, students whose parents pay taxes to one system while the students attend the other. In many cases, students may be choosing the public system over the separate system because some programs, especially high-cost technical programs, are available only in that system. In these cases, the "extra cost" of the program is billed by the public board to the separate board so that the separate, not the public, ratepayers carry the increased burden (Ministry of Education, Ontario, 1991). In other cases, students may choose the separate system for reasons of philosophy; Moslem parents sometimes send their children to Catholic schools because the Catholic system provides single-sex high schools, which public systems usually do not.

For Ontario *francophones* (the Canadian term for individuals who speak French as their first language), three arrangements have been made for schooling. First, where there are sufficient numbers to fill one class or more, French-language sections of the school board have been created. Thus, for example, francophone separate school supporters would elect a special slate of electors to their local separate school board while francophone public school supporters would elect a special group of trustees to their local public boards. These sections, which are paralleled by English-language sections in a few areas of Ontario where anglophones are in a minority, essentially have all the powers of a regular school board—hiring, firing, setting curriculum within provincial guidelines, and so forth—even though they might appear to be a subcommittee of the local board. Second, in two areas, Metropolitan Toronto and Ottawa, French-language school boards have been created. In Toronto's case, it is a public board that covers all of Metro Toronto; it shares the same Metro Toronto "umbrella" board that finances the other six area public school boards (Toronto, Scarborough, North York, East York, York, and Etobicoke). The unified Metropolitan Separate School Board, which provides Catholic education for the whole of Metro Toronto, has a French-language section. In Ottawa-Carleton, a unique type of school board was created, a French-language board with a public and a Catholic section. Such hybrid boards have long been resisted by Catholic anglophones and, judging from reports of its political and economic problems, ought to have been resisted by francophones in Ottawa-Carleton. In any case, it serves the entire City of Ottawa and the neighboring Carleton Region, each of which has its own public and separate school boards. The province has announced the intention to establish two additional French-language school boards, in Simcoe and in Frontenac counties; presumably both will be Roman Catholic separate school boards. Finally, where neither of the above situations prevails, school boards may purchase services from a neighboring school board; this is commonly done where there are very few children who qualify.

The nature of rights to choice under the system used in Ontario is clearly not one of even or symmetric choice (Lawton, 1986). Instead, what I refer to as "asymmetric" choice exists. That is, a francophone Catholic has the choice of three or four systems: the public English, the Catholic English, the public French, or the Catholic French. The Catholic who is not francophone has two choices, the separate or the public board. The person who is neither of these two has but one choice: the public system. Ironically, it is the majority that has the least choice in school systems.

A number of perhaps amusing, or perhaps aggravating, problems have arisen with the expansion of collective rights to the two minority groups of concern. In a small northern Ontario town, the high schools are competing for "open access" students, who are split between the four groups of supporters. With few resources, the public elementary schools suffer because their supporters are "locked" in and their board directs funds to the secondary level, where competition exists. In another small area, where there is currently one high school for all 1,000 students, English and French Catholics are negotiating with neighboring school boards to create their own distinct boards. If successful, there will be three high schools, each with 300 or so pupils, and many students will be bused up to 50 kilometers. Given that the provincial rates of grant from the separate school board are about 80% for operating expenditures and 95% for transportation, it is clear that they are not using much of their own money for this initiative! Finally, in a southern Ontario school board where a community has only two francophone students, transportation costs to a neighboring school board for services are said to have exceeded $50,000 in one year: $25,000 per student.

The asymmetry of choice extends to career lines for educators. The Dufferin-Peel Roman Catholic Separate School Board has ruled that non-Catholic teachers hired after 1991 will not be eligible for promotion (Sarick, 1991). In addition, plans by the Ministry of Education to increase the level of participation of school systems in preparation programs for superintendents have led to distinct programs for francophones and for Roman Catholics.

Choice Within Systems

The emphasis, to this point, has been on collective rights and differentiation among educational structures at the school system level to meet these rights. In addition, there is choice within school systems in Canada. While there are the usual choices that Americans would be familiar with—gifted education, program streams (or tracking) at the secondary level, high schools for the arts, and the like —one is uniquely Canadian: French immersion. This program, beginning early (kindergarten or grade 1), middle (grade 4), or late (grade 7 or 8), immerses the non-French-speaking child in a French environment. French immersion programs have increased in popularity during the past decade or so, to the point where half the children in some neighborhoods are enrolled in French immersion. In some cases, whole schools are dedicated to the program; in others, "dual-track" schools operate with both a French-immersion and an English-language program.

In American terminology, these schools might be considered "magnet schools" in that they often attract students from many different school attendance areas. Several factors lay behind their popularity. First, Canada is officially bilingual at the federal level. Many people support a bilingual Canada and want their children to be bilingual in the interest of national unity and enriched culture. Many also recognize that there is little future with any national agency, organization, or corporation without being bilingual. Thus immersion is a good investment for the future. Second, the federal government promotes immersion by giving provinces grants in support of second-language education. Federal grants go as well to a national lobby group, Parents for French, which acts as an advocate for the program. Finally, many parents perceive a certain elite status for the immersion programs: Usually it is middle- and upper-middle-class Canadian-born parents who enroll their children in immersion programs. One gets good classmates for one's child by selecting immersion.

Immersion has been a sacred cow; if one criticized it, he or she was likely to be seen as being critical of the French, of Quebec, of national unity, and so on. With the decline of belief in the ideal of a bilingual Canada in the wake of political events such as the failure of the Meech Lake agreement and the passage of laws in Quebec that outlaw the use of English and other languages on public signs, however, a frank assessment of immersion is developing. The Etobicoke Board of Education in Metro Toronto announced plans (later dropped due to protests) to phase out early immersion, arguing that (a) it is not suited for immigrant children who speak a language other than English at home, (b) it promotes ethnic (and racial) separation, (c) it requires busing of very young children, which is both costly and difficult for the child, and (d) there is evidence that late-immersion children end up doing just as well in French as early-immersion children and better in English. Another concern that has been raised involves career opportunities for nonfrancophones. Again, francophones tend to be Catholic and have opportunities for advancement in three school systems; anglophone non-Catholics have but one system. Calls by French immersion teachers for French-only immersion schools, and for French-speaking principals, superintendents, and consultants, raise real questions about French immersion's career impact on educators, particularly when combined with programs promoting "employment equity" for racial minorities, women, and the disabled.

Attendance at a French-immersion school often reflects what Ontario school boards usually refer to as "alternate attendance," in that a child who lives within one school attendance area within the school board attends another school within the same school board. Such alternative attendance is freely allowed, if space is available in the receiving school. This policy is in striking contrast to the U.S. norm of mandatory attendance boundaries.

In addition to alternate attendance, "interjurisdictional transfer" is allowed within the Metro Toronto system of public boards; there is more paperwork but, because all are funded out of a Metro-wide property tax (plus occasional provincial grants), there is no fee. Again, there must be space in the receiving school. Finally, "fee-paying" students may be accepted from other jurisdictions. There is no fee to the student's family if the sending school board agrees to pay the cost (as it may if the program is not available otherwise). If the sending board will not pay, then parents are charged a fee set by the Ministry of Education. Hence, by U.S. standards, there is probably a great deal of choice, even within the usual operation of school boards.

In 1990-1991, one large Metro Toronto school board reported the following numbers of transfers to other Metro public boards: interjurisdictional, 141 elementary and 236 secondary; alternative attendance within the board, 2,018 elementary and 2,148 secondary; and fee-paying students from outside Metro Toronto, 82 elementary and 13 secondary. These figures represented the following percentages of the 45,785 elementary and 28,045 secondary students enrolled in the district: interjurisdictional within Metro, 0.3%, and .8%; alternative attendance, 4.4% and 7.7%; and interjurisdictional fee paying, 0.2% and 0.05%. Quite clearly, these choices within the public system have a very small effect on school enrollments, although this is not to say they are not popular with the students and parents concerned. That is, the relatively low percentages may not reflect the displeasure that would occur if the privilege were removed.

Government Funds for Private Schools

Choice in education inevitably raises the question of funding private schools. Americans, on hearing that Ontario recently funded Catholic high schools, often assume there is funding for private schools in the province. That is not so; separate schools, as described above, are a "special form" of the common school and operate under all the regulations and laws that the public schools do, except where religion is concerned. Thus extending funding to Catholic high schools was not a matter of extending funds to private schools but of bringing private schools into the public sector. It would have been much cheaper to do the former, because the tuition fees for the 40,000 or so Catholic high school students in private institutions would have been far less than the operating and capital grants and taxes that are now committed to the separate system.

Some provinces, including British Columbia, Alberta, Saskatchewan, Manitoba, and Quebec, however, provide assistance of varying amounts to private schools. Their decisions to do so have not been of a primarily ideological character meant to increase individual rights but have been, for the most part, a de facto means of extending collective rights to politically influential religious or ethnic communities. Each province has a unique history in this regard, and these cannot be summarized here. The situation in British Columbia, which most closely parallels that in the United States in that the province has only one nondenominational school system and never had separate or denominational schools funded by government, is worth recounting. In 1978, the provincial legislature, pressured by a coalition of Roman Catholic and conservative Protestant groups, extended a modest level of funding to private schools. The subsequent impact of this action has been subject to several studies, at least one involving researchers from both the United States and Canada (Erickson, 1982). It is worth noting, in this context, that the Canadian parliamentary form of government, with a tradition of strict party discipline, makes it possible for majority governments to enact virtually any legislation they so choose. Hence, when a particular group or groups are influential from within and from without government, radical departures are possible.

Comparison With the United States

This extensive discussion of choice in education in Canada can be contrasted with the U.S. approach to choice. The American literature suggests that a concern about individual rights underlies most of the arguments for choice. And it is arguments that we are talking about, in that there appears to be much more talk than action.

The literature on choice in the United States is vast and difficult to summarize, but such a summary is needed to compare the United States and Canada. Several forms of choice that currently exist in the United States will be described. Then, attention is given to current debates about choice and why choice is being seriously considered in some circles as a reform to address current shortcomings of the U.S. educational system.

Choice in schools in the United States operates primarily through the choice of residence. Real estate brochures about housing often illustrate this fact. In these, a county or metropolitan area may be divided into residential areas; for each area, a brochure may describe, among other things, the school districts operating in the area in terms of their enrollment, average residential taxes, dropout rates, percentage of students proceeding to postsecondary education, and so forth. More than 20 school systems may exist in one county—this in contrast to the two or three systems that would be found in a comparable Ontario jurisdiction. For example, London, Ontario, a city of 500,000, has only three systems: the London Board of Education, the Middlesex County Board of Education, and the London-Middlesex Roman Catholic Separate School Board, compared with about 20 in and around Syracuse, New York, a city of similar size.

Even within large city school boards in the United States, "alternative attendance" programs are not common, except where magnet schools are concerned. Even then, these schools often are accompanied by one of the few recognitions of collective or group rights in the United States: the right of racial minorities to transfer schools if racial balance is improved in the process.

Finally, choice operates outside the public system in the United States, with those willing to incur the cost able to send their children to private schools. Although attempts have been made to revoke this right, it is now a right protected by the courts. Note that, in contrast to the "positive rights" that Canada provides certain groups, the right here is a "negative right" in that it prevents the government from interfering with individual rights and choice. This is in the U.S. tradition, where the Bill of Rights is primarily concerned with what government must not do rather than with what the government must do, as in the Canadian Charter of Rights and Freedoms.

The rhetoric of choice in the United States is far more highly developed than are choice programs. One recent work, *Choice and Control in American Education* (Clune & Witte, 1990), includes more than 800 pages. It follows on Chubb and Moe's *Politics, Markets, and America's Schools* (1990), Everhart's *The Public School Monopoly* (1982), and many others. To characterize this vast literature, Weiss, in Clune and Witt, makes the following useful distinction about different types of control over education. Control, she suggests, may be professional, administrative, political, market based, or through values and ideas. Various parts of the American literature have addressed each of these and have led to the conclusion that movement away from professional, administrative, and political control toward market-based or idea-/value-centered schooling would improve the quality of and public satisfaction with American education.

The attacks on the current system come from various perspectives; for example, historian's Tyack's *The One Best System* (1974) ridicules the existing American system of public education in its widely quoted title; sociologist Callahan did the same in his *Education and the Cult of Efficiency* (1962). More recently, political scientists and economists have entered the fray, ranging from general critiques of government bureaucracy such as Niskanen's *Bureaucracy: Servant or Master?* (1973) and Hirschman's *Exit, Voice, and Loyalty* (1970) to specific, research-based criticisms of the educational system per se, such as that by Chubb and Moe, a volume that has been critiqued as unvarnished, or thinly varnished, political ideology. And we have seen sociologist James Coleman switch sides on the issue, from *Equality of Educational Opportunity* (Coleman et al., 1966) in the 1960s—which was used to support forced busing and the like within and among public schools, thus helping to stimulate white flight from cities—to *Public and Private High Schools* (Coleman & Hoffer, 1987), which essentially suggests that voluntary segregation in private religious schools is the answer to U.S. educational ills. Sociologists (including Canadian-born sociologist Donald Erickson, in Everhart, 1982) have come most recently to emphasize the importance of clear mission and commitment ("that vision thing," to use George Bush's terminology) in schools: value communities, if you like; xenophobia, if you don't.

The issue divides, I would argue, into two questions for American researchers: What is right? What works? On the first point, the question of free choice is key. This "negative" right has been granted in the United States—people are free to choose schools for their children, if they have the money. Not granted has been the "positive" right that all people, through government, must fund this choice.

Some would argue that existing choice is no real choice at all even though poor Catholics, Jews, evangelical Christians, and others have shown it can work if the commitment is strong enough to bear the sacrifice. These authors suggest that *equitable* choice must exist and hence that the government must pay: Food stamps for food; vouchers for education. People, especially liberal economists who believe that a social welfare function exits, would hold to this model: freedom of choice but taxation for redistribution to achieve equity in choice. If they choose, they can even quote classic authors from Adam Smith to J. S. Mill to attest that true liberals believe the state has no business in the classroom. Effectiveness is not the issue here, freedom is.

Most recent authors have been concerned about what works rather than what's right. As Witte (1990, p. 4) states in his introduction, all authors in these volumes "support . . . choice and decentralization as an attempt to improve the quality of education for troubled districts by offering them some of the choices already available to most middle-class families." This is American pragmatism at its best. That is, if the economists are right that a free market in education will drive the lousy schools out of business and mean only the best survive, then let's get on with it. If turning over the schools to religious or other agencies improves the test scores and willingness or hard work (Who cares about the religion of his or her heart surgeon, anyhow?), let's get on with it.

Underlying the concern about effective educational systems in the United States is the notion that many schools and school systems have failed to keep their part of the bargain. People pay taxes and send their children to school in part because they expect children will learn something of value—cash value. Education is, in this sense, an investment in human capital, an investment that parents and taxpayers expect to earn a positive rate of return (Lawton, in press). When personal and experts' evidence suggest that schools are not developing this human capital, not keeping their part of the bargain, it follows that people are being robbed. A person's education ought to lead to a product in which the individual has a "property right." A $60,000 K-12 education ought to earn as much as $60,000 invested elsewhere. When this expenditure is forced upon individuals by way of taxes for education, ought not they have some say about the kind of education their children receive? Certainly, the notion that individuals are better than government as agents to decide where investment ought to be made is a matter that touches upon fundamental rights to oneself and one's assets. It is for this reason that pragmatic concerns about "what works" in the United States are intimately linked to concerns about "what's right" for individuals.

Conclusions

What conclusions might one draw from this comparison of approaches to choice in education in Canada and the United States? Not shying away from controversial assessments, I would suggest the following.

Canada's dependence upon the granting of collective rights to achieve national cohesion and social justice has, to date, been a failure. It is well to recall that the process began in 1774, when Britain passed the Quebec Act, granting Quebeckers the right to their own religion, language, and laws in order to keep the recently won colony loyal to the Crown in the face of revolutionary actions to the south. Even a trip to Montreal by Benjamin Franklin, accompanied by Roman Catholic representatives from Maryland and offers of "sovereignty association," were not enough to lure Quebeckers into alliance with the nascent United States. Similarly, in 1867, separate schools were affirmed, guaranteeing collective rights to the religious minorities in the newly confederated colonies to ensure the loyalty of all to the new nation. The process was repeated once again in 1982, when language rights were extended. Yet, while English Canadian children are bused off to their French-immersion classes in kindergarten, Quebec francophones and allophones (whose mother tongue is neither English nor French) are forbidden the study of English in publicly funded schools until grade 4. This is of no concern, of course, to the elite, whose children are enrolled in exclusive private schools where both languages are taught.

Within Ontario, the division of the educational system has encouraged a competition of arguable merit. With the taxpayers' money, public and separate systems compete by extending bus services ever closer to each child's front door and add programs of debatable merit lest their competitor win new recruits. Property assessment offices are set up to ensure every family with a child in the system directs their taxes to the right system. "School Catholics" are created when immigrants, used to the good reputation of Catholic schools operated by religious orders in their homelands, have their children baptized in the church in order to send them to the Catholic system. And French-language school systems begin their own French-immersion programs for the English-speaking children of francophones to "recapture" the child for the French community.

Yet few give Canada a chance for continuing as a single nation for more than five years. If it does survive, it will be in name only as centripetal forces tear apart the body politic and a "coalition of regions" is formed.

The wisdom of the ages suggests, in Lincoln's words, that "a house divided against itself cannot stand." Collective rights divide a nation.

In the United States, the Supreme Court has always been cautious about the extension of public support to private schools because, I believe, it has recognized that such aid will result in the de facto granting of collective rights. Historically, the concern has been that such aid would support religious education and would result in the religious entanglement of government. The potential of similar divisions among linguistic or racial lines is clearly of growing concern. In Quebec, the French-language schoolteachers are among the most vociferous supporters of separation; the schools, some suggest, are nests for inculcating separatist beliefs.

Does this same potential exist in the United States? Could unrestricted, publicly supported choice result in linguistically, racially, and religiously separate schools that would become agents for the development of separatist ideologies? First, let me emphasize that there are many reasons to encourage children from non-English-speaking backgrounds to maintain their "heritage" language, to use the Canadian terminology. Language retention facilitates intergenerational communication among such families; it encourages respect for the child's original culture; it facilitates global communication and, yes, business. But it is naive to assume that language, religion, race, and politics are not intimately linked. It is not accidental that the current government of Puerto Rico, which is opposed to statehood for the Commonwealth, has passed legislation making Spanish Puerto Rico's official language.

At the very least, any movement toward choice must be within a strong centralized national curriculum that defines key elements of a nation's identity and expectations. This is the approach being taken in places such as the United Kingdom and New Zealand, both of which have moved toward school-based management in which community-dominated boards of governors select principals and teachers (Lawton, 1991). Canada, to date, has found this impossible. There is now a minority speaking about a "Canada without Quebec" that favors development of a national curriculum to define what the nation stands for and what it expects. This group does not shy away from suggesting that immigrants who choose Canada are obliged to become Canadian—in language and culture—to a degree that facilitates national unity and development. Beyond that level, the group suggests, language, culture, and religion are private matters.

The lesson drawn from comparing choice in education in the United States and Canada is that it is a topic of such fundamental importance that a much wider view is needed than is provided by concentration on local choice mechanisms in the two nations. Instead, one must look at entire systems, from top to bottom, in a variety of nations, to provide a map for future decisions. One must make sure that, in extending individual rights, one does not inadvertently create collective rights that lead to "a house divided."

References

Callahan, R. E. (1962). *Education and the cult of efficiency*. Chicago: University of Chicago Press.

Chubb, J. E., & Moe, T. M. (1990). *Politics, markets, and America's schools*. Washington, DC: Brookings Institution.

Clune, W. H., & Witte, J. F. (Eds.). (1990). *Choice and control in American education* (Vols. 1, 2). New York: Falmer.

Coleman, J. S., & Hoffer, T. (1987). *Public and private high schools: The impact of communities*. New York: Basic Books.

Coleman, J. S., et al. (1966). *Equality of educational opportunity*. Washington, DC: Government Printing Office.

Constitution Acts (Canada). (1986). [1867 to 1982]. Ottawa: Department of Justice.

Erickson, D. A. (1982). Disturbing evidence about the "one best system." In R. B. Everhart (Ed.), *The public school monopoly*. Cambridge, MA: Ballinger.

Everhart, R. B. (Ed.). (1982). *The public school monopoly*. Cambridge, MA: Ballinger.

Gairdner, W. D. (1990). *The trouble in Canada*. Toronto: Stoddard.

Hirschman, A. O. (1970). *Exit, voice, and loyalty*. Cambridge, MA: Harvard University Press.

Lawton, S. B. (1986). A case study of choice in education: Separate schools in Ontario. *Journal of Education Finance, 11*(2), 236-257.

Lawton, S. B. (1987). *The price of quality: The public finance of elementary and secondary education in Canada.* Toronto: Canadian Education Association.

Lawton, S. B. (1989). Public, private and separate schools in Ontario: Developing a new social contract for education? In W. L. Boyd & J. G. Cibulka (Eds.), *Private schools and public policy* (pp. 171-192). New York: Falmer.

Lawton, S. B. (1991, March). *Implications of school-based management for school finance: An international survey.* Paper presented at the annual meeting of the American Educational Finance Association, Williamsburg, VA.

Lawton, S. B. (in press). Why restructure? An international survey of the roots of reform. *Journal of Educational Policy.*

Ministry of Education (Ontario). (1991). *Education funding Ontario, 1991.* Toronto: Author.

Niskanen, W. A. (1973). *Bureaucracy: Servant or master?* London: Institute of Economic Affairs.

Sarick, L. (1991, April 12). Board limits promotion. *The Globe and Mail* (Toronto).

Tyack, D. B. (1974). *The one best system.* Cambridge, MA: Harvard University Press.

Witte, J. F. (1990). Introduction: Choice and control in American education: An analytical overview. In W. Clune & J. Witte (Eds.), *Choice and control in American education: Vol. 1. The theory of choice and control in education* (pp. 1-10). New York: Falmer.

Index

Kirby, S. N., 108, 159
Knowledge, ready access to, 74
Kolderie, T., 9, 10, 17, 19, 20

Laissez-faire economic advocates, 73
Language skills, 121
Lawton, S. B., 190-205, 191, 193, 195, 202, 205
Learning rate, high school and, 113-114
Learning style, differences in, 5
Legislation, school choice, 11, 28, 34
Levin, H. M., 106, 175
Lewis, M., 173, 174
Liberal democratic tradition, 50
Liberal policy scholars, interest in choice and, 25, 26, 29-30
Libertarians, 11, 16
Liberty. See Individual, liberty
Life chances, 79
Lincoln, Abraham, 172, 181, 203
Literature, achievement in, 137
Locke, John, 51, 52
Louis, K. S., 177, 178, 179
Low-income students: Catholic schools and, 33; competition for schools and, 78; school quality ratings and, 69; vouchers for, 28. See also Poverty

Magnet schools, 10, 19, 30, 31, 197, 200
Mall life, participation in, 154-155
Manhattan, Community School District Four, 4, 31, 89
Manhattan Institute Center for Educational Innovation, 91
March, J. G., 26, 36, 39
Market: common good and, 86; constraints, 75; consumership ideology and, 87; government's role in, 150-151; incentives and, 175; liberal policy scholars and, 30; romanticization of, 94; virtues of, 88, 89
Market control, 11, 162
Market-oriented school choice, 7-9, 58; accountability and, 160; bounded

rationality and, 75-79; business community and, 91, 92-96; gospel of, 92-95; rational choice theory and, 67; rhetoric and, 92-95; school quality and, 69; segregation and, 75-79; social status and, 76-77; sociological theory and, 65-81; stratification and, 96
Market resources, dominant status groups and, 76
Math achievement, 129-137
Mazzoni, T., 28, 34, 181
Mediocrity, 57
Metz, M., 58, 176
Mill, J. S., 11, 50, 51, 63, 149, 202
Miller, J. A., 25, 37, 38
Milwaukee Parental Choice Program, 108-109
Minnesota: chartering schools and, 20; school choice legislation, 34; tuition tax credits and, 108
Minnesota Business Partnership, 28
Minorities, 141; alienation and, 78; Catholic schools and, 3, 139-140; isolation of, 68; school quality ratings and, 69
Moe, T. M., 12, 13, 30, 66, 85, 87, 88, 93, 94, 103, 104, 106, 110, 117, 118, 119-120, 121, 123, 138, 139, 162, 175, 185, 201
Morale, choice system and, 106
Moral evaluation, 77
Moral responsibilities, 48
Moral values, New Right and, 27
Motivation, choice system and, 106
Mueller v. Allen, 108
Multiculturalism, 157

Nathan, J., 6, 30, 36, 91, 147
National Assessment of Educational Progress math examinations, 129-137
National cohesion, 85
National Commission on Excellence in Education, 8, 54-58
National Education Association, 36